DAYTON, OHIO
An Intimate History

by
Charlotte Reeve Conover

Edited by Alexander Kaye

Introduction by Roz Young

Landfall Press
Dayton, Ohio
1995

CHARLOTTE REEVE CONOVER

Original Edition published by Lewis Publishing Co., New York, 1932
Second Edition published by Landfall Press, Dayton, OH, 1970
Third Edition edited and published by Landfall Press, Dayton, OH 1995
Copyright © 1995, Landfall Press, Inc., 5171 Chapin St., Dayton, OH
45429. All rights reserved.
ISBN 0-913428-00-0
Library of Congress Catalog Card No. 95- 78178

The use of the CD'96 Logo is for promotional and educational purposes
only regarding the 1996 Celebration Dayton Bicentennial.

CELEBRATION
DAYTON '96™

To Future Daytonians
May They Carry On

Somewhere, in the bright hereafter of which we all think more often as the years pass, there will be a shining galaxy which we in Dayton will want to join.

It will be composed, not of eminent philosophers or scientists or international statesmen, but those who, in life, had one thing in common: they served the city of their heart with all that was in them.

The earlier members of that group will include Daniel C. Cooper who, a century and more ago, gave Dayton her wide streets and contributed ground for parks, schools and churches; John Van Cleve who, eighty years ago, planted the elms that shade the Boulevard, and saw in imagination, while it was still a rough wooded hill, the place where we lay our dear dead.

It will include Horace Pease, who visioned our classic Courthouse and helped bring it into being; Mary Steele, who was the real founder of the women's clubs in Dayton; Belle Eaker, who mothered the young men through the YMCA; Sinclair and Shuey, who carried out her ideals and their own; James A. Robert, who fostered music and art and reclaimed the river bed.

There will be Robert Steele who, standing at his gate at the corner of First and Ludlow streets, just a few weeks before he died, said as he looked down the vista of the street, "Yes, Dayton is beautiful. I wonder if those who come after us will keep it so."

E. E. Barney will stand in that group because he taught and planted and builded and inspired throughout a long lifetime; there will be William Huffman, Grace A. Greene, William Werthner, B. F. McCann, Margaret Stoddard, Leopold Rauh, Dr. Frank Garland and Electra C. Doren.

At the head of the group of good citizens and gone from us seemingly only such a little while ago, will be John Patterson whose gifts, actual and inspirational: parks, trees, schools, lectures, educational trips, opportunities for recreation, inspiration in civic ideals, will never be forgotten.

And close, very close to him, will be Mrs. Kumler, so close that rarely will their friends, the citizens of Dayton, think of one without the other -- Mrs. Kumler, who founded clubs, led in the social and philanthropic organizations of Dayton, an inspired leader in her home city.

CHARLOTTE REEVE CONOVER

It is a stirring thought to those of us who are yet treading the streets of our city to ask ourselves, "What can we each, personally, do for Dayton?"

Not perhaps in bequeathing lands or dollars (for our bank accounts and our talents may be minor affairs), but someway and somehow, each of us, in his or her own way, may find service to do that that will make Dayton a better place in which to live.

If we do so, whenever and however we can, it will be to honor the memory of those who have gone before.

That is what they would have liked best.

C. R. C.

October, 1931

Contents

Charlotte Reeve Conover

FROM A PORTRAIT DRAWING by
CAROLINE H. VAN BEAN

INTRODUCTION TO
THE 1995 EDITION

When you get right down to it, we all came here from somewhere else.

Some came sooner, others came later. Some came when the big trees were still standing and some came after the streets were paved. Some crossed rivers and streams to get here, others crossed oceans. Some spoke the language, others never really came to terms with the mother tongue. Some were well-heeled, others carried all their possessions in a bundle.

Why did they come? Obviously, the compelling reasons were opportunity and freedom.

In the beginning one attraction was good, cheap land wholesaled by an impoverished post-Revolutionary War Congress to speculaters who retailed it to homesteaders. The Continental Congress, deeply in debt, powerless to tax and whose income barely covered one-third the interest on the national debt, wanted settlers in the West against the continuing British threat.

But the magnet drawing all but the most desperate to the lands north and west of the Ohio River was a new law, enacted for the first time anywhere in the world, proclaiming equality and individual liberties throughout the new territories.

The Ordinance of 1787, just about the last piece of business of the unworkable Continental Congress, established forever that new states would be admitted to the Union as equals to the original ones even though lots of people wanted the new territories to become colonies of the original thirteen. But more importantly this law, also called the Northwest Ordinance, spelled out freedoms that shortly found their way into the U. S. Constitution and the Bill of Rights.[*]

In addition to the sections outlining the governance of the territory, the Ordinance contained a *compact*, in those days a most sacred promise, that is the American story:

Article I guaranteed religious freedom. Article II was a bill of rights assuring habeus corpus, trial by peers, no cruel and unusual punishment,

---

[*] See *The Ordinance of 1787, The Nation Begins* by William Donohue Ellis, published 1987, Landfall Press, Dayton, Ohio.

property rights, representation of the people in the legislature and a provision that no future government could ever annul the contract. Much of this article traced all the way back to the Magna Carta.

Article III encouraged education. Article IV forbade new states becoming a separate nation or a province of a foreign power. It also covered freedom of the waterways. Article V outlined procedures for forming new states, still in effect today.

Article VI prohibited slavery.

The first state to emerge from this vast territoy was Ohio, admitted to the Union as the 17th state in 1803, a scant seven years after the first settlers landed 200 years ago on April 1, 1796 where the Great Miami and the Mad rivers meet. We've been coming here ever since.

The history of Dayton's early years, the first golden age which established our community's place and character, has been lovingly chronicled in this volume by one who lived through much of it. The modern era, unquestionably a second golden age, is recorded in other volumes in this series called the Bicentennial Bookshelf.

It is to our everlasting benefit that there were those who loved this community enough to take the trouble to record not just its progress but its very heart and soul. It is of priceless importance to us to know of and build on our legacy of enterprise, industriousness, innovation and tolerance.

As John Jay Chapman has written, "One of the deepest impulses in man is the impulse to record -- to scratch a drawing on a tusk or keep a diary, to collect sagas or heap a cairn. This instinct as to the enduring value of the past is, one might say, the very basis of civilization."

The reader is cautioned that we have edited, abridged and updated portions of the original 1931 book for purposes of this 1995 version; thus, this version is not a 100% reprint of the author's original work.

That is why we are proud to publish this and the other volumes in the Bicentennial Bookshelf.

Alexander Kaye
Dayton, Ohio
July, 1995

INTRODUCTION
TO THE 1970 EDITION

When Charlotte Reeve Conover reached her 80th year in 1935, she was invited by a group of prominent Dayton citizens to give a special lecture at the Dayton Art Institute. Former Governor James M. Cox acted as chairman. On the invitations was printed a tribute by her friend and fellow Dayton writer, Anne O'Hare McCormick. She wrote, "Charlotte Reeve Conover is the historian of Dayton. Much of this history she herself has lived. Most of the outstanding figures in the local saga were, and are, her friends.

"It is because she is a citizen of the world that Mrs. Conover is so valuable a citizen of Dayton. We honor her because she has labored to keep the mind of Dayton alive. She has struck out into the currents of contemporary thought in order that the community may keep abreast of the great movements and swift changes of our time.

"Athens in the Golden Age was a little town, and Florence of the Renaissance had fewer natural advantages than Dayton. Not size nor wealth, but civilization make a city and civilization is made by citizens like Charlotte Reeve Conover who enlarged life by enlarging the orbit of the intellect and the spirit."

A further idea of the remarkable woman Mrs. Conover was can be gathered from some of her own philosophy on her 80th birthday. "I love life at 80," she said, "but I hate the characteristics of aged people." She said that a man who always voted for the same party, subscribed to the same publications year after year and entertained the same ideas his whole life is a public menace.

She thought there should be a special university course for the aged. The young sponge up knowledge no matter where they are. The old have to be shoved and prodded to learn. The course should be required for all who have lived casually and unthinkingly for half a century and suddenly bump into a 60th birthday and recoil in horror.

After her 80th birthday, Mrs. Conover lost her sight, but she continued to write. To someone who asked her, "When youth, sight and health are gone, is there anything left?," she answered,

"Honeysuckle still smells sweet when you're too old to jump on the running board of a car."

She was born in Dayton June 14, 1855 and died here September 23, 1940. Her father was a prominent Dayton physician. She attended Cooper Seminary and Central High School. She also attended for a time the University of Geneva, Switzerland, and years later after rearing four children, she returned to complete her education. When the officials discussed how so old a person could possibly be admitted, she asked, "Does it never happen in this country that mothers of families want to learn something?" The official answered, "Write yourself down as mere de famille; you may take any classes you choose."

Mrs. Conover wrote a four-volume history of Montgomery County, the story of the Patterson family called *Builders of New Fields*, *Some Dayton Saints and Sinners* and *Dayton, Ohio, An Intimate History.*

The *Intimate History* is urbane, chatty, filled with anecdotes and sometimes gossip. Those who prefer to sit at the table with Dayton families in the 1840s, attend a wedding in the 90s, go for a canal ride, watch a fire burn or be rescued from the 1913 flood will find in these pages life as it was lived in days gone by. The book was first published in 1931 when Dayton had just passed the 200,000 population mark. The telephone book was just half an inch thick and to call anyone on the telephone required the services of an operator. In 40 years since the book came out, although the blessings of modern civilization have invaded the city, Dayton is essentially the same town it was then, and if the author could step into a trolley bus today and ride the length of Main Street, or walk into a city commission meeting, she would have no trouble recognizing the old spots.

In her introduction to the book she said, "Somewhere in the bright hereafter of which we all think more often as the years pass, there will be a shining galaxy which we in Dayton will want to join. It will be composed, not of eminent philosophers or scientists or international statesmen, but of those who in life had one thing in common: they served the city of their heart with all that was in them.

"It is a stirring thought to those of us yet treading the streets of our city to ask ourselves, 'What can we each personally do for Dayton?' Not perhaps in bequeathing lands or dollars (for our bank accounts and our talents may be minor affairs), but someway and somehow, each of us, in his or her own way, may find service that will make Dayton a better and happier place in which to live. If we do so, whenever and however we can, it will honor the memory of those who have gone before."

An Intimate History has long been out of print. Many Daytonians of the present day have not had the opportunity to learn the stirring story and meet the remarkable men of Dayton past pictured so vividly by Mrs. Conover. This edition, complete and unabridged, now makes it possible for us to honor, in the words of the author, the memory of those who have gone ahead.

Rosamond Young
Dayton, Ohio
1970

PRELUDE

Somewhere, buried in the gravel and silt of the river bottom where the Miami joins the Ohio, would be found, if we knew where to dig for it, a leaden plate eleven inches long, seven inches wide and an eighth of an inch thick containing the origins of this city and county as they came into historical and political existence. That historical existence was French. No human eye has seen the plate since it was placed there in August 1749 and none ever will, since the Miami River has a way of keeping what it gets hold of. But the original records, probably in the Bibliotheque Nationale in Paris, have kept the story.

There were six such plates, the inscriptions identical, and they were duplicated in tin. The leaden plates were buried and the tin plates were hung on the branches of trees near the confluence of the rivers emptying into the Ohio. They were called by those who buried them, "proofs of re-possession." The prefix "re" refers to the fact that the ownership of the territory in question had been settled unofficially several years before by La Salle himself who, at the mouth of the Mississippi, with a wave of his arm to the north, appropriated to the Crown of France, all the lands drained by that river and its tributaries. It was a much larger order than La Salle knew at the time but it was something to report to his royal master at Versailles as a token result for what his journey had cost the state.

Whether La Salle's title of possession was held to be weak legally, or whether others wanted expeditionary honors of their own is not plain at this day. But the idea of a colony of French peasants to settle in the heart of the rich Ohio lands was simmering in other minds. One of them was that of Glassoniere, the Governor General of Canada, who had large plans for the development of the whole great middle west in the interests of France. The only one of these plans that materialized is the one we are interested in, which did not turn out exactly as he intended but which resulted in the first appearance of white men on the soil of what we now know as Montgomery County.

Red men there had been in plenty. The lands bordering the two rivers we know best, the Miami and Mad Rivers, were the biggest game preserve the Indians had. They came down the river in canoes from the Indian village at Piqua and up the river in their canoes from Kentucky to kill game and take it home for winter provision. But the brown skins have not counted much in history in the past.

So the Frenchman and his plates are the real beginning. This is the inscription, verified from the record by one plate which was discovered sticking out of the mud by boys fishing for other things and brought to the authorities at Marietta. It was not our plate but it tells the story:

In the year 1749, in the reign of His Majesty Louis XV King of France, We, Pierre Joseph Celeron de Bienville, Knight of the Royal Order of St. Louis; Captain commanding a detachment sent down the Beautiful River (the Ohio) by order of the Marquis de la Glassoniere, Governor General of all New France and Louisiana, have buried this plate at the mouth of the Miami river as a token of the renewal of possession heretofore taken of the Ohio river and of all streams that fall into it and all lands on both sides to the sources of the streams as the Kings of France enjoyed it.

To the nearest tree trunk that overhung the current of the stream, Celeron hung the tin plate with the same inscription and the arms of France upon it.

So that is how Dayton was born. There is much back of it historically, relative to the treaties of Riswick, Utrecht and Aix la Chapelle which there is no time to go into here. But that far off start of our history was a continuation of the vast international struggle between France and England for dominance of the New World. The rich fertile fields of our Ohio valleys seemed to those cramped Europeans, tillers, shoulder to shoulder, of the narrow strips of wornout soil of their native land, a little less than paradise.

Why did it come to nothing? Why have we lost our French accent, so to speak, and kept the remembrance of our French origin only in our geographical nomenclature: Bellefontaine, Des Moines, Detroit and Wabash (originally spelled Ouabache)? In the first place Louis XV was too busy throwing dice at Versailles to care about the far-away interior of North America. It is a long story but we must go back to the Sieur de Bienville and his plates.

There were 244 men in this expedition down the Ohio and up the Miami river, including 80 Indians and 100 Canadians, the "Coureurs des Bois" made famous by Longfellow in *Evangeline.*

Fifty days it took the captain and his men to make that journey from Montreal to Pittsburgh. Starting from Lachine June 15, 1749, carrying their canoes across from Lake Erie to Lake Chautauqua, down the Ohio to the

Great Miami, up the Miami past the Dayton that was to be, across by portage to a French settlement on the Maumee and so back to Lake Erie, this was the itinerary of those doughty explorers.

A historian thus describes the appearance of the little army as it made its way down the waters of La Belle Riviere (the Ohio, so lettered on the early maps of the period): "Soldiers and Canadians in their gay costumes and semi-medieval armor, the half-naked copper-skinned savages, the flying banners of France, all crowded in the frail white birch bark canoes that floated on the surface of the stream like tiny paper shells."

When they reached the Miami it was the largest tributary passed since leaving what is now Pittsburgh and they had but one remaining plate. de Bienville led his forces ashore and in impressive and flowery language addressed his followers and a few savages who had gathered about him. He extolled the honor and glory of their mission and how they would be remembered as thus adding to the glory of France by peaceful conquest of the great Western lands. Then the ceremony of "plate sowing" was carried out, and until the next spring flood carried away the tree with the tin plate and buried the lead plate under tons of gravel, this valley belonged to the King of France.

What these explorers saw of our Miami Valley was not what we see. Our present thin, shallow, useless streams were then the great highways leading from the civilization of the eastern states into the unpenetrated wilderness of the Northwest Territory. An old painting of the mouth of the Mad River, done by some anonymous native artist of the early years of the last century, showed a deep channeled stream opening into another still wider and deeper, both so massed with forestry and bushes that the overhanging branches almost met overhead.

One could imagine the easy possibility of future steamboats stemming the muddy current. It was by means of such abundant waterways that Montgomery County was penetrated and settled. No other way. Progress of the next explorers was on foot, blazing the trees to mark the passage for those who came afterward. On horseback it was still difficult; but when the first wagons attempted to make it, trees had to be felled every few rods to make passage for the body and the wheels.

No modern artist knows how to draw imaginatively the topography of 150 years ago. They sketch some trees and some open spaces, but in 1750 there were few, if any, open spaces. Mile after mile of almost impenetrable forest over all of southern Ohio. Here and there, along the bed of streams where the spring freshets made it difficult for growing timber to find a foot-hold, there was grazing land for cattle.

Unfortunately Celeron de Bienville left no descriptions of the Miami Valley, but Christopher Gist did. Gist was the agent of the Ohio Land Company and the first investor who tried to sell real estate on our territory. More of him later. But he wrote to impress his fellow Virginians of the attractions of the new country he was opening up; that he was "delighted with the fertile well-watered land with large oak, walnut, maple and ash trees."

He told them that "the country abounded with turkey, deer, elk and all sorts of game, especially buffalo, 30 or 40 of which were seen feeding in one meadow." In short, he said, "it needs nothing but cultivation to make it a most delightful country. The land along the Great Miami is rich, level and well-timbered, some of the finest meadows that can be. The grass here grows to a great height on the clear fields and the bottoms are full of white clover, wild rye and blue grass."

This is what the first beholders of our valley saw. Richness of soil, beauty of landscape, green and sturdy woods, abundance of game; buffalo grazing where now concrete bridges throw their arches across the stream, a literal paradise of plenty.

It was to become less beautiful and less peaceful as it became the field for rivalry of possession between the Indians and the settlers and the continuance of age-old antipathies between France and England, of wars that reddened the fields and sometimes the current of the rivers and earned for it the title of "The dark and bloody ground."

The Indians contested every inch of the land they considered theirs by right of inheritance from their fathers. The French never arrived to settle the land they had so proudly claimed. The Indians were pushed westward and the English and Scotch-Irish came in, sturdy younger sons of good families, driving out in Conestoga wagons from Philadelphia and New York. (Ed. Note: The first legal settlers in the Northwest Territory following the enactment of the Ordinance of 1787 were from New England and Virginia; almost all were veterans of the Revolutionary War.)

But it was an epic, an epic that ought never to be forgotten and always be taught to the younger generation that they may receive with humility and carry on with faithfulness the heritage of their long-ago ancestors.

1

Dayton - The Real Settlement

Of course, the "first settlers" were really Indians. Perhaps, to be more exact, they were the Mound Builders whose mysterious relics are to be found scattered over the Ohio country. But our story does not go back to those ancient days and concerns only the men from the eastern states: traders, surveyors, farmers, penetrating the wilderness to make new homes for their families.

The Indians who were already here made the first and most serious difficulty for the newcomers. Most of the country known now as Ohio, Indiana and Illinois was occupied by the Algonquins. The valley bounded by the two Miami rivers was occupied by the Twightwees. Celoron de Bienville referred to our river as *Riviere a la Roche* - Rock River, but its present name is a modernization of the name used by the Indians who lived on its banks.

The two Miamis originate within a few miles of each other, divided by some elevation which sends one current one way and the other another. The larger one was named first, and because of the paucity of nomenclature in the early days the smaller was named after it with the prefix "Little."

On the early maps the territory between them was named "the Miami Lands" and was so called by the first surveyors and land promoters. Back and forth across this territory swept migratory bands of Indians wherever game seemed most plenty. Their camp fires glowed in the woods, their trails meandered along the river banks where now sometimes a disinterred arrowhead or stone axe reveals the fact of their occupancy. But for hundreds of years no one disputed possession with them. Then came Celoron with his rangers and, although he did not know it, the reign of the Indian was over.

Two years after Celoron had guided his expedition up our river, Christopher Gist and two companions passed over the same route on their way to trade with the Indians in their towns near Piqua, Xenia and Springfield. The agent of an English and Virginia land company, he made his errand an excuse for looking over the land values in the Miami Valley, recording the buffalo grazing on the site of Dayton in January, 1751.

The next visitors to our valley were not explorers nor land agents but soldiers, for the Revolutionary War was on and its fringes reached into Ohio, the far frontier. English and Indians on one side and a melange of French, Scotch-Irish and frontiersmen on the other were struggling for dominance of America. A Colonel Byrd, with a detachment of 600 Indians and Canadians and four pieces of artillery, introduced us to the fortunes of war. But he came down instead of up, leaving Canada in the spring of 1780, following the Maumee from its mouth at Lake Erie to the portage across to the headwaters of the Great Miami and downstream to the Ohio. His journey was in the interest of conquest so whenever he found a frontier station he burned it, taking loot and prisoners back to British headquarters.

General George Rogers Clarke was quick to retaliate. He was bent on conquest against the Indians who, from their villages on the Miami lands, were making bloody raids into Kentucky, murdering the settlers, driving off their livestock and making life impossible for the founders of Lexington and Limestone.

Clarke and his Kentuckians, among them Robert Patterson whose name was to mean so much in the future annals of Dayton, destroyed a number of Indian villages and built a couple of blockhouses on the Ohio between the two Miamis, afterward the city of Cincinnati. This was not the only expedition from Kentucky to Ohio; there were many and always with the same object: to punish the Indians and make life safer for the settlers.

But of all these adventurous souls who came to our Dayton vicinity none cared to stop. Why risk it? The woods were alive with Indians who especially frequented the mouth of the Mad River and whose methods of warfare were savage and bloody.

But "Westward the course of empire takes its way." Land was what men wanted and land was what they meant to have. Groups of people here and there in the east, in New Jersey for example, were being first impressed and then engaged to take up land in the west. Returning travelers all told the same story. The eastern states were rich, but Ohio was richer. Land that "tickled with a hoe and laughed with a harvest" could be had for a song.

Among these enthusiasts who had made the trip across the mountains was Benjamin Stites, an adventurer from New Jersey, who happened to be in one of those raids into Ohio and who got a glimpse of the fertile Miami Valley. Charmed by the beauty of the country he hurried back to New Jersey and laid his information before Judge John Cleve Symmes of Trenton, a man of great influence.

Stites' enthusiasm communicated itself to Symmes and they formed a land company to exploit the Miami lands. Congress had recently given such a grant to a company interested in the valley of the Muskingum and Symmes had no doubt his petition would be readily granted. Without, however, waiting for Congress to act on his petition Symmes deeded to Stites 10,000 acres between the Miami rivers thereby causing much confusion later as to property rights among the first settlers of Dayton.

Stites got out a glowing prospectus inviting settlers to select the most advantageous locations at the price of one dollar an acre and promised them deeds when Congress should have made the transaction legal. The current expression "a land office business" is said to have originated in connection with this enterprise. (Ed. Note: the same was said of land sales in Marietta, Ohio's first legal settlement, where the original land office cabin is still preserved at the city's Campus Martius museum. This land rush was caused by the passage by Congress of the Northwest Ordinance which first spelled out many of the freedoms later enshrined in our Constitution and by Bounty Land warrants issued to soldiers in lieu of pay during the Revolutionary War.)

There was a rush of prospective settlers for the bargains in land. The center of the trade was at the mouth of the Miami where Stites and several assistants spent busy days making out grants that were never recorded. It was not a dishonest transaction for Stites fully expected the government to stand by him. Eventually it did, but not until after much distress was experienced by many of the new landowners.

Some of the pioneers came in from New Jersey as far as Fort Washington (Cincinnati), and stayed there in rough cabins around the two blockhouses. A natural hesitancy in penetrating what was becoming known as the "Miami slaughter house" was apparent. It was not an inviting appellation for a real estate boom.

First House in Dayton, Newcom's Tavern, erected in 1796. Interior view shows how it was used also as meeting house, store, court.

An entire party of explorers, attacked at the mouth of the Miami and carried off by the Indians, (a much worse fate if we may believe the early stories than being killed outright), added to the apprehension. Three Kentuckians, Robert Patterson, John Filson and Mathias Denman, became the first proprietors of the land on which the first log forts were built and named it Losantiville, from which it emerged finally as Cincinnati.

Filson, exploring on his own up the Miami, was never seen again. As his bones were never found it was assumed he was carried off by a wandering Indian band. All this sinister uncertainty as well as the furious semi-annual floods in the rivers made an offset to the alluring descriptions in the land offices, and events, as far as Dayton was concerned, dragged.

Cincinnati was definitely settled in December of 1788 but it was to be eight more years before the first cabin was built at the mouth of the Mad River. Nothing was plainer than the uselessness of attempting to create cities and homes on the same ground as the Indians. Small wonder then that the hope and aim of those few already on the ground was to get rid of their unpleasant neighbors. It was literally war to the end with no quarter on either side.

Skirmishes were going on all the time. Indians prowled near the cabins in Cincinnati, picking off with their arrows any settler who dared to go out to till his fields. A gun was left at the end of every furrow and a wife never knew when her husband went out to plough whether she would see him again alive. The old histories, Howe's *Ohio*, Mary Steele's *Early Dayton*, Galbreath's *Ohio*, give story after story of such cruel murders, which left wives and babies burdens on a new community.

Of organized punitive expeditions there were not a few. General Harmar in 1789 with 1500 men, headquarters at Cincinnati, marched past the site of Dayton and somewhere up the valley was badly defeated. Then St. Clair's big promises and preparations and awful, unspeakable defeat. The raw red skulls scattered over the field after this battle reminding an old squaw who told of it of a "field of ripe pumpkins" was not the kind of crop to attract settlers.

Then came General Anthony Wayne, "Mad Anthony" they called him, not so mad but that he saw the weakness in St. Clair's military tactics, improved them, met the savages reinforced by the British at the Falls of the Maumee (August 20, 1794), whipped them unmercifully, leaving them only too glad to give up the sometimes successful but increasingly unequal struggle.

In 1795 the Treaty of Greenville was signed between eleven tribes of Indians on one side and General Wayne on the other, the tenor of which was that the Indians should bury the hatchet and let the whites alone. Thus was settled who's who in the Miami Valley. No Dayton until the Indians understood once and for all that their rule was ended, at least in the area between the Miami Rivers.

After this, events moved quickly. Just seventeen days after signing the treaty, a company of men made a joint purchase from John Cleve Symmes of a large tract of land at the junction of the Miami and Mad rivers. Here we are at last at Dayton. If not paved streets and skyscrapers at least surveyors maps and blazed trees. A member of the new company was Winthrop Sargent, secretary of the Northwest Territory, the land now comprising Ohio, Indiana, Illinois, Michigan and points north.

The map of the United States at that time had the seaboard towns, the Allegheny Mountains, the western rivers in an undefined way and then a blank. All north and west of the Ohio River, then practically unexplored, was called the Northwest Territory. From every returning traveler came the same reports of the extraordinary fertility of this district about to be opened to the world.

Our first legal proprietors, to whom our nomenclature bears witness, were General Jonathan Dayton, General Arthur St. Clair, General James Wilkinson and Colonel Israel Ludlow, but as far as can be ascertained the last was the only one who was ever on the spot to view his purchase. Of the actual occupants only nineteen out of the 46 who subscribed gained their allowances of in-lots and out-lots and came. Nineteen men that is, women not being then counted in the census. When it came to cooking, baking, weaving, carding, baby tending, garden making and washing they counted all right, but officially they resembled the mother of ten who, asked by the census taker, replied, "no occupation."

The names of these first settlers are in all the old histories. Few, if any, have survived until the present census of Dayton. One or two merit remembrance: Benjamin Van Cleve, George Newcom (whose dwelling still stands a noble old relic on the banks of the river where he landed) and Samuel Thompson.

For greater convenience the party was divided into three groups. William Hamer, his wife and eight children in a two-horse wagon started first over the road which D. C. Cooper had cut in the fall of 1795 when he came to lay out the new town. The other two parties set forth on the same day, March 21, one by land led by Thompson and the other by water led by Newcom.

On the banks of the Ohio where now river boats tie up under the suspension bridge, was then a rude craft built by the men who proposed to use it, a pirogue, low, light-draft, with a running board for the propellers to walk on, and a covered section in back for shelter in bad weather. An old account tells how they did it: *the men, each provided with a stout pole with a heavy socket, stood on either side of the boat. They set their poles near the head of the boat and, bringing the head of the pole to their shoulders walked with their bodies bent, slowly down the running board to the stern returning at a quick pace for a new set.*

So, poling laboriously down the Ohio and up the Miami, avoiding as best they might the interlacing branches overhead that impeded their progress and the shallows underneath which strove to catch the keel in the riffles, huddled when it rained into the low shelter at the back (with eight children of different ages if we count right), going ashore at intervals to cook and dry clothes, in terror always of lurking Indians, the boat party came at last to Dayton.

And, in a creaking-wheeled springless wagon often mired in the soft loam of the trail, cutting down occasional trees which blocked the roadway, fording streams where the current swept into the wagonbed, camping at night to cook whatever the men had shot on the way, keeping the children quiet under the canvas top for fear of attracting the ever-present savages, the wagon party also came at last to Dayton.

Is the picture too blackly painted? Were there no pleasures to chronicle in that long 60-mile journey? A faithful historian should tell it all.

In the first place it was a new undertaking with considerably more than a spice of adventure. That in itself constitutes a joy not known to present dwellers in the valley. Unless one travels to the interior of Tibet or South America there cannot be found today such endless allure of the unknown.

Then it was the last of March along the Miami, the charm of which has nearly disappeared with the deforestation and the inflow of traffic. April, with its snowy dogwood mingled with the deep pink of the redbud, the white blossoms of the thorn, the soft grass in the woods dotted with anemones and bloodroot, the wild grape vines adding the sweetest of all the perfumes of spring -- these lent their charm to the journey.

It was on April 1, 1796 that the pirogue pushed its clumsy nose into the loam of the bank where they had been told they would find the town of Dayton. They could not be wrong for the contract said "at the mouth of Mad River" and there it was before them, its full and rapid current swelling the volume of the Miami. Yet where was the town? Just several blazed trees along the bank, one marked "St. Clair" another "Jefferson" and another "Ludlow." Yes, this must be the place Cooper had laid out and named.

Testimony varies as to who was first to put foot to shore. Mary Steele says it was Catherine Thompson. Family tradition has it as nine-year-old Mary Van Cleve. But fathers and mothers 100 years ago could not have been so different from those of today and in imagination we hear them saying, "Mary, you go first." This is guessing but then most history is guessing. It has been suggested there be a monument erected to her in Van Cleve Park, right where her little shoe pressed the soil. The motion is herewith seconded.

The main thing is that they got ashore at last and proceeded to look around. Not a shelter of any kind. Nothing to make home for them but the blazed trees and the street names. But pioneers were resourceful and there were the boat timbers, quickly made into shacks with one side open to the protecting and warming fire. Further up Mad River were some Indians who disappeared soon, leaving the coast clear to the settlers.

Four days later came the land party and then Dayton began to be. What work for those sturdy men and women! All day long the sound of the axe was heard from sunrise to sunset. For they could raise nothing until the ground was cleared. Trees took from the wealth of the soil and afforded shelter for Indians.

Each family had to have its own domicile and all helped in the work. The finest of the new buildings was the Newcom Tavern with its puncheon floor, cat-and-clay chimney and loft above the "room." Each family had its out-lot garden for vegetables besides the in-lot on which a cabin was built.

So here we have the Dayton of the first decade. A row of cabins along the edge of the river where they could see the boats going down filled with merchandise for sale in the south, in which they engaged when commerce was established. A small clearing of several rods where the wheel tracks in the mud indicated the way to Cincinnati; and all around them unbounded woods.

Thickets of hazel bushes made almost as heavy clearing as the big oaks and maples. Thick black loam, while it gave promise of abundant crops where it was cultivated, made weary work for the horses drawing wagons or plows. The wilderness was beautful but threatening. It gave the food they needed but sheltered who knew what dangers.

Bears and wolves and Indians might lurk behind any tree and often did. The worry of it was unceasing. If they did not worry it was because they were so far gone with malaria that they did not care whether they lived or died, and it was the woods and the soil which furnished the malaria.

When one reads accounts of the sickness which prevailed even into the middle years of the last century one wonders how Dayton succeeded in getting established. When the promoters in New Jersey told of the fertility of the Ohio lands they told the truth, but only half of it.

Attempts to visualize and appreciate the hardships of our forefathers must always be accompanied with the realization of what they had to contend with in the ever-recurrent chills and fever, the prostrating weakness and bone-racking pain. There were good days and bad days and in the interim they tried to make up for the idleness, being thankful that the bad days did not come on all the inhabitants at the same time.

Neither must the reader of pioneer annals neglect to supply from his own imagination the part that the women took in the settlement of the new country. The pioneers themselves did not see fit to mention it, for wives were taken a good deal for granted in those days. Nevertheless their role was a strenuous one.

A visit to Newcom Tavern (Ed. Note: now in Carillon Park) will help paint the picture. The first thing likely to strike a visitor is the amazing ingenuity of the people in adapting to the living conditions. Part of their housekeeping utensils had been brought from the east such as three-legged "spiders" in which cornpone was cooked, tin ovens to catch the heat of the fire, tin lanterns with perforations to let the candlelight through and big iron kettles. But by far the largest part of the kitchen equipment was homemade. A square tub on a stand with a hand-worked lever and a hole in the bottom for the apple juice to run out was their cider press, and a good one, too. A broom of shaved down withes on a hickory stick did well enough to clear off a puncheon floor. An upright section of hollowed log, with a wooden mallet standing up out of it, used as a pestle in a mortar, made an excellent hominy mill.

"Slaving over a cook stove" is a modern phrase; slaving over an open fire was the lot of the early housewife. That meant bending over, managing the huge cranes at the side of the fireplace by which heavy pots were swung on and off the blaze. The meat was turned on a spit and had to be kept moving. Biscuits were baked in the Dutch-oven on the hearth. Mush had to be stirred, hominy fried, coffee boiled -- in every instance in a stooping posture, the hardest in the world for a woman. What back breaking work it was to feed hungry men!

Not a history in the libraries even mentions the women's work. The tombstones do indirectly in New England where they point the fact that it often took three wives to last out one Pilgrim father. We may infer that it was no different in the Miami Valley: "Sacred to the memory of Mary, beloved consort of so-and-so, aged twenty-six;" a little further on "to Sarah, aged thirty;" and on to "Josephine, aged thirty-five."

After they died they were "consorts" or "spouses." If they chanced to outlive so-and-so they were registered as "beloved relics of the late. . ." But they seldom had such good luck. Malaria, consumption, hard work, child bearing carried them off. In the old Fifth Street graveyard where as a child the writer once played among the lichened and leaning stones, it struck me that the wives were never "beloved" until they were dead.

All these "relics" came originally from comfortable homes in the east, cheerful willing girls, to be broken before their time, to bear babies in open wagons, to work in the fields as much as in the house, to dread the Indians and never hear from home. This was the fate of thousands of unsung heroines in this and other places who made a path that their sisters might walk the easier.

As to the children -- somehow our sympathies are not so exercised in their behalf. An innate capacity for happiness dwells in every child's heart. The world is his and it is a constant joy. Given a handful of stones and broken dishes, a little girl will play happily all day long; boys can fish and trap squirrels. Work they both had to do, and there was plenty to do, but the work itself was a kind of play. If they had work, they had no worries. Land grants they knew nothing about nor titles to property; malaria they had not yet come to in the chronology of childhood.

Indians, if we except the story of Mary Van Cleve crawling through a hole under the house and running to Newcom Tavern in the night to call for help against some drunken redskins who were besieging the house for more whiskey, were scarcely actualities. There were never any battles on Dayton territory after the Treaty of Greenville and the depredations of the Indians were confined to stealing chickens.

A blockhouse was indeed built at the head of Main Street, but its most war-like use was as a schoolroom for Benjamin Van Cleve and his pupils. Until this unfortunate idea struck the parents it was a carefree life for the children. No books, long days in the woods, fishing in the river, gathering nuts and wild grapes and trapping squirrels. The actual work they did do, which was not inconsiderable, was an education in itself. They felt the importance of being a part in the life of the community perhaps more than children in modern times. They became self-reliant, enterprising and ambitious.

Our rich forefathers! How else can we look upon them? No bank stocks had they nor wealth as the world knows it. Indeed for long stretches of time they had no actual money. But whatever trials were their lot, hunger was seldom one of them. Before they had raised a row of corn or hill of beans, food in abundance was at hand. To how many millions in the world today would that be wealth untold? No money but three hearty meals a day; of clothes a very few and of home manufacture.

No pictures graced the walls of the scanty settlement; they were not needed since every window framed a view of forest, glen or stream; no dishes such as served the tables back in New Jersey, but gourd dippers, horn spoons and platters made of hollowed sycamore slabs. These after all are but the symbols of wealth. The real wealth was temporarily shut up in their natural surroundings; the forest so recently penetrated in which they were to find food and clothes, growing or on wild feet.

From the forest, in time, they were to have turkey dinners, fine venison steaks and rabbit stew. The children were to find and make a fine confection from maple sap and butternuts; buckeyes to string up on a cord like beads for their playtime. Mother was to find sassafras for tea, blackberries for pudding, grapes for jelly and walnut hulls to dye her petticoats.

Out of the forest as the years went by the men would get boards for houses and fences, oak for furniture, maple for lasts, hickory for wheels and hoe handles. We who have the benefit of an added century to give clearer vision know that in the undeveloped wealth of the primitive forest lay some of the great commercial enterprises which have built the city of Dayton.

The river, too, our now useless and devastating river, was to the pioneers a source of wealth. It gave them fish for their tables, fish that broke the seine with their numbers when it was let down and drawn up from the river; it gave them gravel for their roads, sand for their mortar and clay for their bricks. But most of all it was for the first Daytonians the great highway of transportation to the outside world.

The keys to all this wealth, the keys which alone would unlock these marvellous riches were their own stout and willing hands and the gun or axe or jackknife which they grasped. What uncomprehended, unending and inescapable work it meant to unlock that door! If they had known it, would they have stayed, and would we have been here? We shall never know; but having made the journey they settled down to a mixed existence. On the one hand, mud and stumps, catamounts, poison ivy, chills and fever, mosquitoes, rattlesnakes and an occasional wolf to raid the pig pen; on the other the freedom of the air, the water and the land, the magnificence of autumn foliage and summer sunsets, the glory of the seasons as they passed and went; good appetites and sound night's rest.

Best of all was the satisfaction of being the first to build for great things -- greater than they knew.

2

The First Decade

Dayton, which at first narrowly escaped being "Venice" (as Cincinnati escaped being Losantiville), also narrowly escaped becoming a cipher on the map.

Symmes' peculiar optimism and sublime confidence in what Congress would do with his land scheme had unfortunate results. For the first two years the little hamlet was prosperous enough as young settlements go. A large tract of land west of Wilkinson Street had been cleared by the united efforts of all the homesteaders and had bloomed into a sort of communistic garden where peas and beans and sweet corn made welcome additions to the unvarying diet of meat.

Once in awhile an itinerant preacher struggled in the mud up from Cincinnati and held Sabbath services in Newcom's Tavern. The children of the settlement were saying their A B Cs to Benjamin Van Cleve in the blockhouse. Gullies that cut across the streets had been filled up and logs laid across the roadway to keep wagons from sinking too deep into the mire. Fourteen stout cabins sheltered as many families.

All would have gone well if some of the troubles they had come to the wilderness to get rid of had not inopportunely turned up. Two years of excruciating toil looked as if it were thrown away. Two years of stump-grubbing, bear-fighting, Indian-dreading, with full measure of chills and fever, ought, it would seem, to give title to a homestead. Unfortunately the courts ruled differently; the first fruits of the mistaken business methods of Symmes became apparent.

He had agreed to pay the government sixty-six cents an acre, the subsequent purchasers eighty-three, and on this clear understanding the first settlers subscribed. Now it transpired that Congress after all would not honor the Symmes arrangement but passed a law fixing the price at two dollars an acre. Even with long payment plans this meant nothing less than bankruptcy for the early Daytonians, most of them never saw a two-dollar bill in the course of a whole year.

The discouraged citizens held many a meeting before the fire at Newcom's and gave it up as a bad job. Several families moved away. In a town of only fourteen houses it is a calamity for three or four to be abandoned.

The man who proved the best citizen (barring one, years later), that Dayton ever had, came to the rescue. He was a far-sighted, big-hearted, long-headed individual named Daniel C. Cooper. It was he who in the fall of 1795, with another surveyor named Dunlap, had come up from Cincinnati and seen the advantageous location of a region touched by three rivers.

He had made a rude lay-out of streets and went back to Cincinnati to report. Our present traffic advantages we owe to Daniel C. Cooper. Wide straight streets running at right angles with each other and with the river, fixed once for all our topography. If Cooper had not scratched his field notes on a smooth slab of wood the furious rains would have washed pencil marks away. But he preserved his rough notes and there they remain to this day externalized in our spacious thoroughfares.

This was one way in which he saved the town of Dayton. But there was more. He saw the distress and discouragement of the settlers over the land question and determined to find a way out. His own fortunes were, in a way, involved because he owned a large tract of land south of town which he hoped to dispose of profitably sometime. No growth in value unless the town grew. Most of all it was Cooper's utmost faith in Dayton as Dayton which moved him to action.

Therefore a petition from his own hand was dispatched to Congress telling them what a hard time the Dayton people were having, how faithfully they had worked and how cruel it would be to dispossess them after so good a start. We read between the lines that Cooper's personality, as well as his views, was to be respected. Then he took over on his own responsibility the title risk and bought outright from each settler his holdings until practically the whole of Dayton was his. A land office, due to his influence, was then established at Cincinnati and little by little the titles, recorded in due form, were registered proofs of ownership and everybody was at last satisfied. Thus passed the first obstacle to property rights. The later arrivals, buying of Cooper, had titles secure.

Cooper was not only just but generous. The needs of the little community were his first concern. A church the little town must have, for these plain men and women had the fear of God in their hearts; so Cooper presented two lots on the northeast corner of Third and Main for the purpose. Rallying to the work the men of the settlement united to build their church, and while the women cooked a big dinner the log walls of the church went up. It stood on the northeast corner of Third and Main and held the only congregation between Cincinnati and Detroit until later it was exchanged for a lot on the corner of Second and Ludlow, affectionately sacred for one hundred years to the uses of the old First Presbyterian Church.

A burying ground was unfortunately no less necessary than a church, and Cooper provided that, too. Older Daytonians may remember the enclosed block on Fifth Street between Ludlow and Wilkinson with wooden steps leading up and over the board fence outside and where inside sweet briar roses climbed over the sagging tombstones. He foresaw the day when buildings would crowd the business area of the town and gave a city square bounded by Third, St. Clair, and Second "to be an open walk forever," which it still is but seldom gets its proper name -- Cooper Park.

Another area bounded by First and Second, Wilkinson and Perry, was donated by him for a girls' school and Cooper Seminary remained for years (until pushed into the past by the new Westminster Church) a notable institution in Dayton. The boys must have a school and Cooper provided it on East Third facing his park. "The Academy" was the earliest school experience for many Dayton men now long in their graves. If anyone in our city history deserves a monument it would seem to be the man who laid out our streets, saved the first homes for their owners, foresaw both the material and spiritual needs of the growing community and did his best for both.

From 1796 to 1806 the growth of Dayton was slow but steady. In 1803 Ohio entered the sisterhood of states. In 1804 Montgomery County was formed (containing the area of fourteen of our present counties) and at the same time an act of Congress provided that "the temporary seat of justice shall be held at the house of George Newcom in the town of Dayton." Thus we were geographically and judicially placed at last on the map of the Northwest Territory.

The track in the woods leading south became more like a highway,

Bird's eye view of Dayton at an early date; Miami River at Dayton.

though lamentably in need of surfacing and family wagons lumbering clumsily up the trail, bearing household furniture and utensils, were a not infrequent sight. Each settler brought his worldly goods with him, piled his children on top and drove his cattle ahead. All had to come the same way whether squatter immigrants or educated and cultivated families in search of a new home.

There were both. Some were of the sturdy stock with which the great middle-west was eventually populated, "the very best (excepting the Puritans of New England) who ever migrated to America, viz; the Scotch-Irish Protestants, lovers and heroes in civil and religious liberty," as Governor Charles Anderson once characterized them to his nephew, John H. Patterson. But besides them we had patrician emigrants from the cultured precincts of New Jersey. Princeton Presbyterians lay good foundations and from them we profited mightily.

The up-coming Conestoga wagons brought other things besides homesteaders. They brought merchandise, for our business life was making a good beginning. The new Daytonians needed flour and seed corn, farming utensils and stoneware dishes, bonnet ribbons and stockings. First and Main was the business center of Dayton, having two stores kept respectively by D. C. Cooper and James Steele. Money there was none so the word "trade" was a literalism. Beeswax, lard, honey and squirrel pelts were exchanged for spools of cotton and papers of pins.

In time there came a sort of a medium of exchange in the form of skins: bear-skins, doe-skins, buck-skins and muskrat skins. They had standard values accepted by merchant and customer. A bear-skin stood for five dollars, a muskrat skin for thirty-seven and a half cents.

Traveling salesmen were unknown in those days. When a merchant wished to replenish his stock he got a stout horse warranted to ford streams well and swim them if necessary and took the long trail east over the mountains to Philadelphia. The calico and damask, the dishes and millinery which he ordered came by wagon back this way over the mountains to Pittsburgh where it was transferred to a "broadhorn" and floated down the current to Cincinnati and thence by packtrain to Dayton. There are still in secluded and sacred Dayton cupboards, handed down from the great-grandfather generation, beautiful Spode cups and lovely Royal Worcester plates which braved in safety the long journey of seven hundred miles by boat and mule back.

By the time Dayton was ten years old an amount of real commerce had been established, the future which Cooper foresaw when he platted the town at the confluence of three rivers. Cutting down huge oaks and elms to make gangway for wagon wheels is a slow way to supply people with the necessities of living. Here then, were the three rivers, the Miami, Stillwater and Mad River, each draining a different area and all offering passage for flat boats which could embark at Piqua, or any up-country settlement, and go right down to New Orleans. They did, too, many and many of them, loaded heavily, sometimes getting into difficulties due to too low water or too high water, either of which they were apt to encounter in our erratic watercourses.

It was a paying business, if we read the early letters. Our first exports were wheat, rye, tallow, corn, hides and skins. A later commodity was whiskey, when the distilleries vied in number with the flour mills along the river banks. One merchant, Thomas Morrison, a fervent temperance advocate who built his boat in the middle of Main Street in front of the Court House, and whose commercial necessities overcame his principles, records in his diary that together with the barrels of flour and packets of tobacco he included in his cargo three barrels of whiskey. "And I hope the Lord will forgive me that sin" was his closing entry.

A fleet of keelboats floating down the current towards the south always brought an interested crowd of spectators to the river bank along Monument Avenue. They were real freighters too, one described as seventy feet long carrying twelve tons of merchandise. Their departure and arrival depended entirely upon the state of water in the channel. The boats never came back to their owners, being sold with the cargo in New Orleans, the lumber in them bringing its own profit.

The arrival of boats from up stream and the departure of those bound for the south made only part of the commercial activity of early Dayton. Our imports came up the valley by pack train, sometimes numbering a dozen horses or mules, each carrying two hundred pounds of merchandise, coming gayly up Main Street jingling their bells to the shouts of the drivers. Ten days on the road, they had subsisted on game they shot as they came along. How they ever got through is a mystery which must be left to the imagination, as we are told the mud they brought along with them sometimes reached to the saddle-bags.

The very loam which the surveyors knew would raise miraculous crops made traveling in those days a hard necessity. All the old diaries and letters tell of the impassability of the roads and streets of Dayton. Neighbors had to assemble to the help of a traveler and pry his wheels out of the mire. Benjamin Van Cleve, returning on horseback from Chillicothe, where he had been a clerk in the Legislature, laid certain disabilities which remained for twenty years to torment him to that one journey with its flooded streams, frozen edges and muddy banks.

In 1805 the settlers had a new experience. Constant pouring rains continued for nearly a week. Steadily, remorselessly, the Miami rose, filled its channel and poured over the bank at the head of Main Street, destroying much property and reducing the citizens to desperate straits. Old accounts said the water at Third and Main was eight feet deep, which we refused to believe until 1913 when we did!

The real center of early Dayton was Newcom's Tavern. It might be said that it was the only civic center of social and business life for a good many miles up and down the valley. It stood originally on the southeast corner of Main and Monument whence the Historical Society moved it in 1896 to a location in Van Cleve Park. It offered entertainment for man and beast. It was a temporary schoolhouse until Van Cleve took his pupils to the blockhouse; court sat in one room, when there were cases to try before itinerant judges and there was preaching on Sundays in the same room.

The corn crib in the lot behind served several times as a jail when they caught thieving Indians and wanted to scare them into proper behavior. Before blazing logs in the big fireplace sat our civic ancestors discussing crops, a bear-hunt and the price of corn, who was down with ague and who was up, while our maternal forebears climbed over the men's legs to stir hominy or turn the spit.

The outside world was far away. The French Revolution was just over but it is doubtful if Dayton knew it or that the king and queen had lost their heads. News of any public event was weeks percolating the woods of Pennsylvania to the banks of Ohio. The most the pioneers could talk about was the latest arrival of goods for the two stores.

A great advance towards cosmopolitanism began in 1804 when a postoffice was established and the weekly mail came in from Cincinnati. Benjamin Van Cleve was the first postmaster and sorted the mail in his own livingroom. Since not the least of the sacrifices of pioneers consists in the blank silence between them and absent friends we may imagine how welcome this innovation was. Letters came from Philadelphia in a week or ten days and the postage was twenty-five cents, to be paid by the recipient.

Since the government would not accept farm produce or muskrat skins as payment, the precious missive sometimes remained in the postmaster's hands a long time before it was redeemed. Van Cleve is said to have gotten into trouble with the government because, in sympathy with his deserving but impecunious neighbors, he sometimes kept a charge account for postage.

Five stores, three taverns, one church, a dozen dwellings composed Main Street in 1807. On the cross streets other homes were being built. A weekly paper, the *Watchman*, had been established and the population, then about a thousand souls (the fall election showed the casting of one hundred and ninety-six votes) included an editor, three doctors, one schoolteacher, one minister and one lawyer.

Mr. Cooper was more than anyone else the leader in this new prosperity. Besides being surveyor, farmer and merchant he brought in new enterprises, first among them being the milling business. Up to about 1805 all the grinding of corn had been done in hand mortars, a long and laborious process. There are discrepancies in the early accounts as to whether Cooper or Robert Patterson built the first gristmill.

Family tradition inclines to the fact that it was Patterson, since the first mill was on his land. It stood on Brown Street where the Dayton, Lebanon and Cincinnati tracks came into the city and the limestone slabs of which it was built are now in the inner construction of the culvert under the road which carries the stream then known as the Rubicon down to the river.

Old timers tell us how the Rubicon gristmill became a sort of resort and picnic place for farmers bringing corn and waiting with their families for their meal to run through the stones. A grove of fine trees surrounded the mill and the stream came from the hills above to make green the banks and grind the farmer's corn. All city now, inexorable, inevitable city.

Another notable achievement of the first decade in Dayton was the establishment of the first public library. Like the china and the dressgoods, the books came in pack-saddles over the mountains, and up the river. Van Cleve, knowing evidently more about books than his fellow citizens, became custodian and kept the books in his own log house. One of his rules which must have greatly discouraged reading, because of the abundance of tallow and the scarcity of money, was that a fine of two cents must be paid for each drop of grease on a book. It is to be hoped, in the interests of budding culture in Dayton, that the librarian was as lenient as to fines as the postmaster was as to postage.

The Miami being much more of a river than it is now, ferries became a necessity: one at the head of Wilkinson, one at First and one farther down to connect with the road to the growing settlement of Germantown. A rectangular flat-boat propelled by hand-over-hand pulling on a rope fastened to trees on either bank was the arrangement. Boats large enough to support a loaded wagon and team charged seventy-five cents for the passage.

One catastrophe upon which we would certainly like to have accurate information was an earthquake which, in 1811, shook the entire valley. Since it is said to have lasted, in its gradually receding vibrations, nearly a month, there should be some official account of it, but lacking newspapers, reporters, photographers and the seismographic observatory at Washington, all that remains is the scattered comments in several personal diaries according to which it must have been terrifying and destructive.

The earthquake, the sharp June frost which killed spring vegetation, and the migration of squirrels sweeping over field after field leaving nothing in their wake, gave early Daytonians quite enough excitement to vary the ordinary monotony of their days.

Dayton was beginning to train her citizens to walk on the newly built sidewalks, they who so long had plodded in the mud. An editorial comment, very unusual in those days in which the only news seemingly worth printing was news from distant points, appeared in the *Centinel* of Cincinnati to this effect:

It is with great satisfaction that we can announce to our readers the rapid strides of population on the frontiers of the country. The banks of Mad River display at this moment hopeful appearances. But yesterday that country was a waste, the range of savages and prowling beasts; today we see stations formed, towns building and the population spreading. At the mouth of the river on the eastern side now stands the town of Dayton in which are already upwards of forty cabins and houses with the certain prospect of many more. . . . a mill will shortly be built . . . . two stores of goods will be opened there in the course of the spring. Thus we have a certain prospect of a flourishing frontier that in case of a renewal of Indian hostilities will be shield to the older and more popular settlements within the Miami Purchase.

Canny Cincinnati! Glad Dayton was growing so as to protect the "older and more popular settlements" from the Indians! And the "town on

Mad River!" How changed our point of view in a hundred and twenty years!

Immigration to the west was greatly accelerated by the opening of the Mississippi, the purchase of the Louisiana territory and the admission of Ohio to the Union. By 1805 it was estimated that no less than thirty thousand people a year were settling in Ohio, a goodly portion of them drifting toward the fertile Miami lands. More people meant more business and the figures begin to be impressive. The small news sheets beginning to appear in Dayton and Cincinnati carried such notices as this: "Subscriber will pay cash for one hundred thousand weight of good cornfed pork," "Wanted, five thousand bushels of wheat," "Whiskey and corn at market prices."

The great need was that latest product of the twentieth century -- organization, which they had not yet got to in their social economy. Among the farmers it was every man for himself. The same man who grew the corn took it himself to market. A carpenter who built furniture or door-casings, built also the boat in which to float them down the rivers to the market. The Dayton merchant bought pork and packed it, bought wheat and had it ground, had barrels made to hold both, had the boat built, loaded it and acted as skipper from here to New Orleans where he set up a retail trade until his stock was disposed of.

Flat-boats could not be floated up stream so the Dayton merchant had an eleven hundred-mile journey back to headquarters, not infrequently on foot, as one old diary tells us. Sometimes he went around by water to Philadelphia and there bought goods for the return journey, going through the same process of buying a wagon to Pittsburgh and a boat to Cincinnati and again a wagon to Dayton. McBride tells us that the round trip from Cincinnati to Pittsburgh usually consumed about three months.

It seems never to have occurred to the early farmers and merchants how much time they could have saved by some form of cooperation. It is the more strange because so much of their activities were cooperative. Together they put up each log-cabin, one set of men felling the trees, another notching the ends of the logs, another lifting them in place and thus in one day a pioneer family would be housed. Together they cultivated their truck-gardens, side by side they defended their homes against wild animals or Indians, but separately they continued for twenty years, until the canal was opened, to both raise and market their produce.

It was ruinously wasteful, of course, but the one thing that seemed never to have impressed the first Daytonians was that things might give out. Food was so plenty, wood so abundant, the water supply so unending and time, our most valued possession, so absolutely not-to-be-considered that they continued cheerfully to waste trees, top-soil, game and time with no regard whatever for their descendants.

The reason why Dayton, by the end of the first decade, was growing finely, was because her citizens were beginning to realize that in addition to the advantages noted by Cooper and Symmes there were others. Cooper had stressed the fertile soil as an inducement to settle. But the loam was only top-soil and underneath it lay a deposit of gravel, a priceless material for road-building and without which Montgomery County would never have been interlaced with turnpikes, bringing intercommunication and traffic possibilities.

For commercial purposes the gravel beds were so much pure gold. In fact gold itself would have been of far less practical value to the first dwellers in our city. Road material -- building material -- what could have been more valuable?

The soil above was composed of leaf-mold from centuries of seasons. Old letters reveal the astonishment of the pioneers as the first crops came up and were luxuriant beyond hope. They had never seen such peas and beans and corn. Assurance of untold riches lay in the first ten inches or so of the ground in the valley; below that there was untold promise for the material of their houses. Another advantage of a gravel sub-soil is the drainage it affords. Under the city at a depth of a few feet runs a constant stream of water acting as a natural filter. It gave a supply of good drinking water sufficient to Dayton needs until the population had increased to such a figure that a scientific water supply had to be established.

Log houses were good as far as they went, but the settlers, some of them from the finished sections of the east, longed for more civilized surroundings. Their first use of the gravel was for mortar and Newcom's was the first mortar-stopped house in the valley. The others were clay-daubed between the logs. The next houses, after sawmills had been built, were of board construction and the third and last were of brick. To all of these the gravel beds contributed.

But it was in road-making that the gravel proved such a blessing, which we can only faintly figure when we read letters from Daytonians in the first half of the past century describing a trip up from Cincinnati in a private or stage coach. One traveler was sick and bruised from the fatigue of being thrown from side to side of the vehicle as it pitched in and out of almost bottomless mud holes. All this was put to an end when the citizens got around to excavating the gravel and applying it to the roads.

The value of the rivers as a means of transportation has been noted but there was another more immediately advantageous in a new community; they were the only sources of power. Steam had not been invented and would have been no use to such isolated communities as the Dayton of 1806. Electricity had not been thought of. Their own stout arms and the few horses they possessed were the only available power until they had harnessed current of the lazy Miami and its tributaries and taught it to run under huge water wheels. These turned the stones to grind the corn into meal, the looms which converted their wool into yarn and the saws which made boards out of logs. Therefore, as soon as mill machinery could be brought across the mountains, mills began to appear all up and down the valley. By 1830 there were more than fifty gristmills along the Miami between Dayton and Franklin each with an annual output of over two thousand barrels of flour.

But this is ahead of our story. It is merely to illustrate that when Cooper and Symmes in placing Dayton where they did, thus foresaw clearly the future possibilities of the place, and they were wise men. The soil, the river and the woods -- Dayton's material wealth. That they did not see far enough into the future to know that the rivers would be not our precious possessions but our greatest nuisances, being of no modern use whatever either for power or transportation, that our woods would disappear and no longer count in our lives, that our soil would deteriorate under wasteful cultivation, is not to belittle their vision. It was sufficient to the needs of their generation.

Sometime later when the pioneers, literally, knew their ground better, they discovered another treasure -- limestone. It was invisible at first but one of the early settlers, Robert Edgar, found white stone sticking out of the ground on his farm south of town, probed it far enough to know it was suitable to quarry, hustled to Cincinnati on horseback (to get ahead of a neighbor who had also seen it but had no horse), bought the quarter section and came home a rich man -- in prospect.

The deposit is practically inexhaustible. For many years the quarries out on the Beavertown Pike were scenes of activity, and what came out of them went into many structures in Dayton, including the old and new courthouses, Steele High School, culverts all up and down the streams, the bridge piers to all the bridges, sidewalks (sending their blinding white glare up into the eyes on scorching July days and giving out the heat like cook-stoves all night), stone curbing and horse-blocks, the old jail (since demolished) on South Main Street and front steps to the houses.

It was also used for the arched bridge over the canal on Jefferson Street, a remarkable piece of masonry noted in its day because it was built on a slant over the bed of a canal. Now destroyed to give place to the Patterson Boulevard.

"Dayton Marble" it was called and continued to be not only our greatest domestic utility for many years but an export as well, until the invention of synthetic stone from Portland cement put a quietus on the quarries. The poorer qualities of the stone are still used in the manufacture of cement and lime.

NIAGARA ENGINE, No. 1 OF DAYTON, O.

First fire engine used in Dayton, about 1825.

The Old Courthouse, built of "Dayton Marble," amidst elms and buggies, circa 1878.

3

Weddings and Wars

In the chronicle of the childhood of our city its recreational and social life must not be lost sight of. It was not all sickness and hard work. Wherever human beings, especially young human beings are, there will be an outlet for the spirit of fun.

The first significant fact that strikes the historian is that whereas the present generation so often makes work out of play, our forebears made play out of work. There was nothing else to be done. A party for a party's sake was not to be thought of. There was no time for aimless merry-making, no strength when the day's work was done, no illumination, no clothes. And how silly to come together just to talk and eat!

But that is not saying that the young folks of those primitive years did not find opportunity to have a good time. Trust young folks for that, whenever and wherever they live. And, after all, the chances were not lacking in those first Dayton homes for jolly parties.

Every household needed quilts. The neighbors got together and made them all at once and it was a quilting bee. Corn had to be husked in the fall and a husking was a frolic. Sap-boiling in the sugar-camp drew the young people together and they made the most of it. The elders gathered for cabin-raising, road-making and bridge-building; the women had to be there to cook a big dinner, which made another chance for a jollification.

On the whole it would seem that making play out of work is more to the point than letting play, for its own ends, degenerate, as it so often does, into boresome weariness. The only occasion when people came together with no work to make a reason for it was a wedding. What more fitting than to chronicle the first wedding in Dayton?

It was when Benjamin Van Cleve brought his bride, Mary Whitten, to his home. His worldly goods consisted of a "horse creature," a wagon and saddle, a cow, a sow and pigs, two lambs and an ewe; hers were a bed which her parents had provided her and some cooking utensils. The garden on his in-lot in Dayton already contained growing corn and vegetables.

With this plenteous outfit the young people determined to begin a life together. They were, as the bridegroom said, "not rich but contented and happy." The wedding took place in the country at the bride's home, where the tables for a bounteous feast were set out of doors and to which every frontiersman came for miles around, his wife sitting behind him and holding on tight when a stream was to be forded. The officiating minister was an itinerant preacher, always an honored guest at early homes.

After the ceremony and the dinner, all the company, family, guests and preacher accompanied the young couple to their Dayton home, a log cabin on the corner of First and Jefferson. It was the cabin which later became post office and public library all in one, and it was, moreover, a center of frontier hospitality as long as the Van Cleves lived.

No one knew the conditions and advantages of the Miami Valley as did its master. Prospective settlers went there first and got all the information they needed about their intended dwelling place. This wedding occurred in 1804 when Dayton was eight years old.

Another, some years later, was that of Henry Brown and Kitty Patterson, the former a personable young soldier and merchant, most active first in the War of 1812 and afterwards in the growing commercial life of Dayton; the latter a charming and vivacious daughter of Colonel Robert Patterson who founded Lexington, Kentucky and came to Dayton in 1804.

Lexington was an older settlement and the Pattersons had lived in a luxurious stone dwelling, but Dayton was the frontier and things were different. Here they had a large log house with three spacious rooms below and four chambers above, a porch in front facing the river half a mile away. Main Street had not been extended to make what is now the Cincinnati Pike. It was Brown Street, then known as "the big road" which formed the connection. West of that, in the declivity following the windings of the river below the Bluffs, and probably the bed of the canal built later, was "the Miami Road." Here, where it curved from west to north stood the house Robert Patterson had prepared for his family.

More shall be written of him later, our concern now being the weddings that the new home saw. First there was to have been the silver wedding of Robert and Elizabeth Patterson, prevented by a flood which covered the roads and kept more distant guests away.

Then two weddings when the older sisters were married; and at last Catherine met her fate in the person of Henry Brown and became engaged to him in 1810. He was described as being:

Straight as an Indian, of robust build, dark long hair, full beard, a man of quiet and dignified bearing. His business kept him much in the saddle and for comfort and convenience he wore "short Clothes," that is, hunting shirt or jacket buttoned to the chin, knee-breeches and buckles, cap, stockings, and moccasins. For Sunday, or when he courted Catherine, he wore an open jacket or cloth coat, doe-skin vest, ruffled shirt, high collar and stock, brass buttons on coat and vest, buckles to fasten breeches and stockings at the knee, buckles on his shoes and beaver hat. This was the prevailing style of dress for busy men of that day.

Both families being so numerous and widely known, the wedding festivities lasted three days: one day for the guests to assemble from Kentucky, from up the rivers and from Cincinnati; one day for the ceremony and the banquet (set out in the open with the blacks to wait upon them); and one day for the infaring of the young couple in their new home.

The bride, we are told, wore a Quaker gray silk, very becoming to her fair beauty and which had been purchased in Cincinnati. Side by side, with the wedding guests following, they rode to the home on Main Street where they were to live so happily. The young men had prepared a big bonfire in the middle of the street to add to the welcome, but Henry Brown, suspicious of ultimate happenings, generously provided the crowd with a barrel of very, very hard cider. It was soon disposed of and the young couple left in peace.

The Brown home was notable because it was the only brick house in Dayton at the time and for years a landmark. Standing just north of the courthouse on the corner of the alley leading to Ludlow Street, it lifted, for many years a broad gable towards the south on which was inscribed the date of erection, 1808.

Later the house was reconstructed for business purposes and occupied by the *Journal* office; still later it was demolished to make way for a three story block built on the site; lastly the site was occupied by the Union Trust Building.

The Brown home must have been a startling innovation and improvement, if we may take the word of other writers describing the homes in that distant day. They were frankly utilitarian, with lean-to kitchens, a well-sweep, a brick oven, the wood-pile and sometimes even a pig-pen in full view; there was no undue hesitancy about hanging the family wash boiler on a hook outside the kitchen door. We read that most families still had their private vat in the back lot for the curing of skins with tanbark for leather. Even Henry Brown saw to it that there was a well-filled smoke-house for his bride to begin housekeeping with.

Now Daytonians began to imitate eastern fashions as they percolated over the Alleghenies and affected flower gardens behind neat paling fences and porches surrounded with what they called "pinies and laylocks." They painted their houses white and their shutters green, and laid flat limestone flags around to the back door.

DAYTON, OHIO! What an important place it was to those who lived there! And yet the majority of the people in the sparse and scattered United States had never heard of it. Now, if you mention the name to an inhabitant of Tuscany or Bavaria he is likely to reply "Yes, that is where the Wright brothers come from."

It is a pity that this story of our parent city cannot be confined to weddings and quilting bees, a pity, too, that a community having wrung their homes at such a cost from the wilderness should not have been allowed to remain at peace to enjoy them. Freedom from Indian raids and British harassment was thought to have been guaranteed by the Treaty of Greenville.

For fifteen years the Dayton settlers possessed their souls and their land in serenity and quiet. Then rumors, vague but disquieting, began to circulate through the medium of travelling merchants coming from those far off portions of the state near the Canadian border, rumors to the effect that the Indians were not keeping to the terms of the treaty but breaking them wherever possible, being incited thereto by the British, who furnished them arms and ammunition. Not much inciting was necessary since the Indians were making the fight for their very existence and the defeat by Wayne still rankled in their hearts.

Dayton people gathered at Henry Brown's store to hear the latest news which, when it came, was neither new nor authentic. All doubt, however, was at an end when the *Centinel* printed an order for the First Division of the Ohio Militia to meet in Dayton on the "usual parade ground" (a wide common east of Cooper Park on Third Street), "armed and equipped as the law requires."

This was the opening of the War of 1812, an old story and often written -- a tragic and sorrowful story. Can our imaginations picture it? How twenty companies (fourteen hundred men in all) were suddenly quartered on a village of half that number; how, lacking accommodations, they slept in the rain on the ground without blankets; how the Governor of the State begged for covering and how the women responded by depriving their own families; how many took pneumonia and went home, or farther; how this ignorant, untrained, ill-furnished army was put under command of General William Hull who turned out to be a coward and a traitor; how at last they marched up the Troy Pike and disappeared into the distance.

Every school-boy knows the sequel. That army which was to protect the homes of Southern Ohio, numbering all told twenty-five hundred men, together with horses and ammunition, was surrendered to the enemy of less than half their number without striking a blow. This was the news brought to Dayton, after many weeks, by a weary muddy horseman describing the terrible fate of the army that had so proudly marched away ten weeks before.

Imagine, if you can, the situation in Dayton. Every man of conscription age had gone to the war; only those over age or younger were left. It was the same in every settlement up and down the valley. The countryside was depleted of its workers, its fighters, its horses and supplies. Yet here was the necessity for all three once more upon them. It was Saturday noon when the sad word arrived. But did they sit down and mourn over it? Not at all. That is one thing that in her history Daytonians never do. If the work was all to be done over again they were there to do it.

No one slept that Saturday night. They were busy getting the word by mounted messengers to every little hamlet on every road leading out of Dayton, sounding the call for more men, more horses, more arms (anything would do from a horse pistol to a pitchfork), more supplies. Will it be believed that by ten o'clock Sunday morning (the only occasion recorded when the church was not open) seventy men marched grimly out the same road on the same errand that Hull's army had gone so many weeks before.

No time was to be lost. Other companies kept coming in from outside points, all taking the same direction north. In all this excitement and preparation there was one strong element of hope. It was "no old woman, thank God," as one pioneer put it, who commanded the new army of defense, but General William Henry Harrison.

The enthusiasm for him and his command ran high when the troops from Kentucky and Ohio marched in review past him in front of the court-house. Public confidence was not misplaced, for all that Hull failed to do Harrison did. Straight to Fort Wayne he marched with the enemy disappearing before him in a panic. After some days came the battle of Missisin-ewa resulting in a deadly defeat for the enemy and a costly victory for our forces. As usual in war it was the victors who were as badly off as the vanquished. Nevertheless the campaign ended finally in the surrender of Detroit and that broke the back of the war once for all.

Hull's surrender was reported on August 22d; it was on September 12th when Harrison's army went to the rescue and late in November when the limping relic, two hundred wounded, starved, shivering and frost-bitten soldiers out of seven hundred came slowly down the pike at three miles an hour, the wagons bearing the wounded dripping with blood which froze into icicles.

Here again was work for willing Dayton and in which we know the women had as large a part as the men. A tent hospital on the grounds of the courthouse was improvised by Dr. Steele and there the sufferers were cared for until they were ready to go out again into life or down the muddy road to the Fifth Street graveyard.

This is only the story of the War of 1812 as it affected Dayton. The rest of it is in the school text-books and belongs to the history of the United States. In it you will read of the Battle of the Thames on September 5th, 1813, when Tecumseh, the great Indian chief was killed; Perry's glorious victory on Lake Erie which was the final stroke in our favor. In December, 1814, a treaty of peace between the United States and Great Britain was signed at Ghent, since then for over a century there has been peace on the Canadian border.

Other things besides weddings and wars were going on in the Miami Valley in its second decade. We find accounts in the newspapers of meetings held in Dayton and Franklin relative to the unsatisfactory condition of the river. It seems that fish and flour were both interrupting commerce; that is, the dams built to turn the current into the mills and the nets stretched from bank to bank to catch the fish, were proving obstacles to the passage of boats which could not wait for the proper stage of water. All this was done by private individuals for the sake of personal gain. One indignant correspondent wanted to know if a man would be allowed to fence off a part of the public highway for his own uses and if the Miami was not a highway what was it? All of which sounds strange to our modern ears.

But they were in deadly earnest about it and, although the papers of that day never proceeded to record the progress of a public enterprise, we may assume that the Navigation Board, which was appointed, did get to work and do something about obstructions in the river, because a new line of keel-boats was replacing the flat-boats. Nothing more is needed to prove the difference between the Miami of 1820 and the Miami of 1920. For keel-boats draw much more deeply than barges and in our day the channel which then accommodated boats fifty to seventy feet long will now hardly float a skiff. It suggests the idea that what we call high-water was then the normal stage and our normal stage was their low water.

It was presently discovered that some difficulties in Miami navigation could not be settled by committees. The man-made obstructions were, perforce, removed and the channel dredged of accumulated mud and gravel, but the next freshet undid the work and left things as bad as before. In short, each spring and fall brought new problems to the boatmen, there were always new channels to navigate.

Those whose imaginations refuse to think of the Miami River as a navigable stream should read the *Dayton Watchman* with its account of the third week in March, 1815. For weeks there had been a drought. The downgoing boats settled hopelessly in the mud on the bottom of the river at the head of Wilkinson Street where stood big warehouses, packed to the roof with merchandise waiting to be moved.

More boats from up river edged gingerly down past shallows and riffles and could go no further. There, tied up along the bank in discouraged idleness, lay thirty freighters of all sizes and shippers began to wonder if they would ever see profits on cargoes they had so laboriously collected. Practically all of the commerce in Southeastern Ohio lay bogged in that basin.

Then it began to rain. Rain that raises the river has not always been welcomed by Daytonians, but this time it was. As it continued to rain their spirits rose as well as the river. The big hulls began to lighten and lift themselves under the buoyant power of the current and the populace also began to move. Word that "the boats are moving" brought all of Dayton to the river bank.

Boatmen, storekeepers, millers, distillers, farmers, teamsters, school boys, mothers and babies all had a more or less personal interest in the hegira. Some boats held four hundred barrels of flour, forty-four of whiskey and a thousand pounds of bacon. The total value of cargoes in that fleet of boats was estimated at not less than one hundred thousand dollars.

Such activity with wheelbarrows, laden mules and wagons, everybody of proper size helped in the loading of the boats. And as one by one the hulls swung out where the current could catch them a shout went up from the bank, and not until the last one had turned the corner of the river where the Dayton View bridge now is did the crowd go home to prosaic occupations.

Some of these boats came to grief on sand bars and dumped flour into the water, but most of them got to their destination in safety. One editor in commenting on the losses by the foundering of loaded boats said that in ten years they would pay the cost of one-sixth of the length of a canal from Mad River to the Ohio River, a revolutionary sentiment but it deserves notice because such was beginning to be whispered here and there by firesides and in taverns all through the area.

The first word was *canal* and the second was *steamboat*. Both were hailed with the same hospitality that the word *airplane* was in the year 1900. Those who made a point of discussing either were held to be the wildest visionaries. The Lord made rivers to be used as waterways; the founders of Dayton had put the city there because of it. Why say more?

But the two words continued to be discussed, the former with more pertinacity as time went on and the latter quite uselessly because the Miami River never saw a steamboat. The canal idea stuck. Its implications were what carried the day, water at the same stage everywhere and at all seasons.

Another idea called visionary by the obstructionists of the day was a weekly passenger and mail service between Cincinnati and Dayton. How was it possible to make such an enterprise pay with the few people that would ever want to be going to Cincinnati in a week? But ideas are tough things and sustain any amount of adverse discussion.

The roads were still bad but improving, as they always do under the inevitable demands of wheeled vehicles. When passengers were exasperated to the proper pitch by the number of ribs they sacrificed to the jolting on the trip up from Cincinnati the beginnings of the Dixie Highway were laid and as usual it was a Van Cleve (John, son of Benjamin) who started the enterprise.

When enough passengers got wet crossing fords they demanded more and better bridges. In 1818 the first weekly coach service was started between Dayton, Franklin, Middletown and Hamilton and in 1819 the first bridge was built over the river at Stratford Avenue and Salem Avenue. The roads were toll roads and the bridges were toll bridges. Tollhouses stood at equal distances which protected against violators of the law by leaning poles like a well-sweep across the road which the toll keeper could lower and raise at will.

The writer, as a girl, penniless as to small change but mounted on an agile pony, has been known to edge around the far end of the pole and escape before the toll-keeper got up from his breakfast table to sound his maledictions at the vanishing horsewoman. Three cents was not much for the privilege of riding under the pole but paying it was not exciting. Twelve cents was the price for a loaded wagon, six for an empty, the proceeds being used to keep up the roads. The tollgates lasted to sometime in the '70s.

On Third Street in front of the courthouse (which in 1818 was a two story building flush with the sidewalk) was the starting and arriving place for the Cincinnati stages. Twelve persons could be accommodated in each vehicle; three on the back seat, three on the front, three on smaller seats between the two and two beside the driver. At first there were no springs, later these were supplied. Eight cents a mile was the fare and fourteen pounds the allowance per person for baggage. The Cincinnati coach left Dayton at five o'clock Friday morning and arrived at its destination late on Saturday evening, Friday night being spent at Hamilton.

With such innovations as these, and the weekly example of what could be done in the way of rapid transit, the canal project was reopened. Or rather it came to the surface, for in the minds of some prominent men like Robert Patterson, James Steele and Henry Bacon it had never been absent. The two latter men were merchants and to get their goods out from the East with the least delay and danger of disaster was a prime requisite. They talked of it after business hours in the store and at their homes (log houses on First Street), but being wise men they forebore to risk their reputation for common sense in the community and so got somebody from the outside to propel the new project.

At a Fourth of July dinner at four o'clock in the afternoon in the backyard of the courthouse, one of the speakers was named Stephen Fales, not a Daytonian, and his subject was "The Contemplated Canal from the

A lock in the canal south of Dayton.

Jefferson Street canal bridge, graceful as it was utilitarian. (Photos by Dr. H. S. Jewett.)

Waters of Mad River to those of the Ohio." The fact that the canal was to connect Mad River with Cincinnati was proof that they still held to Mad River as the geographical reason for Dayton's existence and that it still accommodated freight boats of one kind or another.

On June 29, 1821 a meeting was called at Reid's tavern to appoint a committee to act with other committees of the contiguous country for the purpose of raising funds to pay for a survey for such a route. The committee consisted of H. G. Phillips, G. W. Smith, James Steele, Alexander Grimes, and J. H. Crane, chairman.

Events were working for them in other sections of the country. The Miami Erie Canal had been partly completed and Governor De Witt Clinton of New York State, the great canal promoter of that time, was to come out to Newark and dedicate it.

This was a chance for Dayton and they took it. James Steele and Henry Bacon rode up through the woods to Newark to invite the Governor to come to Dayton and "boost" the canal idea. But the early Daytonians never used slang, much less in connection with so important a person as the Governor of New York. Most dignified and punctilious were they in their long-tailed coats and beaver hats.

The Governor was duly invited to a dinner in Dayton and he came. A detachment of horse, with the canal promoters at their head, went as far as Fairfield to meet and escort him to the city. This time the dinner was at Compton's Tavern on Second Street. His speech must have been effective for it started others to discussing the canal.

One speaker had a lovely plan for the canal to go down the middle of Main Street, a forty-foot wide waterway with a wagon road thirty-four feet wide on either side and twelve-foot sidewalks. The *Watchman* said editorially in the next issue, this would make Main Street the handsomest thoroughfare in the State of Ohio. The earth taken from the excavation, it was explained, would fill every hole and level every street in town.

We all know that plan fell of its own weight, but the canal continued to fill the public mind. A law passed by the Legislature in 1825 authorizing the canal was the first step and from then on progress was steady. The contract was given that same year and 1829 saw its completion at a total cost of $567,000. At one time a steam canal boat was given a trial but its waves washed the bank away and it had to be abandoned.

One can but weakly visualize what the canal was to Dayton. It put Dayton definitely at the head of navigation, since wagons coming down the valley could shift their cargo to a boat and send it straight to Cincinnati. The canal basin on Second Street was a crowded and busy place, the banks piled with merchandise as the river bank used to be. The last keel-boat went down the river sometime in 1828, and the warehouse being carried away by the flood, the new center of commerce became definitely the canal bank.

No sooner was the route open than traffic became at once heavy, speaking not satirically but actually, for we read that in the month of April, 1829, seventy-one boats arrived at the Dayton wharf and seventy-seven departed. For a little city of only two hundred and thirty-five dwellings and three churches this was indeed "big business."

Naturally, it was not long before passenger service followed the freight. It became both a pleasure and a practical necessity to travel by canal. The company built big boats glistening with white paint with seats and awnings on deck and luxurious bunks within. Silk curtains hung at the windows and a long table filled the middle of the saloon, for passengers had to eat five meals between Dayton and Cincinnati.

Often a Negro fiddler accompanied the crew and dances were held in the evenings on the broad smooth deck. When a boat thus planned came up to the basin at Second Street, what wonder that the town came out to watch it tie up! Old men who were boys then told boys who are old men now how gay it was and how thrilling to see the horses, gayly harnessed with ribbons and bells, draw the boat up to the wharf.

Let not the present day citizen smile at the transportation achievements of our ancestors. They had really done a big thing. They had linked up the northern part of the state with the southern on the western side. And what odds they worked against we can but dimly guess. In 1825 the population of Ohio was barely 700,000, the tax duplicate for the whole state was $58,000,000, the per capita tax $83. That is, the wealth of the whole state then was less than the wealth of a single county now.

The population was sparse and the citizens all poor. Comparatively few people travelled and comparatively few food products were carried to markets. But these men of vision and action undertook an enterprise of which the estimated cost was two and a half million dollars. In fact they spent a million dollars a year for sixteen years on what was the greatest developing agency in Western Ohio. And the irony of it was that on the day the canal was finished it was obsolete. Railroad talk was in the air and in 1825, railroad and canal talk was like aviation talk today.

4

Railroads, Markets and Other Things

Practical men in the Dayton of that day saw even farther than the stage coach and the canal boat. That they met opposition goes without saying and from the same sources which had opposed the canal. Lack of imagination is, as Emerson calls it, "a mortal distemper."

The inevitable objection was that there never would be enough people going in any direction to justify the amazing expenditures involved by these innovations. But the argument was fast losing its force, for increase of population was the first result of the canal and the stage coach. But the people who can't see ahead, can't see what is going on right under their eyes, so this juxtaposition of cause and effect was slow in getting accepted.

A notice in a July issue of the *Journal* of 1831 invites the public to inspect a sample railroad which had been installed in a large warehouse on East Third Street. A circular track of wooden rails had been laid out around the inside of the building carrying a small car and a locomotive. "It will be," says the paper, "a rich treat to the friends of national and State improvement. The locomotive works with great celerity and precision, drawing a splendid miniature car in which two persons may ride at the same time. Ladies and gentlemen" (there seem to have been no men and women in those days) "are respectfully invited to call and ride. Price twenty-five cents. Children half price."

The railroad in Dayton in 1831 was therefore not yet a utility but a mere curiosity. However, things were certainly moving. In 1821 they had been paying a bounty for wolf scalps; in 1831 they were paying twenty-five cents to ride around behind a steam locomotive on a track in a big shed. If that is not progress, what is?

However, the application of the new invention to practical needs moved slowly, in fact so slowly that Xenia got ahead of us. A road begun at Sandusky had ended, for want of funds, at Springfield, which was Dayton's great chance if she could but see it. Meetings were held and speeches made by far-sighted residents like Daniel Beckel, T. J. S. Smith and others, urging the citizens to complete the road and belong to the great outside world but there was little money and no enthusiasm. Cincinnati seemed to have both, at least enough of both to reach as far as Xenia with a railroad, which she promptly did.

Then Xenia woke up, connected the two ends of the line, and lo! the north of Ohio and the south met and Dayton was left out in the cold. Much fun was poked in private letters and public print at the "Granny Rip Van Winkles" who did not know a good thing when they saw it. The sting remained for many years as Daytonians had to drive over to Xenia to take the Pennsylvania to New York.

Either the sarcasm or the economic needs of the Miami Valley at last triumphed and in the end, 1849, we connected with a line of our own to Springfield and within a year five railroads were coming into Dayton: the Miami and Lake Erie, the Dayton and Western, the Cincinnati, Hamilton and Dayton, the Greenville and Miami and the Dayton and Union. At last Dayton was a railroad center.

The first station was merely a brick building at the north side of the tracks at Sixth and Jefferson streets where the trains stopped to let passengers off and on. Sometimes in the early '50s a real station, or depot as it was called, was constructed on Sixth Street west of Ludlow. According to the testimony of a citizen who saw it in the building, the depot was a long brick shed astride the tracks with three open arches for the trains to enter under a barrel-shaped roof.

Each of these openings had a heavy wooden door with large hinges. The Dayton of that day was strictly Sabbatarian and the railroads had to follow suit. Therefore no Sunday trains; every Saturday night the doors were closed and padlocked until Monday morning. At first the passengers, in order to mount, clambered up from the ground to the steps leading into the cars; later a raised platform on the south side with ticket office and baggage room was a welcome addition.

The three arches were at some later day transformed into one large arch. This archway, with smaller blind ones at one side, a row of busses and a pump outside, constituted the old Union Depot, which for us in the '70s and '80s marked the beginning and the end of all our trips away from home. With the lack of imagination and foresight already noted, the city authorities arranged the approaches to the depot on the south side of the building, away from town, so that departing and arriving guests had always to cross the tracks to get anywhere.

The following incident reported by William F. Scott, an early resident of Dayton, but absent for a long lifetime after leaving in 1856, will serve to illustrate conditions in the Dayton of that day:

One day, on leaving the Rogers school (1852 or 1851) I heard much noise and saw a crowd gathering at a point just south of the tracks and midway between the station and Ludlow street. The crowd surrounded a man who was crying and shrieking. He had been struck by a car when crossing the tracks and had one leg cut off at the ankle, a horror to see. He was well dressed, probably not an employe of the road but there as a passenger or on other business. There could not have been a doctor there or sent for because they were putting him on a dray, a two-wheel, one-horse, low platform cart with a long skid tail and no springs. He was sitting up when I last saw him on the rear end; two or three men got on and sat or stood so as to support him. The only pavement then was gravel macadam and I can still hear the piercing shrieks as the dray got into motion.

Now where was the dray going? To a surgeon? To a hospital? Was there a hospital? If there was had it no ambulance or surgeon for emergencies? True there was at that time no way to reach a hospital except by a messenger afoot or on horseback so perhaps the dray may have been the quickest way after all. But Lord! What a situation!

It ought not need a story like this to remind us to be thankful for our modern appliances to help the sick and suddenly hurt. The correspondent who sent in this story should see what would happen on South Ludlow Street today if there was such an accident. Within not more than five minutes a sounding gong down the street would herald the approach of the police ambulance. Traffic would give way to it; the officer in charge would administer first aid to stop the pain and in another five or ten minutes the sufferer would be between the sheets of a comfortable bed in the hospital with all the advantages of modern surgery at his disposal.

East side of Main Street looking north from Third to Second in 1850 (above); Main Street bridge, built in 1839, in flood of 1866.

From railroads it is not such a long jump to markets, which properly to consider we must go back in our story. The first Daytonians did not need a market because each family was, in a way, self-supporting. Each had its own vegetable plot, it shot its own game or butchered its own pigs, cured its own hams, raised its own chickens and made its own maple sugar. But the growth of the town gradually changed these primitive conditions and made necessary a public place where supplies might be purchased.

The first market, opened as a part of the Fourth of July festivities of 1815, was a long wooden building on Second Street between Main and Jefferson, with butcher stalls inside and stalls for garden produce outside under the wide projecting eaves.

Market was held two days in the week, on Wednesday and on Saturday, from four to ten a. m., not ten to four. Those were too late hours for thrifty housekeepers. Butchered meats would not keep many hours and they wanted their steaks and chops fresh. And it was the men of the family in those days who went to market. They could be seen coming down First and Second streets at five o'clock in the morning wearing silk top hats and carrying the family basket.

If the chronology of the narrative be here criticized, it will be explained that to the first market in 1815 the customers probably wore leggings and coon-caps like Henry Brown, but to the later market in the '30s and '40s he certainly wore a silk hat. Witness old cuts and old letters.

What could he buy, this gentleman in correct afternoon dress at five o'clock in the morning? And what did he pay? Well, if word had come that friends were driving up from Cincinnati (and in those days they thought nothing of coming down suddenly on their relatives or friends, six to ten at a time) he could get a pair of venison hams for fifty cents or a turkey for the same. An old poem in the *Piqua Register* says:

> *A good half dollar still a turkey buys*
> *Though (clip their wings!) 'tis said that fowls will rise.*

Which shows that market prices were practically equal up and down the valley. He could get beef at three cents a pound, butter at twelve and a half cents, eggs eight cents a dozen, and chickens (undressed) seventy-five cents a dozen. Profuse and redundant plenty, that's what it was in the Dayton of those early days. No taxes, no poor land, no middlemen, no freight rates. Flour two dollars and seventy-five cents a barrel, pork one fifty to two a hundred weight, wheat forty-five cents a bushel, who so lazy or inefficient that he could not live at that rate?

Another market (when the Second Street lot got too valuable) was built on Sears and Webster streets on ground donated by Cooper; later it was installed on Main Street below Third. This was held to be a fatal business move, for Dayton already had its caste prejudices. North of Third Street was where "the best people" lived; south of Third Street did not count at all. It was called "Cabintown" and held in deep disesteem.

In spite of opposition, part of which had to do with local partisan politics, the market was moved bodily down Main Street to its new location, bearing a sign which read: *Bound for Cabintown.* The new location was boycotted for a time. We suspect that roasting ears and watermelons had in time something to do with the decision to accept the City Hall Market without reservations. Dayton markets have always been good, whether held in a shed on Second Street or in a palatial "Arcade" under a glass roof. What the proverbial warmth and hospitality of Dayton homes has to do with it and which is cause and which effect must be left to the reader.

An era of picturesque interest was initiated when the first fire companies were organized and the first fire engines installed. Both were sorely needed, Dayton having suffered great and serious losses from fire.

It was in 1824 when, owing to a disastrous fire on Main Street with the loss of two thousand dollars worth of goods, a fire engine costing two hundred and twenty-six dollars was ordered from Philadelphia. Not a steam engine, be it understood. It was fifteen years earlier than the first locomotive and enterprise of that day could see no farther than a handworked pump.

It might have been an improvement on trying to put out a burning building by throwing water on it by single individuals, but there were drawbacks. There was a large reservoir which had to be filled from buckets at the public pump. It was provided with long handles on each side which, when worked up and down by men and boys, threw a considerable jet of water on the fire. But it took some time to fill it, especially if to prevent freezing, the tank had been put away empty from the last fire.

Fire companies were formed and every man or boy in town belonged to one or another of them. In the night one was apt to be called out of a warm bed to fight a fire and the only thing that brought patience was the thought that the next fire might be nearer home, in which case favors might be returned. The old "Safety" engine gave way to another one of the same type before steam engines came in. Called a double-decker because of its two sets of handles, with twenty men on a side, it threw quite a considerable stream of water.

It was in 1863 that the first steam engine was purchased and with it came to an end the volunteer fire companies. Abuses of an astonishing kind had crept in, such as rival companies which in their ambition to be first at a fire actually placed obstructions in the way of their opponents. Sometimes, to maintain supremacy they got into a free-for-all fight, so that in time Daytonians dreaded a fire more for the fire department than for the fire itself. But the old system before its decadence had its excitement and its charm. The very best citizens in the town belonged to it and, when old men, would tell their children of their prowess in "running with the engine." As late as 1880 the fire department consisted of part paid members and part, what were known as "call men." Not until nearly 1890 did we have an expert fire department on a full pay basis.

It is interesting to try to picture the Dayton of those early years; the stages arriving and leaving on Third Street, the canal boats filling the basin and discharging their loads, passengers climbing aboard the cars on wooden rails at the old depot; housekeepers filling their baskets at the City Hall Market, mud in the streets, doctors driving around in their buggies to see patients miles distant, deep gutters at the side of the roadway and wooden bridges crossing them, two or three vehicles to a block the excess of traffic on Main Street, the bell of the old First Church or the Wesley Chapel calling people to service, Keifer and Conover selling prints and bonnets on the corner of Third and Main and offering customers a drink of whiskey out of the free jug on the counter, camp-meetings on the river bank, parties on the canal boats, high school graduation ceremonies over across the river in Steele's woods, the girl graduates walking in a procession wearing white sunbonnets, all this we can but guess at from the stories and reminiscences of the old people who have long ago been laid away in Woodland Cemetery.

Woodland Cemetery! That reminds us of John Van Cleve and again of Robert Steele, to both of whom we owe that lovely dwelling-place of the dead on the hill above Dayton. Business and homes had surrounded the old graveyard on Fifth Street whose space became too restricted for future interments. The green hills lifting their heights above the city to the south appealed to Van Cleve as the place he would like to be laid when he was gone and his opinion was shared by others who together purchased, surveyed and planted what we now know as Woodland Cemetery. No other city cemetery in this part of the Middle West has a more beautiful situation.

In the early '30s the waves of the trouble that brought on the Civil War began to touch Dayton. We were not so far from the Southern border and as a consequence fugitive slaves were able to reach our city.

A cut, kept regularly in the newspaper offices and used for advertising purposes, testified to the frequency of such occurrences. It pictured a Negro with a bundle under his arm and the inscription, "Fifty Dollars Reward," etc. People get used to anything, so not much attention was paid to these occasional notices.

No man in Dayton would willingly give back into custody a Negro fleeing for freedom even to gain the sum of fifty dollars. To disregard it was, of course, to break the Fugitive Slave law but men did break it over and over again.

The most notable example was Dr. Adam Jewett's residence on Jefferson Street, an "underground station," i. e. a place either in the cellar or the barn where a runaway slave could find food and shelter on his way to Canada. If the poor fugitive could get far enough away to the north it did not pay to have him arrested and sent back. Those who thought the slave law was a pernicious law gave all the help and comfort they could to the runaways and settled with their consciences the best they could.

Things were brought to a crisis sometime in the summer of 1832 when Federal officers came into town and arrested a quiet inoffensive colored man, known as "Black Ben," and took him to Cincinnati in order to return him to his southern owner. An effort was made to buy the Negro and keep him where his faithful work had made him many friends, but the offer was refused.

Knowing what was inevitably in store for him when he got back, Ben eluded the officers in the night, leaped from a high building and was killed. What that self-inflicted martyrdom did for the cause of abolition can only be guessed. It certainly struck fire in Dayton. Soap-box orators on the street, fervent preachers in the pulpits, all awoke their hearers to the iniquity of one man owning another.

The slumbering question of human rights grew to large proportion in that time of agitation. Not long after the notice of the arrest and death of

Black Ben appeared in the *Journal*, the announcement was carried of the first meeting of the Dayton Abolition Society. Luther Bruen was the president and the members met at the home of Peter P. Lowe on South Main Street right where customers who have forgotten what anti-slavery agitation was about, or never knew, go to drink soda water at Elder and Johnston's lunch counter.

From 1830 to 1845 a renewal of business activity and civic advance was shown in Dayton. The bend in the river from west to north making an elbow suggested the advantage of a mill race.

Steele's dam was constructed north of town, a part of the current deflected from the main channel and made to flow across what is now Riverdale to unite with the main stream a half mile further down. It made a not unattractive tree-bordered stream and gave power to several mills, most notable among them being Tate's Mill on what is now Riverview Avenue and Forest. All remains of the old mill have long ago disappeared but in its day it was a great productive center.

Stillwell and Bierce's knife factory also took advantage of the water power and for a while it looked as if that part of suburban Dayton was to be given over to factories and mills. This did happen in another place when the hydraulic was taken out of Mad River on the Springfield Road and turned through the center of Dayton to unite with the Miami below the fair grounds.

Mills -- flour mills, paper mills, woolen mills -- followed its route, making that central part of Dayton permanently a manufacturing locality. But as the steam engine replaced water power, the mill-race was converted into a boulevard, the gabled mill and the ugly factory gave way to McKinley Park with its contiguous apartment houses and its planted masses of foliage and that part of Dayton was saved to beauty.

Cooper it was who, with his usual generosity, gave the land for the hydraulic, and it is interesting to discover in his mind a combined sense of beauty and practical needs. It was he who, when the troops were quartered in Dayton in 1812, set the young recruits to building the levee. His plan was a rare combination of moral and physical prophylactics.

The river menaced the town at every freshet; the soldier boys were on the dangerous ground where forced idleness makes surely for mischief. It does not appear what authority Cooper had for the measure but he put every homesick and idle recruit to digging. In time an embankment made

The levee built by Daniel C. Cooper, trees courtesy of John Van Cleve, as it once looked.

its way down the river edge from the head of Main Street, where the rising ground made a natural protection, across the end of Monument Avenue (then Water Street) where the river turns across the ends of First, Second, Third, Fourth and Fifth streets, covering the part of town needing security.

Whether Cooper had any legal right or not, this was a fine fore-sighted, public-spirited thing to do. Other men saw the possibilities of the levee as a public park. Van Cleve planted elms and maples throughout its length and, under the spreading trees with the river flowing lazily (or fero-ciously, according to the season), at its foot it became the favored walk of Daytonians.

Adult persons there are in Dayton today who, as they read refer-ences to the Levee ask: "Where was it, anyway?" Their ignorance is not inexcusable for the topography of that part of the city has greatly changed. For their information it must be explained that what is now known as Rob-ert Boulevard, the winding parkway, was originally the levee now levelled down to the adjacent territory. (Ed. Note: Robert Boulevard in turn was replaced by I-75 which did little to enhance the site's natural beauty.)

The remaining plot laid out in building lots and sold for residences belongs to another part of this history. The Levee itself became the prettiest and the longest pleasure walk anywhere around. One could always meet one's friend there on pleasant sunny afternoons. To this rule one exception held. Dayton was aggressively Sabbatarian in the old days.

The Levee was a pleasure place since no one could possibly have anything useful in view while walking there. Pleasures of any kind were wrong on Sunday, therefore the Levee was a place to be avoided by good church members. One little boy in the '50s, William Scott, committed a double sin: he walked on the Levee after Sunday school and while thus engaged he whistled. To whistle on Sunday was bad enough, but to walk on the Levee and whistle was to make him an early candidate for hell and he was so advised by an elderly friend of the family who met him while engaged in these pernicious occupations.

This lands us straight in the middle of the question of religion, or what passed as such in the earlier part of the last century.

A highly to-be-praised sentiment of loyalty to fine ideals of living, strict probity of conduct, fealty to the Ten Commandments, definite stan-dards of law and order and personal rectitude that as a leaven would be highly appreciated by the best of us in these modern days. The men who by hard work dug this city out of the wilderness and built its foundations had their fundamentals in the old Puritan times and manners. They had no compromises with what they called "sin." As might have been expected, and as fanatics always do, they carried it too far. Like the elder who reproved the little boy for whistling on Sunday they were against pleasure of any kind. If a thing was beautiful or pleasurable, and had no other meaning, it was to be avoided at all costs.

It is an astonishing thing to realize how much the minds of our early citizens were occupied with religion. Rather, may it be explained, with a kind of barren self-centered theology which made the safety of one's own soul take the place of public service for other people's needs.

The sources of information to an historian are mainly two: old letters and old newspapers. Of both in Dayton we have been bereft by the flood. Those files of old news sheets still remaining in the Public Library are difficult to decipher in spite of the nothing-less-than-heroic efforts of the staff of librarians after the ravages of the flood of 1913. But when we have laboriously examined the pages, brown with dried mud, we find little to reward us. Local news seemed in those days not to be of interest. Instead of a view of the small town which we would love to have reproduced we read indefinite European news, advertisements of strayed or stolen hogs and a silly continued sort of sub-novel or a sermon.

The same thing with family letters. Here at least we should find a picture of domestic life in the early '30s, accounts of daily happenings as recounted by, perhaps, a mother to a daughter or a father to a son. Something to help us reconstruct the life of that distant day. Letters were letters too in those days and we marvel that, with the difficulty of the mechanical part of it, they should have so diligently persisted through three closely written sheets of foolscap paper. The fourth side was the one that carried sealing wax, stamp and the address, being folded so as to carry in the mails. (Envelopes were a long time coming in.)

These crowded pages should tell us of family affairs, of family happenings, of the price of food stuffs, etc. But they seldom do. Most of them, from the formal greeting, "Beloved Mother," or "Respected Father," to the signature of the writer, contain disquisitions as to the state of the soul or on infant damnation. They were strong on infant damnation, a dreadful doctrine of a dreadful God. The implication is that as theology filled their letters it also filled their time and their minds.

Besides the business or profession by which the husband maintained his family, and the housekeeping cares with which the wife was occupied, there was little other interest except in religion. Social life was limited to occasional tea parties or picnics; lectures, even after the Lyceum was established, were of necessity few and far between.

Shows of any kind seldom penetrated into small centers where the toll roads in and out must have used up all the profits. No one traveled, few had libraries, there were several violinists but they seem not to have given concerts -- in fact the cultural life of all small towns in the early days was practically nil. Therefore the one outlet for their cultural and emotional side was the exercise of religion.

Preaching services were at first conducted by itinerant preachers and were held in the houses of the citizens. Then the First Presbyterian Church was built as has been told. Camp meetings were held on the Commons below Sixth Street and in the woods across the river to which wagon loads of people came for miles around. The whole town went to church. A non-church-goer was branded as an infidel and felt his unpopularity to the point of losing business by it.

When they went to church what did they hear? A monstrous doctrine of an angry God instead of the good news of a loving Father. Sin was anything that was pleasant or lovely. Right living was to spend your time thinking of your soul and patronizing your neighbors who did not have the inside track with God.

An early record notes that: "The first minister who preached in the settlement (Dayton) was the Rev. John Kohler of the Methodist Church on Sunday, August 12, 1798. Topic mainly hell."

Like Jonathan Edwards of New England fame they conceived that the greatest pleasure one would have in the hereafter would be leaning over the ramparts of heaven and beholding the sinners writhing in the pains of hell. We have progressed far since those days in many things but in none farther than in the new, and yet everlastingly old, conception of religion, "To love God and thy neighbor as thyself."

In 1830 the population of Dayton was two thousand nine hundred and fifty-four, being a gain of one thousand two hundred and thirty-seven in a little more than two years. In 1833 the population was four thousand. Curwen, in his first tiny history of Dayton published in 1850 and describing the primitive simplicity of urban life in the first decade asks: "What would those first Daytonians think if they could have foreseen that on the site of those first log cabins on the river bank there would at last arise a city of *four thousand* inhabitants?" Ah! what would they indeed?

Wolf Creek in winter.

5

Politics and Pestilence

In the '30s and '40s Dayton was afflicted mainly with politics and the cholera. Which was the greatest scourge would be hard to say.

The canal was a grand institution but it had its disadvantages and brought other things besides passengers and freight to our shores. The worst cargo it imported was the cholera. It was in the summer of 1833 that a whole boat load arrived from Cincinnati suffering from some mysterious digestive disorder.

The captain would not bring his passengers up into the middle of town, but discharged them onto the bank of the canal at the foot of Ludlow Street. Twenty-five patients suffering from cramps and fever were taken to one house (it is to be wished we knew where) and put, with utter disregard of the first principles of prevention, into one room.

It must have been a warehouse for no Dayton private home at that day could accommodate so many. Of course there was no board of health, no hospital, no provision whatever for the care of contagious diseases or of any other kind.

Every mother of a family was a nurse perforce, and the only one, except kind neighbors who were angels in disguise in the last century. Anyhow, here were several dozen people, helpless and suffering excruciatingly, to be looked after somehow, someway by people already overworked. A doctor and two nurses (the latter untrained of course) volunteered to care for the patients.

In two days both nurses were dead and the doctor himself down with the same complaint. Every day saw a funeral procession wending its way to the Fifth Street graveyard. There could be no doubt about it; it was the cholera, and nothing else, that had invaded Dayton. Such diseases are better understood now and two precautions stand out: sanitation and segregation. Neither was understood or practiced in 1833.

Cesspools in close proximity to wells, open gutters carrying roadwashings to the river, no kind of supervision of the removal of refuse, open garbage pails at every back door, all these were the usual thing in the Dayton of that day. These combined to give a warm welcome to the cholera germs and they made the most of it.

With dreadful suddenness people were taken ill at breakfast time and died before sundown. Panic invaded the city. Those who had private carriages (there were only two in 1820 so probably they were quite few in 1833) left for Cincinnati as fast as they could, a useless procedure because the cholera was just as bad down there. Strong men died and little children died, mothers died leaving helpless families; it was a time of terror such as only those who have been through it can know.

Sporadic outbreaks continued to occur for several years and in 1849 another violent epidemic was experienced when two hundred and sixteen lives were lost out of the small village in one short summer. With the point of view of the day this calamity was charged up to the Lord, when the responsibility of it really belonged to the authorities themselves. A proclamation from the mayor set apart a day, not for cleaning up the streets and alleys, but for fasting and prayer, beginning: "Whereas it has pleased Almighty God to afflict our beloved city by sending the pestilence among us," etc., etc. What blasphemy!

Local and national politics took hold of the populace with as much violence as the cholera. The epidemic broke out at election time and people caught it from each other. Because they had so few interests, politics took as strong a hold on them as religion or the plague.

Read the accounts of the Jackson campaign as it was carried on in Dayton in 1833. Bonfires and processions, hundreds of people coming in from the country, banquets at the hotel, flag-raisings on the Common, speeches in the square, bitter denunciation of candidates and more bitter opposition for those who upheld them; business men refusing to do business with men of the opposite party, neighbors not speaking on the street, vitriolic attacks in the newspapers and even in the pulpits, oh, the cholera was only a very little worse. The difference being that while they died of cholera they did not die of politics, they only raged and fought and forgot about it when election was over.

In the Jackson campaign some amusing incidents occurred as when his election was celebrated by a barbecue on the Common east of the canal. The ox that participated had been too long out of cold storage and was eaten, not by the fervent patriots of the occasion, but by dogs which, attracted by the odors of burning meat, gathered to pay their tribute to the Presidential candidate.

The Harrison campaign of 1840 was a remarkable occasion and need not at all be treated with satire. What Dayton did at that time was a great thing for a small town and merits a story of its own.

The national situation was this. In 1836 Martin Van Buren had been elected over William Henry Harrison. The former was an aristocrat with the standards of his class. Believing in the amenities of life, he had refurnished the out-of-date White House with carpets, mirrors and curtains, all offensive to the opportunistic spirit of the time.

Harrison was a plain Ohio farmer, a gentleman, too, but not the brand of the man who sat in the bedecked White House. Harrison was not only a friend of the people but, since the War of 1812, had been the idol of the nation. An attempt to make political capital out of his plain tastes and antecedents was made by the Baltimore *Republican*, which said editorially of Harrison: "Give him a barrel of hard cider and settle a pension of two thousand dollars on him and our word for it, he would sit the remainder of his days contentedly in a log cabin."

This was enough! It was not the first time, nor the last, in the history of politics that a slogan has proved to be a boomerang and done more harm to its friends than to its enemies. The implication in the editorial was enough for the Great West, the West of the plain people, grown up in log cabins and on hard cider and proud of both. Harrison was dubbed the "Log Cabin Candidate," and his followers the "Log Cabin Boys," and they made the campaign rallies the occasion of "cabin raisings." It was a throwback to the time when the greatest fun of the early settlers was to gather from near and far and raise a cabin for the latest arrivals.

The Whigs did a modern thing; they brought out a newspaper in behalf of their party projects and called it the *Log Cabin*. These ancient sheets, yellow with age and brown with flood water, are still the greatest treasure of the Dayton Public Library. Local politics of the day are to be seen in its pages, the scare-heads in bold face type, the whoop-em-up slo-

Old county jail and workhouse, built in 1845, at the corner of Main and Sixth Streets (above); Huston Hall, southeast corner of Third and Jefferson Streets, destroyed in fire following 1913 flood.

gans which in spite of their antiquity have a familiar sound -- "National Prosperity: Civil Liberties: Our Noble Candidate."

To this sheet, more probably than to any other influence, was due the election of Harrison to the Presidency. A glance at it will show that they took their politics seriously in those days. Never would they have conceived such a necessity as is implied in the modern slogan: "Get out the Vote." Here is the invitation which was printed in the issue of July 25, 1840:

LOG CABIN CANDIDATES.

For President -- WILLIAM HENRY HARRISON.
For Vice-President -- JOHN TYLER
For Governor of Ohio -- THOMAS CORWIN, 'The Wagon Boy"

To the People of the United States, more particularly to those of the WEST, and most particularly to all in the MIAMI VALLEY.
You are invited by your fellow citizens of Montgomery County to convene with them in a GRAND COUNCIL at Dayton on the anniversary of our gallant PERRY'S VICTORY, on September 10th, 1840. COME ONE! COME ALL!

Take in the breadth, depth and height of this pronouncement! Here was a little city of less than seven thousand souls all told, few of them rich, many of them poor, having but two small hotels and no railroad, bravely offering to entertain "the people of the United States" within her borders for three whole days.

Did they come? Ask the old *Log Cabin*! For days preceding the event crowds began to gather, swarming into Dayton by stage and canal, on foot, on horseback, in private vehicles, whole families, troops of soldiers; they came from all the land in the Miami Valley, from Illinois and Missouri; twelve canal boats filled with delegates arrived from Mississippi and Louisiana. The turnpikes showed a black procession by day and an illuminated one by night with the camp fires of voters coming to greet their beloved candidate, until the total, according to the careful computation by local engineer Luther Bruen reached a hundred thousand.

How did Dayton take care of them? We can search it out in the annals of that day and the testimony of private letters. Many camped by the roadside, tying their horses to a tree, seeking provisions in the neighboring farms and cooking over an open fire. Those who had the means filled up the two hotels. When the Swaynie and the National had no more bedspace the private homes took the overflow as best they might.

Preparations had not been lacking. For weeks and weeks house-keepers had been making ticks and filling them with fresh straw. As the house kept filling up with these improvised beds, the pantries bore shelves loaded with hams, baked fowl, loaves of bread, jars of preserves, pickles and honey. In the H. G. Phillips house beds were laid side by side down a long upper hall and that family took care of one hundred guests at night and three hundred for dinner.

Notice was given to the effect that a stranger might knock at any door that displayed a flag and receive dinner and bed. There were but seven hundred homes in Dayton at that time and it is told that six hundred and forty-four of them displayed flags.

This was great, but greater still was the entry of the procession bringing to Dayton the hero of the hour. It came by way of the Springfield Pike. The Log Cabin hero and his staff spent the night at Harshman's Station, four miles east of Dayton. On beginning the trip into Dayton the next morning they were met by a welcoming procession which, with the floats and carriages in the Harrison crowd, was said to measure four miles in length. With carriages three abreast, and scores on horseback, the head of the procession was coming into town by the canal basin while the end of it was still leaving Harshman's.

This is the way the *Log Cabin* reported the scene:

The huzzas from gray-headed patriots as the banners borne in the procession passed their balconies, the waving handkerchiefs of the thousands of fair women, the glimpses at every turn of the eye of the fluttering folds of six hundred and forty-four flags, the soul stirring music, the smiling heavens, the emblems and mottoes, all added to the intensity of the excitement. Every eminence, housetop and window was thronged with eager spectators whose acclamations seemed to rend the heavens. Second Street at that time led through a prairie and the bystanders, by a metaphor the sublimity of which few but Westerners can appreciate, likened the enthusiasm to a mighty sea of fire sweeping over its surface gathering and heaving and rolling upwards till its flames licked the stars and fired the whole heavens.

Making all allowance for the heated enthusiasm of the day, that procession must have been remarkable. An immense log cabin on wheels, with the usual accompaniments of a coonskin nailed onto the logs and a barrel of hard cider, was drawn along the road by six horses.

A ball as large as a one-story house represented the states rolling up for Harrison. It had been trundled along from the top of the Allegheny Mountains and bore the legend: "This ball we roll with heart and soul." Twenty-six little girls, seated in a big canoe, carried each the banner of her State. A live wolf, covered with sheepskin (signifying the hypocritical designs of the Democrats) occupied a wagon all to himself and was said to behave as well as the rest.

The reception in Dayton proved worthy of the occasion. A long banner at the corner of Main and Second streets had on one side a log cabin, on the other a ship in full sail with the inscription, "Roll on the ball" and "Perry, September 10th, 1813" At the corner of Jefferson hung a white silk banner with the words "Jefferson Street honors him whom Jefferson honored." On Third, at the courthouse, "No standing army" and "Resistance to Tyrants is obedience to God."

As the journey had taken all morning the first thing on the program was dinner at eleven o'clock at the Swaynie House, whence later the distinguished guest was escorted to the "Common," east of St. Clair Street, where the soldiers had camped in 1812. It was there that General Harrison made a speech which, according to the accounts of that day, could be heard clear to the river and by an audience of not less than one hundred thousand people.

After the speech more presentations of banners and a plough from the Tippecanoe delegation with which Harrison was expected to "plough up the thistles and briars of the last administration." The ladies of the city presented a white silk banner painted by the artist, Charles Soule, but could not make the presentation speech themselves, so Judge Daniel Haynes came to their assistance.

Not since then, until the Wright celebration, in 1909, has Dayton seen such a crowd and such wild enthusiasm. But the glory must go to the earlier date, not because the occasion was greater but because Dayton was smaller. Nothing that can ever happen here can mar the grandeur of the Harrison campaign rally, nor equal the all-embracing hospitality of the little town.

Little has been said so far in these pages on the subject of education and schools, but that must not indicate that the parents and citizens of Dayton were blind to such needs. Earlier chapters told of Benjamin Van Cleve's school in the blockhouse and this chapter with its lugubrious heading will be a good place to tell the school story and mitigate the horrors of "Politics and Pestilence." They might have epidemics both of cholera and politics but they never lost sight of the fact that the future of a community depends upon the education given to its children.

Conventions are thought-breeding and action-bearing occasions and one of them, a school convention, was what happened to Dayton in August, 1836, a noteworthy occasion because it brought an entirely new idea into the minds of citizens. This was no less than the plan of free public schools.

Up to this time "dame schools" were carried on for the girls, and schools, taught by a man, for the boys, the expenses of both being paid by the parents. Now it seemed, from indications in the outside world, that the proper thing to do in a democracy like the United States was to install schools in buildings owned by the community, to employ teachers paid by the community, and make education absolutely free to every child no matter what the financial status of his parents.

It was no less than revolutionary. Nevertheless, after three days spent in listening to distinguished school authorities, the convention not only advocated free schools but also the establishment of free normal schools that the cause of education might never lack trained teachers.

Among the attendants at this meeting was Rev. W. H. McGuffey, whose name will always be connected with a set of readers which he compiled and which were used for fifty years or more in the schools. These six readers, with their excerpts from the classics, are answerable for the first appreciation of real prose and poetry which many people had. In the dearth of libraries and book stores, the McGuffey readers brought to the young people and to their parents as well the treasures of Shakespeare, Scott, Dickens and Tennyson.

The concrete results of this meeting may still be found in the pages of the *Dayton Journal* which gave a full report and its support to the school plan. Resolutions to the effect that such schools should be established, that normal schools should make teaching a real profession, that geology and physiology should be introduced into the curriculum and that a periodical should be published called *The Teachers Magazine*, will not make the impression now that they did then because now they are the veriest commonplaces. At that time, when teaching was a haphazard sort of profession which anybody could carry on provided he knew his A B C's, such pronouncements as came from this meeting were too advanced to be accepted without protest. The date should be remembered, it was August, 1836, ninety-five years ago, and it was the seed-planting of our Dayton Public School system.

To read of the efforts of our fellow citizens of an earlier day towards the cultural things of life is touching and impressive. Far as they were from the sophisticated East, limited as they were for funds, burdened as they were with the hard conditions of living, these plain men took time from their absorbing duties and reached out for the higher things of life. They were not willing to live by bread alone, nor that their children should.

We have already told the story of that first library on its wooden shelves in the home of Benjamin Van Cleve. The books were paid for with coonskins and packed across the mountains on muleback. Little by little, under the influence of the reading aristocracy of the little town, other collections of books were gathered and kept like the first one in private houses and circulated among the citizens. That they were treasures and constantly read goes without saying.

One tangible result proved to be the Dayton Lyceum Association organized in 1833; its object was somewhat pompously proclaimed as, "the diffusion of knowledge and the promotion of sociability." Meetings were held every week "for lectures, essays and discussions of all subjects except theology and the politics of the day." There was no way, it is plain, to avoid having the literary programs degenerate into affrays ending in broken noses except by the wise provision "except theology and the politics of the day." This Lyceum lasted several years and was supplanted by the "Mechanics Institute" with its library (a combination of the scattered books) reading rooms and a course of lectures each winter

H. G. Phillips, building at the time a three-story block on the corner of Main and Second streets, was much commended because he had especially planned a room for library purposes. One of the earliest impressions of the author is standing with her father in the middle of the biggest room she had ever seen lined completely with books. It was described as being "elegantly and handsomely furnished, second to none in Ohio."

An old cut published in the *Daily Gazette* May 27, 1854, shows impressive Corinthian columns, gilt chandeliers, book shelves, globes, reading tables, and six gentlemen all with their hats on. The implication of the latter point must not be lost. Reading was done by gentlemen in correct afternoon dress; those who lived on First and Second streets and elegant residential Jefferson, not by the Irish on the Commons south of town. Anyhow they justified their ornamental existence by taking "noblesse oblige" literally. They shared the little they had of leisure and the results of reading with their fellow-citizens, hats off!

Of this early library in the Phillips Building one thing may be certainly noted: The books were all good books -- Shakespeare and Milton, Defoe, Hugo, Lamartine, Scott, Irving; there was history, essay and travel; but little fiction perhaps, for novels were looked at askance seventy-five years ago.

One reader, Dr. J. C. Reeve, in a letter of October, 1854, says: "The Phillips Building is a fine block. I don't think it has its equal in Cleveland (where he had come from). Right across the hall from our office is the library room. I think I shall subscribe immediately; it is five dollars per year and six payments entitle one to a life ticket. They have a good supply of books, among them Miss Pardoe's *Court of Louis Fourteenth.*

As for the lectures which were given every winter in the Mechanics Institute, history fails to record them and the minutes are lost. But we know who could have given lectures, and interesting ones, too, on history, botany and ornithology, architecture and art. For they were lovers and readers of books: John Van Cleve, Robert C. Schenck, Wilbur Conover, Peter Odlin, E. W. Davies, Robert A. Thruston, E. E. Barney, Charles Anderson, Judge Haynes, J. D. Phillips, Joseph H. Crane.

From this magnificent beginning, the Dayton Library has progressed, first into the upper story of the City Hall, and then in 1888 to the center of Cooper Park, so that having been housed in its infancy under the roof of Benjamin Van Cleve it is in its maturity still under the spiritual charge of another of the pioneers who gave the ground on which it stands.

A great deal was made of the Fourth of July in the early years of Dayton. The "spirit of 76" was kept alive in very practical ways. Take the celebration of 1816 for example. First they met and appointed a committee of arrangements, then they decided on somebody to be toastmaster, then they notified the "ladies" that their patriotic duties would include providing a big dinner.

On this particular occasion Isaac Spining was president for the day, and Van Cleve read Washington's Farewell Address; patriotic toasts were offered and one hundred persons sat down to dinner. At four o'clock the ladies and gentlemen assembled "in the adjacent woods" (Perry Street, probably, considering the date. Ten years later it would have been Steele's Hill across the river) and had supper.

A ball at Colonel Reid's Inn in the evening and vocal music at Mr. Bomberger's finished the perfect day. They took everything hard in those days. With the seriousness of children they perpetrated politics, religion and merry-making in a way that makes our modern activities seem tepid. Perhaps it was the way to make life worth while as they went along.

The thrilling news of the year 1823 is that the first menagerie came to town. It consisted of a moth-eaten African lion, a leopard in the same condition and an elephant. Some difficulty was experienced in finding a place to keep the elephant, he being too tall for the prevailing type of wood shed, so a barn was commandeered and the little boys saw the show without a ticket by peeping through knot holes.

We hazard the guess that just as much of a show was the first camp meeting, for a thousand persons were in attendance and there were many baptisms in the river. Real shows, that is the theatre, were not yet a part of Dayton's recreational interests but the beginning of such was probably the "elegant comedy called *Matrimony*" which the paper announced "would be performed at the home of William Huffman on St. Clair Street. Tickets fifty cents." April 22, 1816.

This same year we find listed on the City Council the names of D. C. Cooper, Joseph Peirce, H. G. Phillips, O. B. Conover and George Grove.

In 1817 the Sunday School Association, the first religious organization not a church, was organized by the Rev. Bacchus Wilbur, pastor of the First Presbyterian Church. Mr. Wilbur was a very prominent and popular preacher, so much so that there were quite a number of babies named after him, most of whom for reasons of their own, dropped the given name in adult life. The dues of this organization were twenty-five cents a year, and the roll held such well known names as Mrs. J. H. Crane, Mrs. W. R. S. Ayres, Mrs. Hannah George, Joseph Peirce, Sarah Bomberger.

In 1821 a severe fever, perhaps an exaggerated type of the malaria which had so discouraged the first dwellers in Dayton, made its appearance in Dayton in epidemic form, and among those who were carried to the Fifth Street graveyard were Joseph Peirce and that stalwart defender of Dayton's prosperity, Benjamin Van Cleve.

Main Street river bridge and the buggies of yester-
year.

6

The Early F. F. D.'S

It is said that history and biography are one; that the life of an individual is the narrative of the times in which he lived. If this be true of large general things it is no less true of our city of Dayton. More than in most places the citizen made the town; one cannot write of one without the other.

Therefore it seems high time to introduce the reader to some of the First Families of Dayton. First in occupation, first in constructive ability and first in ambition for the town they had founded. But we must hasten to say that space denies the mention of all, or of a half, or even of anything but a partial minority.

In this chapter will be considered only those who came here in the first two decades, from 1796 to 1816, and of these merely the most outstanding individuals, the ones except for whose personal service Dayton would have perished from the earth. Those who are interested to find a full list may consult John F. Edgar in whose *Pioneer Life in Dayton* are many interesting details of the first families. Mary D. Steele in her *Early Dayton* goes further into facts regarding pioneers.

Benjamin Van Cleve will easily head the list of the F. F. D.'s on all three counts for he was almost the first, if not the very first, to set foot on our shores; he devoted his whole life to furthering Dayton projects and his loyalty was never questioned. It is impossible to write a page about the first Dayton years and leave him out. No one merited more than he the name "pioneer."

A boy of ten when his father drove the family wagon over the mountains on all but impassable roads, the wheels lurching in and out of the half-frozen mud holes, reaching frontier taverns with exhausted horses and frost-bitten children to find every bed full and obliged to sleep in the wagon, Benjamin Van Cleve certainly knew what privation was. A boy of twelve, looking from their cabin door on the farm lot near Cincinnati, he saw a savage dart from the underbrush, scalp and kill his father who was ploughing. Van Cleve knew what terror was.

A stripling of fifteen, when the flat-boat reached the bank at the head of Main Street, Dayton, he knew what adventure was in search of a home. Taking his father's place as best he could with his mother and the younger children, hewing trees, hunting game for food, Van Cleve knew what self-discipline was. Self-taught he must have been, for there were few schools and no time for schooling in his crowded life. Yet he stood always for the higher things and quoted the classics.

His various activities from first to last would make a stirring book. He was schoolmaster, as we know, county surveyor and engineer; was appointed by the President of the United States to explore and mark out a road from the Miami to the Western Reserve; a faithful diarist almost to the point of an historian; assistant to his uncle who was quartermaster in St. Clair's Army (at fifteen dollars a month) during which time he was sent to the War Department at Philadelphia with important secret dispatches (and allowed forty dollars for his personal expenses during a whole winter).

It is told of him that during this, his first trip to the eastern coast, he found time to read everything he could lay his hands on and bought twenty-five volumes out of his own scanty sources. How many of those books found their way onto the shelves of that first public library of Dayton would be interesting to know.

This entry in his diary makes Benjamin Van Cleve our historical if not legal ancestor.

April 1 1796. Landed at Dayton after a passage of ten days William Gahagan and myself having come from Cincinnati with the Thompsons and McClure's families in a large pirogue.

Bad luck came his way at first. He spent twenty dollars for a cow and it died. He gave eighty dollars for a yoke of oxen and one of them was shot. He farmed a whole year and at the end of it was forty dollars in debt. He raised a good crop of corn but it was destroyed. So when orders came to survey the United States Military lands between the Scioto and the Muskingum rivers with Israel Ludlow he was glad of the chance to go.

The weather was bitter cold and game hard to shoot because the crusted snow left no traces; for five whole days they had but four meals and those scanty, no bread at all. The expedition over, Van Cleve was glad to get back to civilization which was Dayton.

His bad luck was waiting for him there in the shape of rheumatic fever contracted while digging a sawmill pit for D. C. Cooper. Thereafter we know what his life was: storekeeper, postmaster, schoolteacher, hunter, librarian, promoter of frontier welfare and commercial prospects. Outside of his home town, Van Cleve was clerk of the first Ohio Legislature. In 1896 twenty-nine persons of various degrees of consanguinity could be counted in Dayton and neighboring communities as descendants in direct line from Benjamin Van Cleve.

At the intersection of Main Street and Brown, now called Far Hills Avenue, stands a relic of one of our most influential First Families of Dayton. It is the original home of Colonel Robert Patterson whose migration with family and flocks and herd from Kentucky into Ohio we have already chronicled. The cabin, built of logs hewn by the owner himself was to be the home of his bride, Elizabeth Lindsay, when he brought her out from her Pennsylvania home into the wilderness. Twenty years ago it was discovered by the writer in an obscure backyard in Lexington, Kentucky, being used as a tool-house but keeping its identity as the first house built in that city and the home of its founder, Robert Patterson.

His grandson, John H. Patterson, had it removed and brought to Dayton where it probably will remain for the rest of its existence. It was built in 1787. The land it now occupies is a part of the original grant and has changed hands only once in a hundred and thirty-six years, from D. C. Cooper to Robert Patterson, thence to the Patterson heirs.

Its original owner being a "F. F. Lexington" became on his arrival a "F. F. Dayton." Although no longer a young man he transferred his interest from the roads, schools, libraries, tree-planting in Lexington to similar activities in Dayton. It was in the nature of a personal celebration when the Patterson family one summer afternoon in 1829, went down to the canal bank near their home to watch the first boat go by. Their father was not with them for he had passed away two years before, but so valiantly had he worked for the canal that it seemed his own accomplishment and his noblest monument.

Robert Patterson lived in Dayton from 1804, when he came, to 1827, when he died, and all those years participated in promoting everything from gristmills to church and library. On his farm land now stands the huge factory for the manufacture of cash registers. His descendants are Mrs. Julia Patterson Crane, Frederick Beck Patterson, Mrs. Dorothy Patterson Judah, Mrs. Roger Woodhull, Mrs. Caroline Patterson Bush, Jefferson Patterson, Mrs. Mary Patterson Davidson, Robert Patterson and family, Robert Dun Patterson, Jefferson Patterson Crane and Joseph Halsey Crane.

The leading name in Dayton during its first years was that of George Newcom who piloted one of the parties from Cincinnati to Dayton in 1796. He built his cabin on the southwest corner of Main Street and Monument Avenue, and later replaced it with a stout two-story structure. It is a monument also to the loyalty of that almost forgotten organization, the Dayton Historical Society, which rescued it from the destructive axe of a contractor, stripped off its plebeian sheathing of clapboards, restored its ancient log walls to view and moved it to a better location

The renewal of interest in our town history aroused by the celebration of our centennial in 1896, brought from remote garrets some of the original furniture and implements that had been used in the Newcom Tavern a century before and placed them in the cabin where they recall to the vision of today the primitive life of our forefathers.

Up to 1805 Dayton lacked a lawyer. Circuit judges came and went, trying cases in the Newcom Tavern, but a lawyer of her own she never had until Joseph H. Crane, a boy of twenty-one, but already admitted to the New Jersey bar, came to Dayton. He and his descendants must surely be counted among the early F. F. D.'s for, in 1809, he was elected to the Ohio Legislature, served in the War of 1812, was made prosecuting attorney in 1813 and judge in 1817

Like other citizens of that time, he contributed to the cultural advantages of the town, was on the committee to buy the first books for the public library and it is said he would not yield to the popular demand for light literature but purchased only the best. He took his place at the head of his profession and gathered around him men that acknowledged him as leader. It was said that, more than any other, Judge Crane molded the character and directed the ambitions of young lawyers, so that the spirit of integrity came to be a characteristic of the Dayton bar.

Of this early group of lawyers many took foremost places. Charles Anderson became Governor of Ohio, four were judges, two members of

Congress and ten of the Ohio Legislature. Forty years ago Mary Steele wrote that "Dayton received an impetus in the right direction from the cultivated and far-sighted men who came during the first ten or twelve years of the town's history which is felt at the present time." That declaration is as true now as when it was written.

The Steeles were F. F. D.'s from the beginning. James Steele, having come from Kentucky in 1805, was another of those public-spirited pioneers who gave time and labor and money to schools, libraries and churches. What they once called the "new" Presbyterian Church, erected in 1839, was due largely to his efforts.

He was associate judge of Montgomery County and for four years a member of the Ohio Senate. When his friend, Henry Clay, ran for the Presidency, James Steele was one of the electors of the State of Ohio. From 1815 to 1822, he was first director and then president of the first bank in Dayton, on North Main Street, since demolished to make way for the Steele High School. This bank under his leadership had the honor of being one of only three banks in the United States to continue to pay specie to its depositors during the financial panic of 1837.

The name Peirce is so interwoven in the early days with that of Steele that they can scarcely be considered apart. Connected by both marriage and business, both families contributed much that was valuable to our community. The Peirces were of Quaker stock and carried out to the letter the principles of plain living and high thinking. Joseph, the progenitor of all this large relationship, was born in Rhode Island and brought as a child of two to Marietta with his father, who was aide-de-camp to General Horatio Gates in the Revolutionary War. The boy spent his childhood in the stockades, which in those days were the only safe dwellings for mothers and babies.

In 1805 Joseph Peirce came to Dayton and entered into partnership with James Steele, a connection which endured throughout his long life. The store was on the corner of First and Main; in it was kept a miscellaneous stock of wearing apparel, farm utensils, dishes and food supplies. Large orders were shipped by the firm to the army in the War of 1812 for the liquidating of which the government took its time, being like the individual of that day, chronically hard up.

Mr. Peirce was president of the Dayton Bank. He fell a victim to a mysterious fever which was prevalent in 1821. Two sons survived him, Joseph C. and J. H. The first married Louise Smith and died without issue.

The second married twice into the Bruen family. The children are all gone; a grandchild surviving is Elliott; great-grandchildren are J. P. Davies, Mrs. George Wood, Mrs. Coolidge, Mrs. Morrison and Mary Frances Peirce.

The Peirces bring us by natural transition to the Bruen family with whom they are so closely connected. Luther Bruen was known for two things, his skill as a surveyor and engineer and his strong sentiment against slavery. Happening to be in Yellow Springs, in 1804, he stopped on his way through Dayton to Cincinnati to pay his respects to his uncle, Isaac Spining.

Here he met pleasant relatives and saw good prospects in the new town. He made shoes for the whole family, that being his métier, and from the family branched out to the general public, built a store, worked hard, laid up money, and by 1810 had bought a large tract of land across the river. The Peirces bought property in the same neighborhood and friendships followed.

Luther Bruen was a fanatic on the subject of the abolition of slavery, a most unpopular subject with public feeling mounting on both sides of the question. It was a time of free opinions freely expressed, sometimes in harder things than words. An abolitionist was in danger of physical violence from people who did not respect the Quaker position. Luther Bruen built a meetinghouse where he induced radical speakers to come and discourse, at the risk of their skins, sometimes, if not of their lives.

He taught and preached the sin of one man holding another in bondage. The incident of the arrest and subsequent self-destruction of Black Ben has already been told. This was the impetus that abolitionism needed in Dayton and following it we find a notice in a Dayton paper calling those who believed that slavery should be abolished to meet with Luther Bruen at the meetinghouse on Main Street below Fourth and organize into an Anti-Slavery Society. The end of this story is the Civil War but twenty years before it broke out Luther Bruen, having done his bit, was dead of the cholera which swept over Dayton in 1842.

Daniel C. Cooper, who belongs chronologically in this connection, has already been treated in a previous chapter, but he was not the only early local patriot from whom the young town benefited. There was, for instance, Horatio G. Phillips from New Jersey, whom Cooper induced to try his fortunes in the growing frontier city of Dayton, and who did come, in 1805, bringing with him the gifts of business enterprise, civic acumen and social prestige. He married Eliza Smith Houston and brought her via horseback through Pennsylvania, by flat-boat from Pittsburgh to Cincinnati and wagon to Dayton, the standard wedding trip for those early brides. Mr. Phillips was wise in the choice of both his wife and his business partners. She gave to the little community the grace and culture of her personality and her granddaughters and great-granddaughters still call her blessed.

His business associates were Alexander Grimes, Daniel Beckel and Samuel Edgar. The contributions of this far-sighted trio to Dayton were the founding of the first Dayton bank, the promotion of the Dayton Hydraulic Company, the establishment of the village of Alexandersville, named after one of the partners, and the promotion of various extensive business interests all up and down the valley.

The children of Horatio Phillips were Jonathan Dickinson, who married Luciana Greene; Elizabeth (Mrs. Worthington); and Mariana (first Mrs. Robert Thruston, afterwards Mrs. John G. Lowe). From one generation to another the members of the family have been ornaments to the life of the city. The son, J. D. Phillips, followed in his father's footsteps; a man of culture and taste, he was as generous as he was socially delightful and his gifts to public things were known to only a few friends.

The first public library was especially indebted to him for its quarters in the "new" Phillips block on the corner of Main and Second streets. The Phillips House was built by him and named in honor of his father. It was for eighty years the center of social and business life in Dayton and the best hotel in this part of Ohio. It is now destroyed.

J. D. Phillips had one son, Horace, and four daughters: Mrs. A. D. McCook, Mrs. J. P. Davies, Mrs. J. Harrison Hall and Miss Sophie Phillips. Mrs. Kathleen McCook Craighead, J. P. Davies, the Misses Alice, Eliza and Agnes Hall are grandchildren; Mrs. Katherine Houk Talbott and her nine children, and their twenty-eight children, are third and fourth generation descendants of the Phillips family.

One cannot think of banking and business interests in Dayton in the early years and not recall the name of Jonathan Harshman. He also was an 1805 settler who purchased forty acres in Mad River Township where he proceeded to erect on the banks of that stream a flour mill and a distillery, one in those days being just as legitimate and respectable as the other.

He accumulated great wealth and his eight sons and daughters, who invariably lived in the biggest houses in the town, were wont to recall that their father hung the door of his first cabin home himself and put in one four-light window. His later home, which was a palatial one, and his mills formed what is still known as Harshmanville. Mrs. Harshman was Joanne Rench, the sister of his partner, John Rench, and his children were Elizabeth (Mrs. Huston); Catherine (Mrs. Valentine Winters); Jonathan, who married Abigail Hiveling; Mary (Mrs. George Gorman); Joseph, married Caroline Protzman; George, married Ann Rohrer; Susannah (Mrs. Daniel Beckel); and Reuben D., married Mary Protzman. From this union are all the Renchs, the Winters, the Beckels, the Hivelings, the Hustons and the Huffmans.

Abram Darst was another 1805 settler, coming from Virginia. He built his home on the west side of Main Street on the site of the Rike-Kumler store on a lot for which he paid Benjamin Van Cleve seventy-five dollars. Here he carried on a successful business for many years.

His children were ten: Julia (Mrs. James Perrine); Christina (Mrs. William B. Dix); Mary (Mrs. Jacob Wilt); Sarah (Mrs. W. C. Davis); Martha (Mrs. George M. Dixon); Napoleon, married Susannah Winters; Phoebe and John. Abram Darst's descendants have also multiplied and replenished the earth to good purpose, their names being Perrine, Barney, Dixon, Wilt, Dix, Bimm, Shaw, &c.

Among the first, if not the very first, ministers who came to Dayton was Dr. James Welsh, who was pastor of the First Presbyterian Church, also a practicing physician and kept the only drug store. There was room enough for all three occupations in 1804. On Sunday he preached and on week-days he administered "Yellow bark, oil of vitriol, paregoric, Venue turpentine and polypodium, a famous worm medicine purchased by the late King of France," as his advertisement stated it.

Dr. Welsh was also a public-spirited man and had a hand in most of the advanced measures intended to make Dayton a rival of the big cities in the East. He imagined that growing real estate necessities would make a suburb advisable and so he laid out one to the north and west of the city and called it Dayton View. A ferry was also established by him from the foot of Salem Avenue to the end of First Street, but the public never believed in such radical adventures and rejected all inducements to go so far out to live. In 1821 Dr. Welsh applied to the court to vacate his plot.

He was one of the incorporators of the Old Academy, the first school for boys in Dayton. He and Dr. John Elliot, who succeeded him, were both retired army surgeons. Both seemed to have some of the difficulties of a later day, as witness a notice which appeared not once but several times in the local press of that day:

I must pay my debts. To do this is impracticable unless those who are indebted to me pay me what they owe. All such are once more for the last time called on to come forward and make payment before the 25th of March next, or disagreeable as it is, compulsory measures may certainly be expected. Signed,
    JAMES WELSH.

In our enumeration of the very earliest settlers we must not forget those who bought land west of town, far out in the country it was at the time, now the busy section of Dayton known as the West Side.

The three outstanding names were Isaac Spining, William King and John Harbert Williams, all Presbyterians who helped build and foster the church when it was a log cabin on the corner of Third and Main and after it was removed to the corner of Second and Ludlow. All bought large farms which have long since been swallowed up into city streets.

In 1803 Isaac Spining was appointed one of the two first associate judges in Ohio. Like most of the professional men of that time he combined law and business, being another of the adventurous voyagers who made the journey to New Orleans with a load of flour, only having more initiative than others he took his flour around the coast to Boston because he could not get the price he wanted in New Orleans. Three granddaughters are the only surviving descendants of Isaac Spining: Miss Bessie Mulford and the Misses Emma and Margaret Stewart.

John Harbert Williams was a strong force in building up the West Side. His descendants are Mrs. John H. Campbell, Miss Nancy Williams and Fowler Smith and family.

William King, another of those who came up from Kentucky because he was opposed to slavery, arrived in Dayton in the spring of 1801 and began his career by joining the Presbyterian Church. With a strong streak of the Covenanter in his disposition he maintained to the last of his life, which was a little less than one hundred years, the principles of temperance and uncompromising morality. His descendants bear the names of Osborne, King, Scott and Brenneman and only a great-granddaughter, Marian E. Brenneman, survives.

Among the western-bound adventurers from New Jersey was a young man named Obadiah Burlew Conover. He came from Monmouth County, New Jersey, near Middlepoint, the same part of the state that the Schencks came from (populated in the beginning straight from Amsterdam) where half the stones in the graveyard are marked "Conover" and the other half "Cooven-hooven" that being the Dutch version of the name. The Schencks and the Cooven-hoovens intermarried, both in Holland and in New Jersey.

It was either in 1810 or 1812, the records differ, that Obadiah Conover alighted from a horse on Main Street and became a first citizen. He had learned the trade of blacksmithing, that being a most necessary craft in a frontier post, but also he planned to carry on a shop for the manufacture of ploughs, wagons and other farm necessities.

Looking about for a location, he thought he saw a good one, how good lie did not know. It was on the southeast corner of Third and Main opposite where they were planning to build a courthouse. He purchased, supposedly of D. C. Cooper, the solid quarter of the block bounded by Main, Jefferson, Third and Fourth and built a shop on the corner and a house back in the lot. It was a log house and a log shop.

The first step toward business was to make a surface on the quagmire that Main Street became when it rained in order that horses could come up and be shod. Some time in the '80s when excavations were going on for the installation of a sewer system, the workmen disclosed a quantity of walnut logs far below the surface which were laid down in the second decade of the last century by Obadiah Conover and sundry fellow citizens who wished to improve the commercial facilities of the town.

In time the two buildings, the shop and the house, were changed to the more fashionable clapboard finish, and then property values increasing, the residence was changed to Fifth Street. The store prospered and was rebuilt two stories high with a board awning as pictured in Howe's *History of Ohio*. This old wood-cut shows the sign Keifer and Conover, for the stock had expanded to include groceries and dry goods.

By that time (1843) a son, Harvey Conover, a partner with Daniel Keifer (the father of Mrs. John Stoddard) who together conducted the store. In the '50s the frame store was replaced by a dignified four-story brick building which was for fifty years the center of things in business Dayton. The leading law offices were under its roof, principal among them being the firm of Schenck and Conover, afterwards Conover and Craighead.

In the old store, as a part of the regular stock in trade, was a cellar full of kegs of whiskey and even when Conover's became the leading general store there was always a jug of the beverage on the counter at the back where customers were wont to refresh themselves.

Whiskey was a common table beverage and not confined to meal times. Every farmer had a still and old wood-cuts in the Dayton papers of that day called attention to the fact that they were Dayton made and for sale, like ordinary utensils, on the corner where the Phillips House was afterwards built.

In 1827 the temperance question began to be agitated for the first time in the community. Obadiah Conover was a man of strong convictions and a Presbyterian conscience. He believed that an honest man should live up to his principles. If whiskey was the bad thing it was represented to be (and of its evil effects he could not doubt), then it must go. So, ignoring the loss of profit involved, he had the kegs brought up, the bungs drawn and every gallon emptied into the deep gutters on the corner of the street.

Years later when this moral hero had been sleeping under his monument in Woodland for over half a century there came up the question of renting a storeroom in the building for saloon purposes. Recalling this story of her grandfather, one of the heirs declared that this incident placed the stamp of total abstinence upon the property and that if ever a saloon be allowed under that roof the name *Conover Building* should be given up. It did not get in but other influences did, namely commercial changes. The building was sold during the first years of the present century and another built which bore another name, and that of Conover, which had been associated for ninety years with the corner of Third and Main, was lost forever.

All through the years when Obadiah Conover lived and did business in Dayton, he took his place as an ardent Presbyterian and upholder of the Old First Church. His name will be found on the records of the schools, the library, the Sunday school and other public matters. He married a daughter of John Miller, who came to Dayton in 1799, and had three sons and two daughters: Obadiah M., Wilbur B., and Harvey; Harriet (Mrs. Hiram Strong); and Martha (Mrs. Collins Wight). Descendants include Mrs. Hannah Strong Frank, Alfred Swift Frank, Mrs. Fowler Smith, and Collins Wight.

The contrast between the business section of today and that of the early years of the last century is to be found in a yellowing letter written in June, 1829 by John Van Cleve to Samuel Bacon. After some social gossip about the latest engagements he goes on to say:

If you were dropped down in Dayton you would hardly know it. Great improvement is going on. The streets are all busy, drays running, hammer and trowel sounding, canal boat horns blowing, stages flying -- everybody doing something. The corporation has gravelled nearly all the streets in town and are now about erecting a new market house on Main street opposite Obadiah Conover's store. The first idea was to build the market house in the middle of Main Street. I did not like that so well. I am sorry to see Main Street have anything in it which will obstruct the view.

Property is selling very high. A third of an acre at the head of the canal basin sold for $2920. The corner of Fifth and Brown streets was divided into twenty-seven building lots and sold for $220. The three lots behind the Presbyterian church (property afterward owned and occupied by Simon Gebhart, Lewis B. Gunckel, Martha Perrine and Chas. E. Pease) sold for $1800.

If the "dropping down into Dayton" could be put back just one hundred years and made operative on the writer of this letter and the recipient, would they "hardly know it?" We think not.

7

The '40s and '50s

In 1840 Dayton boasted only a little over six thousand people. Considering the meagre population they succeeded in getting a good deal of interest, not to say excitement, out of life.

First there was the Harrison campaign, the story of which somehow wandered into a chapter previous to this. Then the Clay campaign, more cholera, church revivals and the deep and growing public occupation with the question of the abolition of slavery. Those who think that prohibition makes hot-headed adherents, and the opposite, should read what they thought in the '40s about abolition.

A church in Dayton who brought an abolitionist from the East to preach on the sin of men keeping their brothers in bondage was as nearly wrecked as vigorous hands could do it. The stove was jerked out, the pulpit hacked and even the Bible torn to pieces.

Threats were made that every speaker on that subject would receive the same treatment; notwithstanding which threat, or maybe on account of it, Rev. Thomas E. Thomas came up from Hamilton and in the most prominent place Dayton offered him, the courthouse steps, denounced the sin of slavery.

He was rotten-egged by the crowd and felt like what indeed he was, a modern martyr. It was the old conflict still going on under other names, the conflict between the rights of humanity and the rights of property. The slaves were property; to suggest freeing them was to interfere with personal possessions, which has always inflamed human passions.

Dr. Hibbard Jewett was one of the most uncompromising abolitionists of those heated years and in a letter to James Steele, then State Senator, he asks his assistance to obtain redress by an act of Legislature which would compel the corporation of Dayton to pay for the damage caused by the mob to his premises. He says:

I, for the sin of lodging Dr. Birney (a noted abolitionist speaker) had my house assailed, my windows broken, my family and furniture bespattered with rotten eggs and my life threatened in case I should ever shelter him again or any other lecturer.

One visitor whom they did not stone was the Honorable John Quincy Adams, a guest of Dayton in 1843 and welcomed by a committee to whom he replied in a speech of thanks from the balcony of the National Hotel on Third Street.

Small items in the press of that day reveal to us the smallness and frugality of the town. The mayor received a salary of a hundred and fifty dollars a year. The total amount of the school fund was $2,482; it was used for the upkeep of four schools, two in school buildings and two in rented rooms. The first school board was composed of four members, Robert W. Steele, E. W. Davies, Ebenezer Fowler and Wm. J. McKinney.

There was a flood in 1847. The river broke at Bridge Street (Stratford Avenue) where Cooper's levee was weakened by citizens scraping dirt from its inner surface to fill up their lots or holes in the streets. It happened in the middle of the night, fortunately moonlight, and people opened their houses to receive those whom the water had rendered temporarily homeless.

Following the catastrophe we read indignant denials in the papers that the damage had been anywhere near as great as was computed by ignorant and jealous outsiders; that whereas it had been put at a million dollars, it really would not exceed five thousand, all told, and that merely for spoiled carpets and furniture.

We read of a meeting in the City Hall which was "literally jammed," the occasion being, according to the *Journal*, "to encourage the enrollment of volunteers for the war with Mexico." For the politicians at Washington were at their old tricks of fomenting trouble between us and our neighbors. Nine companies were formed in Dayton and started out for the scene of the fray in a canal boat, a large crowd being gathered at the

Basin to see them off. It was an iniquitous war, if ever there was one, and is generally so conceded by all honest historians.

Thomas H. Benton offered a resolution in Congress calling attention to the fact that the annexation of a certain portion of Mexican territory to the United States as contemplated by the treaty of Texas, would be a "direct act of aggression on Mexico for all the consequences of which the United States would have to stand responsible."

It is an honor to be remembered that our representatives both in the Senate and the House were opposed to the war and upheld the Benton bill. They were the Hon. Thomas Corwin and the Hon. Robert C. Schenck, the latter one of our bravest generals in the Civil War.

Once in a while we get, thanks to the painstaking care of family descendants, a personal account of an epoch which beats mere official history hollow. The present instance is that of an exuberant girl of seventeen who lived on Main Street on the present site of Rike's store and whose brother was a student at Gambier College. He was Samuel Darst and she, Martha Jane Darst, afterwards became Mrs. George Dixon. She says she "loved to write" and it is fortunate for us that she did, because in her weekly letters to her brother we get a unique picture of a cross section of life in Dayton.

Public happenings, family news, the weather, the latest styles, what "gentleman" called on her and how late he stayed, election returns, the Mexican War, rumors of engagements, picnics on the canal, all was grist to her facile mill. Her letters punctuated the months of 1844, 1845 and 1846, and she promises her brother that as soon as the postage gets down to five cents she will write him every day. Dayton was either very gay or very dull according to how many days passed without a party:

Dayton is very gay but I don't know how long it will last. On Tuesday was the grand Clifton picnic. Our streets were filled with buggies, carriages and rockaways from seven till nine. The National turned out its loafers by the dozen. All the First Street girls were there of course; the Misses Nesbit, Smith, Phillips, Morrison, Judkins and Miss Darst, Julia I mean. They stayed all night in Springfield and came home Wednesday morning at ten o'clock. It was a great day and will long be remembered in the annals of Dayton.

Today the military companies have a grand parade. I hear them out in front of the house now. Oh. There they go! Oh, how beautiful Captain

Bomberger's company looks in its new uniforms of the "Blues" with their white pants and blue coats.

(By the kindness of Reuben Harshman:)

They are going to begin a new front to our bridge in a week or two and fix it so horses if they get frightened wont fall over the bank as a fine horse and wagon did last week.

We have a new regulation about our bell. I think the people must like to hear it ring for it rings at five and seven and at six and nine in the evening and at twelve and one in the middle of the day. It rings in the morning for the benefit of the mechanics for they all work on the ten hour system and the bell is to warn them when to commence and when to quit their work.

(Since she writes of the bridge and the bell both in the singular it must mean that in the '40s there was only one of each in Dayton, the Main Street river bridge and the First Presbyterian bell.)

We are going to send you some pantaloons and some neck handkerchiefs. I suppose when you first see them you will not like them but I assure you they are the most fashionable goods worn this summer. Mother says you will have to get along without boots. We are also going to send you a pair of rubbers but they are not to be worn in the house, only for out of doors.

I never saw so much interest in any election before. The evening the returns came in there were bonfires at every corner and the street looked as bright as sunlight and the shouting and hurrahing from both parties made sleep impossible. All the talk is of the war and there is nothing else heard. News came this morning to the companies that they must march right off. . . . A great many have volunteered, the fife and drum is heard from every quarter. I declare it makes one heart-sick to think how many young men must go and the anxiety that only half may return.

This philosophical remark did not prevent the next statement:

Brother has just come home to say there will be war for certain. Hurrah for America! I say.

I suppose you have heard of all the fires we have been having. The latest was the ten-pin alley but the people are so much opposed to ten-pins that they would not turn out as they generally do at a fire.

The Whigs had quite a jollification last night. There were a thou-

sand in the procession, marched over to French-town where they were addressed by Charles Anderson. They had splendid transparencies. One was a coon eating up a rooster with a motto "He crowed too soon." Another, "Louisiana, Whig to the core." You know all this fuss is about the Louisiana election. They sent to Cincinnati for six hundred torches but were disappointed in getting them, but they had fire-balls flying in every direction, tar barrels burning at the corners of the streets and the Dayton band out. The Transcript *and* Journal *offices splendidly illuminated. The procession marched through the principal streets and stopped at the Court House where our white-headed senator gave them a splendid speech. The whole concluded by some fine songs. The nearer election comes the more enthusiasm there is.*

(This with a date in February.) *The weather for the last three weeks has been delightful, the streets filled with ladies without shawls and carrying sunshades. The ladies look quite dashing these days in their cross-barred coats and white hats with feathers which are all the rage. The ladies walk out without their shawls just as if it were springtime. The fashion now is to have the bonnets very short and tipped over on the face and the hair in "coon tails" hanging out from under the bonnet. I have mine arranged so. But I suppose you wont care about this.*

Yesterday a large picnic came off at Ludlow Falls attended by the "white hat gentry" as we call them, from the white fur hats they wear.

We are sending you two pairs of pantaloons but cannot tell if they will fit. We hope the fine cashmere ones will. Mother says the laundress must not wash them in soft soap or they will shrink. . .

Last night they had a learned pig performance in the hall and I will send you a bill of the performance. The young folks talk of nothing else. Brother went to Yellow Springs yesterday. He thinks it must be nearly equal to Niagara Falls.

Parties given by the gentlemen are all the rage now. Several have been given under the title "Bachelors Ball." Alexander Gebhart went east last night to be married to a Miss Snyder of Somerset, Pa. It is also said that the great beau, Mr. Craighead, is engaged to his cousin in Pa. What has got into the men of our city to get their wives in the East? It shows very bad taste I think for certainly the Dayton girls cannot be beat.

Went down to the boat to meet sister and a party going from Toledo to Nashville. *Mr. Barney has begun his school; there are twelve scholars, eight of them boarders. I have received two philopena presents, one of them Young's* Night Thoughts, *beautifully bound.*

We are having a great time about politics. The Whigs have a meeting to nominate a candidate for squire. I suppose you know the Transcript *has come out Whig. Father would never look at it before but as soon as he saw it had changed he subscribed right off.*

The following passage shows what people went through in pre-vaccination days:

I suppose you have heard of the melancholy death of P. B. in Cincinnati. He died of the small-pox, the worst case in the fifteen hundred that are down, the doctors said. His mother went down two weeks before he died and waited upon him. He was put in the third story of the house with no one near him but his mother and a colored man who had the small-pox. She had to pay three dollars a day for help and was not allowed to leave the room even after he died. She had to dress him put him in the coffin and screw the lid down herself.

He was blind and deaf all the time but when be could speak he implored his mother not to cease praying for him. He was buried two hours after he died.

An accident this morning created great excitement. A little boy, one of a party of movers was thrown off a cart full of things and the cart ran over the boy's chest in front of Smith's Tavern. He was badly hurt but his parents put him in the wagon and drove off.

Maria Demorest and Dan Mead "Launched their bark in the sea of matrimony" last Tuesday night. I was there. It was large and pleasant. The bride dressed in white satin and (as all brides do) looked lovely; her husband (as all husbands do) not so well. They did not follow the usual custom but like sensible people stayed at home.

Bony (her brother Bonaparte Darst) *was in Cincinnati last week and brought me a splendid silk dress for a present. He paid $19.75 for it.*

Plenty of fun here as usual. We have in existence now a little one-horse theatre in the City Hall, admission twenty-five cents. It is crowded with the "lower crust" every night, . . . The Virginia Minstrels have been exciting our easily-excited community with their Lucy Lang. *The elite of our city were there, all the ladies and gentlemen but sad to relate it proved to be so vulgar that it put all the ladies to the blush and some of them sneaked home, so I heard. I was not there myself.*

May 9th, 1846: The river is higher than for ten or twelve years. About a thousand people have been watching it today (Sunday). McPhersontown (Riverdale) *is almost completely covered so that all on that side of the river have moved out, some at two o'clock in the morning. They take their things in canoes from their doors. Mr. Tate has had one hundred men working hard all day trying to keep the race bridge and head-gates from giving way. If they go his mill* (junction of Riverview and Forest avenues) *will be carried entirely off, then he will be a ruined man. About an hour ago I heard it would be impossible to keep the head-gates from giving way* (Steele's Dam). *I tell you it looks frightful up there. One of the long bridges this side of Troy had floated off. A stage with fourteen passengers was caught in fording Mill Creek all drowned.* (This proved to be a mistake.) *Later -- the river has fallen and Tate's Mill is saved.*

Great excitement about the Millennium. They say tomorrow or the next day the world is to be destroyed. Well, if it is you will never get this letter. . . . They have immersed fifteen people since last week. They meet twice a day at the Campbellite church and pray. Mr. Butterfield is almost crazy about it. He has sold all of his tools, given up his jobs, settled up all his business and is now ready to depart as the last trump sounds. . . . Mr. Barnes preached to a crowded house, a sermon to refute the Millerite preaching but one of our physicians says if the world does not come to an end this week he will burn his Bible.

John (Darst) *returned this morning from Cincinnati. He is perfectly delighted with the city, went to see everything that was to be seen. . . . He took five dollars with him besides paying his stage fare and* spent every cent of it. *He visited the theatre twice and the museum.*

The case between Holt and Comly is still pending. Tom Corwin made a splendid speech today; the Court House is filled from morning till night.

All is excitement about the return of the volunteers (Mexican War). *They are expected about three this afternoon. To look at the street it is like a convention; hundreds of people in from the country. All the bells are to be rung, the cannon to be fired and McKinney to make a speech at the National; a splendid dinner to be served at the Market House on Main Street. Tonight every house will be illuminated; every window in "The*

Four-Story" (the only four story building in Dayton, site of Rike's store) *will shine. I do wish you were here.*

There was a large party at the Phillips' last week given for Mrs. Beckel and Mrs. Edgar. I was invited but could not go. Tableaux at Ralph Hart's tomorrow night and a large party at Dick Phillips tonight.

I am really going to Niagara Falls. We are getting ready as fast as we can, expect to start the first of next week. I can hardly realize it all and will not believe I am going until I am on the boat and feel it starting.

In one of her not infrequent philosophical moments Martha Jane gets this off: *I think there is no greater accomplishment for a young lady or gentleman than to be able to write and compose a good letter.* In which sentiment we heartily concur.

Not all the letters of that era are fun-provoking and witty as Martha Darst's. Here is one with a different note in it, from T. J. S. Smith, a lawyer (grandfather of Fowler Smith) to his brother in June, 1840:

You remember a case of cholera occurred in our city whilst you were here. After that we heard no more of it until about a week since when a man from Cincinnati with his wife stopping at one of our taverns had a severe attack but in a short time was considered convalescent. The next day the landlord, Klein was taken with it and died in a few hours. The next day, Spohn, the undertaker who was a boarder at Klein's and assisted in putting the corpse into the coffin and drove the hearse was taken with it and died in the course of a few hours. The next day the ostler at the tavern was taken and died in a few hours. The day following Snyder, a hand in the Empire office who also boarded at Klein's was taken and died in a few hours and last night the wife of the Cincinnatian first taken died after an illness of a few days. After Klein was buried his wife, taking it into her head that he had been buried alive, hired a couple of Germans to disinter his body and examine it. They did so and were both taken with the cholera but are supposed to be convalescent. And strange as it may appear, three countrymen, two from adjacent counties and one from our own, who stopped at this tavern, two of them overnight, the other only for dinner, went home, were taken with the cholera and died in a few hours. What wonderful fatality! And how clearly it indicates the strongly infectious character of the disease! The tavern is closed and the city council have been employing means to cleanse and disinfect it.

The country people have such a dread of the city that our markets are very poorly supplied and we shall probably have to live on short allowance.

The outstanding event of this period of Dayton's history was the building of the courthouse. On that same corner had been a three-story brick building flush with the street, built in 1806 and used for both church and judicial purposes, where the furniture in the court room consisted of a few three-legged stools and a bench. This building was sold at auction in 1845 for eight hundred and sixty-four dollars.

In the spring of 1847 were laid the foundations of what Curwen in his first small history called "the most elegant and costly building of the kind in Ohio." It is indeed a remarkable edifice and grows more remarkable as the citizens of Dayton have grown in appreciation of fine things. That a group of men at that distant day, when foreign travel was unheard of, when books on art were few and architecture as a profession was very rare, could evolve such a structure will always be one of Dayton's sources of pride.

Its origin is somewhat obscure. Just who was mainly responsible for its style is debatable, but it is certain that Horace Pease had in his library the book of steel engravings depicting the Acropolis of Athens. Just below the famous ruin of the Parthenon is a temple to Theseus, a hero king who lived about 460 B. C. In style this was a type of Doric, built of Pentelic marble, and it was this temple which suggested to the county commissioners, through Mr. Pease, the type of building that the courthouse should be.

It is not, of course, an exact replica of the Theseum but maintains throughout the same dignity of form and beauty of structure. Our white limestone was the material used to build up the imposing pillared facade. The building is fire-proof throughout, the only wood used in its construction being the inner doors, window sashes and furniture. It is of vaulted masonry throughout, with a self-supporting stone stairway winding up from the entrance hall to the second floor.

The central apartment is the Probate Court room, elliptical in form, the shorter diameter being forty-two and the longer fifty-two feet in length. The whole is lighted by an elliptical dome, the eye of which is forty-three feet from the floor. Beneath the court room is an elliptical crypt supported by columns and arches. The design, together with the tentative sketches for ground plans was given to a Cincinnati architect, Mr. Howard Daniels, who prepared the working plans and specifications.

The Phillips House, built in 1852, destroyed in 1926.

Main Street and City Hall in 1860.

The courthouse was conceived in 1847, begun in 1848 and finished in 1850. It cost one hundred thousand dollars, a great sum for those financially narrow days, stands as we now know it and please God will for many years to come, a monument not like its great Grecian prototype to a long forgotten pagan king, but a monument to the public spirit, careful planning and artistic instincts of the men who built it.

The erection of so notable a building fixed the corner of Third and Main streets as definitely the center of the growing city. Increasing demand for a good hotel suggested that the proper site for such a building was across the street on the south side of Third. J. D. Phillips, who owned the corner, took the hint of circumstances and built a hotel which was known as a social center and the best place for man and beast in southern Ohio. It was named the Phillips House after the father of the owner, and its familiar outline, now obliterated by time and increasing real estate values, was for eighty years, as much as the courthouse, the center of Dayton.

Old letters written in the fall of 1852 speak of the prestige that was coming to Dayton from the new hotel. Nothing evidently equalled it between the Gibson House in Cincinnati and the Forest City House in Cleveland. The opening ball on October 14, 1852, was a social event that thrilled the Miami Valley up and down its entire length.

The *Daily Empire* said of the hotel that the order and beauty of its arrangements, the courteous and liberal style in which it is conducted, were the subject of general remark among the strangers that were present from Cincinnati, Indianapolis and Columbus.

"At the grand opening the three full stories of the Phillips House blazed with candles at every window. Carriages drawn by spans of horses deposited the guests at the Third Street entrance whence they mounted the stairs to the parlors on the second floor and then into the long dining room decorated as a ballroom."

On both sides of the entrance and across the street at the courthouse, uninvited outsiders watched with envy the girls tripping into the lobby with their escorts. The girls of those days, when they donned ball dresses, were worth looking at. No such skimpy outlines as the girls show now, but ample draperies and flowing skirts, They simply billowed and swam with the breadths of filmy material of their gowns.

For the elderly ladies silks that "would stand alone" were de rigueur, both girls and matrons encased in outlines four or five yards in circumference at the hem, the hoops which distended them giving a swinging motion to the skirts which, I have been informed by the beaux of the period, was very fetching. The skirts of lace or tulle garlanded with festoons of fluttering ribbons or artificial flowers we may well believe were compelling. And the white shoulders that rose out of the bodices of these gowns were also worth looking at. Mind, I did not say necks or backs but shoulders, and there is a vast difference, all in favor of the early fashion.

The coiffure of the day was low in the back with sometimes one curl escaping on one side and resting along one of those smooth shoulders emphasizing its smooth whiteness, while in front the tresses were parted and drawn softly down each side of the cheeks. There were pearls, of course, and not a few diamonds, little fans and bead "reticules" to hold the handkerchief. The slippers were square-toed and without heels, held on by crossed straps of velvet over the ankle. But they shouldn't be mentioned in the description of a toilet of eighty years ago, for only the tiniest tip was visible under the flounce of the skirt. No one ever saw as much of a girl's foot as the ankle. It was not good form.

The men of the day deserve mention and they shall have it. Pomaded hair worn quite long, high collar wrapped with an immense stock that looked when unfolded like a small shawl, tight waists and full-skirted coats with flaring tails worn over "pantaloons" which, if one could change the first syllables to "bal," would better describe them. These garments tapered suddenly to the feet and were strapped narrowly under the boots. So the beaux with their figured waistcoats, glued hair and little pointed boots were, as well as the belles, ravishing to the eye.

We investigate the columns of the daily papers of that day to find if society reporters practiced the same enthusiasms as they do today. The *Journal* editorialized on the Phillips House ball to this extent: "The ladies were elegantly and richly dressed and *all* (that word italicized he had no mind to get into trouble) looked very beautiful." Of the gentlemen he recorded that they were "polite and attentive and mirth, good cheer and good humor reigned supreme throughout the evening.

"The dancing was kept up until a late hour, or rather an early hour in the morning and old and young participated in the festivities with a hearty good will. Five hundred guests filled the dining room and presented a most enlivening appearance as the gay company threaded the mazy measure of the dance." (Oh, that reporter used the whole dictionary to tell the story of the Phillips House ball) "and displayed the elegance and grace which lends attraction to such a scene" (not forgetting the caterer and the band, he sends two bouquets flying in their direction). "The supper arrangements exhibited a perfect acquaintance with all that was required and no expense was spared to make this part of the entertainment a fitting accompaniment to the other arrangements. The tables were loaded with the choicest viands and delicacies. The cotillion band of Monsieur Ernest gave gayness to the fete."

"Threading the mazy measure" meant something in those days when square dances were the vogue. The cotillion first came and ten years later the quadrille. They were danced to four-step time and the leader "called the measures."

"Choose your partners," caused some palpitations on the part of young ladies not so sure that a black coat would be seen coming their way. A square, two facing two both ways, was formed and repeated all around the room. "Salute your partners" (but he always said "pardners"). Extreme bows on the men's part and low courtesies from the girls whose billowy skirts rose around them as they sank to the waxed floor.

"Right and left" "Ladies chain" (but he meant ladies change) and each lady crossed over and swung the partner of the girl opposite. "Allemand left" meant to turn to the left and go hand over hand from one partner to the other until you came to your own partner and place again on the floor. It was a contraction of "A la main," but the callers did not know it and the Phillips House dancers did not mind. "Chassez all," when each couple joined hands and skipped to the measure of the violins until the caller shouted "Places!" and it was all over until next time.

Of course there was the waltz but the less said about it the better, those days, for it had been imported from Paris and was considered "fast." For thirty or forty years round dances were forbidden by proper minded parents and thundered at from pulpits, but it was evidently included at this festivity because the paper speaks of "the dance and the waltz."

The list of managers and the executive committee included the names of everybody, men that is as ladies' names were not seen in print in the '50s, who was socially eminent in the city. Merely to read the list recalls the Dayton of the past. At the time of the destruction of the Phillips House (1926) it was humorously suggested that another party should be held to commemorate the fall of that one-time popular hostelry and that the only guests should be descendants of those who attended the 1852 ball. Colonel Edwin A. Parrott's name would be the card of entrance, for all the Parrotts still form quite a numerous clan in Dayton.

Henry Perrine was in the heyday of his society life at that time but he lasted full forty years afterwards and was always an indefatigable party-goer, the "perennial bachelor" of the smart set. He was, when I emerged from school into the social ring in the '70s, much more solemn and ponder-ous but still dancing with every society bud that came out, for by that time he had learned to waltz, or thought he had. A part of his procedure was to get himself hopelessly entangled in his partner's long train and have to stop in the middle of the floor and disentangle himself. I speak from personal and painful experience. The Perrine descendants are still numerous and would make a party in themselves.

Samuel Craighead was one of the beaux of the '50s and, with his wife, led in much social gayety. They both lasted until my day, when Mrs. Craighead had become a dowager with a seat along the wall which she filled like a throne and kept the tone of the young people what it ought to be. Alas! there are no Mrs. Craigheads now and too few of her descendants.

Daniel Beckel was another gay young buck of the executive com-mittee whose own home with its four daughters, when they came along a generation later, was a center for the club dances of the '70s. The big house on lower Jefferson Street is empty of girls and dances and will soon go the way of all dignified old homes when business pushes on them.

John G. Lowe's name as leader of ceremonies would let into the modern party several of the same name, all with the charm of manner which came as a heritage partly from him and partly from his wife, who was Marianna Phillips. There seems to have been little going on in the '50s and '60s, either social, civic or military, that Colonel Lowe and his wife did not have a hand in. The same must certainly be said of one granddaughter now, Mrs. H. E. Talbott, who with her flock of children and grandchildren would make an overwhelming party if nobody else came.

Charles Harries and Daniel Mead were both active in the Phillips House opening, and many other things beside. The Mead House on First Street with its carved woodwork and spacious rooms has now given place to a four-story garage. The early Meads would not have known what a garage is, let alone a "ramp," but the modern Meads do and drive up it too. The Meads, the Harries and the Lowes have all intermarried in the eighty years since the Phillips House party and their descendants would surely be in any festivity to continue the social life of Dayton.

Among the list of directors it is painful to observe, considering the strict principles which we have elsewhere chronicled, the names of some good and leading Presbyterian elders. I do not refer to the lighter and more worldly variety of church members represented by names like Valentine Winters, Peter P. Lowe, T. A. Phillips and William Harries, who valued their social obligations and observed them.

But what about deacons like Henry L. Brown, William Barnett and Peter Odlin? What were they doing with such frivolities as "ladies to the right, gentlemen to the left" or "promenade all?" There seems a discrepancy somewhere. We can only account for such a lapse from grace by explaining that the Phillips House was a big municipal affair sure to reflect credit on Dayton and they felt it their duty to support such a worthy undertaking. I have frequently heard such special pleading and doubtless it has its logic. Anyway the deacons were there, all of them.

It is interesting to speculate upon where the things came from which made the Phillips House so "well-appointed and chastely elegant" or where the dresses were purchased that "graced the ladies' fair forms." Across the street was the dry goods store of Keifer and Conover. In the advertisements of the day we find they called attention to "rose-colored silk for ball gowns, also taffetas and velvet ribbon." Again we find this: "V. Winters is now receiving and opening the largest and best selected stock of dry-goods in the city." (So the Keifers and Conovers had competition.)

Then Van Ausdal advertised "lace curtains, carpets and bedding;" G. W. McDaniel, "Fall and winter stocks of clothes, vestings and cassimeres; also shirts and collars. Under the Phillips House fourth door from Third." Here, evidently, is where the showy and dashing young gentlemen, our grandfathers, got their frippery for the Phillips House ball. Now the store, after the vicissitudes of eighty years, is dust and bricks and mortar. So is the Phillips House and everything in it gone into the past to make way for a modern Dayton which we fear will neither remember nor care about those lovely, leisurely, fastidious, courteous and friendly days.

It was on a Saturday afternoon in warm September, the 20th, 1858, (Ed. Note: it was Sept. 17, 1859) that Abraham Lincoln stood on the steps of the courthouse and spoke to the citizens of Dayton. Slavery was his main topic and he kept a big crowd listening to him for fully two hours.

The framers of our government, he said, found slavery existing but looked forward to the time when it should cease. The word slave is not found in the Constitution. He made an eloquent defense of the rights of free labor -- no white laboring man should be compelled to toil in competition with a slave. (There were enough Abolitionists in the audience to greet this declaration with a cheer.) The free white man had a right to claim that the new territories into which their children might go to seek a livelihood should be free from the encumbrance of slavery.

Hon. Lewis B. Gunckel wrote (in 1902) of this historical occasion:

In 1856 at the first Republican National Convention, an Illinois delegate nominated Lincoln for President. . . . Some two years after that Lincoln came to Dayton to speak. I was on the reception committee. When we called at his room in the Phillips House and knocked at the door there was a hearty western response, "Come in." Opening the door we were surprised to find him in his shirt sleeves and his wife brushing his hair. She afterwards put on his collar and cravat, he talking to us meanwhile without any apology for his undignified appearance. His speech was a surprise to everybody; a close logical argument without anecdote or illustration and yet so clear and so intensely interesting that although the audience stood upon the Court House steps and pavement not one person left until he closed.

In commenting upon this occasion the newspapers differ slightly. The *Journal* reported that five thousand people listened to him. The *Empire* (Democrat) said editorially: "Instead of tens of thousands of persons being assembled in our city to hear Mr. Lincoln and the streets deluged with people as one of our morning contemporaries prophesied would be the case, a meagre crowd of barely two hundred was all that could be drummed up, and they were half Democrats, who came out of curiosity. Mr. Lincoln is a seductive reasoner but his speech was a network of fallacies and false assumptions."

It was during this, his only visit to Dayton, that the now famous Nickum portrait was painted. Photography had but lately come in and the one photographer in Dayton was Mr. Cridland, who had a gallery on Main Street. The business in hand being finished, Mr. Cridland bethought himself of two young artists in a studio across the hall. The younger, Charles W. Nickum, he summoned to bring his brushes and paints and make a sketch of this stranger whose virile face so strongly moved him.

Mr. Samuel Craighead, who was present, told the artist that his subject was leaving for Cincinnati on the four o'clock train so he must work fast. So it was begun. Mr. Lincoln, amused that anyone should want to

This is the portrait young Charles Nickum drew of Abraham Lincoln on that famous day of Lincoln's Dayton visit, Sept. 17, 1859. The original sketch has long since been lost, but fortunately this photographic copy was found by Lincoln expert Lloyd Ostendorf of Dayton. (Photo courtesy Lloyd Ostendorf.)

paint his portrait, remarked to the young man, "Keep on; you may make a good picture but you'll never make a pretty one." The result shows a portrait with which we all are familiar, the one most often reproduced, and the only one without a beard.

In June the following year Mr. Craighead met Mr. Nickum on the street and asked if he had ever completed the picture of the friend whom he brought to the Cridland gallery.

"Yes."

"Where is it? I want it. That is the man nominated for President. That was Abraham Lincoln!"

"Then," writes Mrs. Nickum, "the little portrait was hunted up, framed and carefully cherished ever since. It has many admirers. The first offer to purchase it came from the editor of the Philadelphia *Public Ledger*. An article in the *Ledger* bewailed the fact that so few good paintings from life were made of Lincoln. Mr. Nickum wrote to the editor of his portrait and was offered to name his price. But the portrait was not for sale.

"At an examination of the Lincoln portrait at the Metropolitan Museum of Art in New York City one critic said he believed it recently done and mellowed by a new process. But when a revenue stamp was discovered on the back, put there when it was framed, in the '60s, he was silenced."

(Ed. Note: A photograph was taken by Thomas Cridland and a portrait by Charles Nickum was started that day and finished the next, according to Lincoln scholar Lloyd Ostendorf of Dayton. Both were unfortunately lost. A year later, Ostendorf claims, Nickum used oil paints to color a Mathew Brady photograph of Lincoln, by then elected president, and it is this colored photograph, still in the same frame made for it by Mr. Cridland, that is in the collection of the Dayton Museum of Natural History. The photograph, pictured on the back cover, shows a remarkably young-looking, handsome Abraham Lincoln, about to become president of the United States. It was right after his election that Lincoln started to grow his famous beard.)

8

The War Years

The '60s were the Civil War years. No one who lived through them will ever forget the scenes then enacted in our quiet streets. The great drama was played out many miles from Dayton, in the halls of Congress and on the battlefields of the South.

Here in Dayton we were behind the scenes. But our share was as vital to us as the greater action of the war itself. The story as a whole has been many times written in the different histories of our times and much valuable data as to events and personalities is to be found in the local histories. It would seem therefore pardonable if I should put the story down as it appeared to me, a child of seven when the war broke out.

Our little city nestling in the valley with its surrounding belt of river and green hills looked serene and quiet in those days, but there was a seething undertone of which I was only dimly conscious. Men came and talked with my father and I knew there was something ominous in their talk.

New words were being heard that had never been heard before: "Rebels," "Secession," "Union," "Traitor," "Red, White and Blue." The flag seemed to take on a sudden new significance. People took sides. Even the children were drawn into it and I sensed a certain hostility because my father was known to be an anti-war Democrat.

It was a warm April day in 1861. The streets were suddenly rent by a cry that came from newspaper boys with an extra issue which said, "Sumter fired on!" What was Sumter and why was it fired on? I ran into the house to seek my father and found him sitting with head bowed in hands before the fire in the sitting-room, an attitude of the deepest sorrow. "What is it, father?" I cried. "What has happened?"

"It is war," he replied. "Civil War! Brother against brother."

I was a little girl; I had read no history; I knew nothing of politics or slavery or the great issues of the day, but the bowed shoulders told me more than books. It was the impact of sheer tragedy that we were facing and which I only dimly understood. I was to understand better and better as time went on.

The excitement grew with each dispatch from Washington. Higher and higher rose the sentiment for war. If you were an abolitionist you were all right. If not you had best bury your head and keep still. Recruiting offices opened and the older boys at school began to enlist. There was a great deal of the hurrah side of war manifested -- flag raisings and marching with banners. New songs were on everybody's lips: *The Union Forever, Hurrah Boys, Hurrah!; The Red, White and Blue; We Are Coming, Father Abraham, Three Hundred Thousand Strong.*

The bands played them and we sang them. Everything centered on the courthouse steps. Boys in blue, girls in big hoops and little round hats atop their curls, filled the streets. I know now that in less than two days after Lincoln's call for troops Dayton had answered by sending two companies of militia. I saw them march to the depot and one would have thought they were going to a festival instead of to a war.

Indeed, I well remember how sure people were that the South would be put down in no time, and that in a few weeks the boys would be back home again. I know now, too, that it was the sagacious foresight of Salmon P. Chase, then Governor of Ohio, that made possible the quick response of Ohio with its well organized and finely equipped militia. As a State we were far and away ahead of other states. Dayton likes to live up to big promises and she did then.

Two regiments were equipped here and at Camp Chase on the Springfield Pike, three miles east of town. Every time a contingent of forces entrained, there were the same scenes of excitement and patriotism. People worked themselves into a frenzy. The two newspapers: the Republican *Journal* and the *Empire*, Democratic, were vitriolic in their attacks on each other.

We began to know what mob spirit was. One night we awoke to hear hoarse voices and to see the light of flames in the vicinity. It was the *Journal* office on Main Street just back of our house. From a bedroom window I watched with a younger brother. The glare, the shouts of men, the terrified neighing of horses taken from a threatened stable and tied in front of our house, all filled me with terror. A fire is a fearful thing, but when combined with political hatred and partisan bitterness it is indeed something to appall the soul.

Fear and antagonism did not stop with incendiarism but led to actual murder. My father was called to attend the editor of the *Empire*, who was shot as he was coming home from market. There was nothing to do for he died almost instantly, a war casualty that had no glory in it.

Longer and longer grew the war story. The months dragged on. We heard of Chickamauga, Bull Run, Stone River, Chancellorsville. Notices of the dead were posted at the courthouse corner and we feared to look. War funerals wended their way out Brown Street to the cemetery, with the dead march as an accompaniment and flags at half mast. More and more we saw women in black.

Then came a piece of news that took us as a family in. There had been a great battle at Pittsburg Landing and my father as a surgeon was called to minister to the wounded. It was not a pleasant time for a wife to be left alone with three little children.

Nothing but the assurance that doctors were safe because their work kept them behind the lines was any comfort to me. I am afraid I was not much of a patriot. He came home to us safely, in time, with awful tales of the horrors of war, and then we moved into another home. And always the bitter hatred of anybody that thought out of the stream of common opinion pursued us as a family. Because my father was a personal friend of Vallandigham I was subjected to a sort of persecution from my schoolmates.

A state election was on hand with Brough the Republican candidate and processions and meetings in order. I was jerked to the scene of one public demonstration and told to say at the top of my voice:

> *Hurrah for Brough and Abraham!*
> *And a rope to hang Vallandigham!*

Well, I wouldn't. Wild horses could not get it out of me. Whereupon I was shut up in an empty outbuilding and the girls all went home to supper. Rescued by a frightened and irate father I told him I had stood up for our side. He kissed me and laughed.

My mother had her own particular ordeal. Late at night. Father

117

away on an all-night case in the country. Mother sleeping with the children in the sitting room downstairs. Fanny Stacey (otherwhere described) in an adjoining room. Steps and voices outside. Through a lifted shade a group of men could be seen pointing towards the house

The door bell and the curt question: "Is the doctor home?"

No answer possible except the true one: "No."

"When will he be back?"

"I can't of tell."

Then quiet for a time. Then voices and steps sound from the side porch and it was thought best to waken Fanny to be what moral support a very deaf, very timid, person could be. Her immediate reaction to the situation was to crawl under the bed where her hair, catching in the bed springs, kept her a prisoner. At last the crowd dispersed and the last remark heard by my trembling mother was "We'll burn this hell-hole down next."

Other less personal occurrences crowded the next few years. A bazaar was held in the Beckel House for the benefit of the soldier families. A cantata was given in Huston Hall, directed by James Turpin for the same purpose. Patriotism grew as the news indicated that the North would be victorious. And at last it was. Another event to hold the attention of childish minds. At two in the morning our doorbell was rung, not to ask about the doctor but to tell us that Lee had surrendered.

The war was over and won! Then again we heard the guns of victory fired, this time from the Commons; again heard the bands and saw the red and white and blue bunting covering buildings. Great rejoicing, and then great sorrow. The wires spoke again and they told us of the assassination of President Lincoln. Decorations came down, the music changed to a minor key, everybody was seen in tears and crepe, America had lost her best friend. This was how the Civil War seemed to one who had no idea of its meaning, a faintly colored sketch that the bigger and better histories do not give.

Dayton was, during these war years, as for some time after, a small middle-western city, or rather, a mere country town, past its village life and not yet emerged into cityhood. Then, as now, the corner of Third and Main Streets was the center.

To me it was more. It was the center of the universe. My imagination could impossibly picture anything more portentous than the buildings that graced that locality. There was the courthouse with the pillars, the Phillips House, then in its pristine magnificence. Busses were always backed up to the sidewalk in front of the Third Street entrance, embodying in themselves a hint of far-off places like Cincinnati or Cleveland. There was Keifer and Conover's store on the southeast corner and the Harshman and Gorman bank on the northeast, with Odell's bookbindery above it. How imposing it looked to my eyes and how meagre it really was!

The business section of Dayton, in that day, began and ended in the two squares between Second and Fourth Streets on Main. A few stores spread out on Third each side of Main. There were dwellings between the Phillips House and the church on the corner of Ludlow and between the Courthouse and Ludlow.

The section west of Wilkinson was entirely residential. Miss Eaker lived in the big box-like house on the corner which afterward became the Young Men's Christian Association and now has given way to something else. The imposing pillared home of Valentine Winters graced the middle of the block but no one remembers it when looking at the Federal Building on that site. The Youngs lived on that block and the Gebharts, the Loom-ises, the Keifers and, in the house not yet occupied by the Bicycle Club, dwelt the Willey Smiths and later the Craigheads.

Perry Street was the last real cross street and the Brady home on the corner the last good residence on Third. Beyond that the houses were small and scattered, interspersed with vegetable gardens and corn patches. The street led on to the levee where it went up and over the top and down into a gravelly river bottom before it again rose to meet the bridge.

This bridge, a dark, covered, timbered structure, the only kind they knew how to build in those days, only crossed the main current of the river. As soon as the river rose, as it did regularly spring and fall, it swept over the roadway between the bridge and town, making an impassable thor-oughfare. It could be forded, of course, and always was, the horse plunging along in and out of the holes in the gravel bottom. If the river rose to any considerable height the people on the west side of the river were quite cut off from town until the river went down.

There were not many of them. Cornfields began immediately as one crossed the bridge. One building only remains in my memory and it is not a fragrant memory. On the levee opposite the end of Fourth Street stood Finney Sprague's glue factory, supposed to be too remote from civilization to trouble the noses of Daytonians, but I can smell it yet. On Third Street I remember field after field on either side of the soft dirt road, but no dwell-ings except farm houses. On the corner of Summit was a blacksmith shop.

Grace Methodist Episcopal Church before the move to Salem Avenue (above). The First Lutheran Church is another beautiful structure that gave way to progress downtown (right).

So much for the west side of small old Dayton. On Main Street, stores ceased and homes began just north of Second. The roadway, wide, empty, muddy in winter and dusty in summer, plunged into the dark mouth of the old wooden bridge. Once across this bridge one was again in the country, except for a handful of small houses on either side of the road called McPhersontown. Beyond that, nothing but cornfields, unless they were wheat fields, until one reached West Milton, Covington or Ludlow Falls, for this was the Covington Pike of dear memory to those who wanted a drive in the country.

Just over the bridge a mud road slanted down to the left (now Riverview Avenue) and followed the curve of the river. It was a pleasant drive, sunny, quiet and warm, the huge sycamore trees that lined the bank leaning out over the current and holding on to a precarious roothold in the soft loam. Long ago they were carried down in a flood and no one thinks to plant more.

Along that bank in the '60s was the only rope-walk in Dayton. It was owned by a man named Kilworth. His starting point was in a shed near the bridge from whence he carried the strands of hemp to a point at some distance, twisting as he walked and slowly manipulating the strands. When they had been twisted long enough and hard enough and suddenly released they formed, of their own accord it seemed, a nice smooth rope. This was an operation watched with extreme interest by bystanders.

Main Street toward the south stopped being a business street suddenly and at Fourth came out frankly as a leading residential section. On the west side were four large homes with shady yards and pleasant entrances. They belonged to the Peter P. Lowes, the John G. Lowes, the Lytles and the Coblentzs. On the east side, the Lutheran Church presently raised its beautiful tower to heaven but has now been scattered to the earth, to give way to commercialism.

Jefferson Street for its full length was a thoroughfare of stately old mansions. The Cleggs lived there, the Beckels, the Parrotts, the Voorhees, and the Gormans. First and Second Streets, from Main West, presented an unbroken vista of lovely well-kept homes. From east to west one could count the names of families who have made Dayton what it is: Harries, Simms, Walters, Bimm, Parrott, Bunstine, Steele, Phillips, McDaniels, King, Smith and the old Cooper Seminary, where all the girls went to school, then Crane, Barney, Babbitt, Rench and others down to the levee; after these came the rise to the top of the levee and the green pastures along the river. Second Street held Gebharts, Greens, Perrines, Peases, Edgars, Neals, Gumps and so on again to the river, always the end of everything as far as Dayton was concerned, the boundary beyond which was Montgomery County.

An old resident of Dayton, having moved to California, and having heard that a business building then lately erected on the corner of Ludlow and Second Streets was probably the precursor of more, exclaimed in dismay: "But where are Dayton people to live?" Her idea was that being forcibly exiled from a home on the blocks bounded by First and Second, Ludlow and Perry Streets, a Daytonian would fall off the earth.

Let us return to the perhaps dry enumeration of what constituted Dayton in the '60s. East Third Street soon left behind the buildings of the center of town and led to open spaces, beyond which were Harries Station and Harshmanville, five miles away. Fifth Street crossed the canal and reached a semi-suburb called Oregon, of which there was nothing much, except the Darst mills, a fire engine house, some small stores and then the inevitable wide-spaced "commons" full of gypsum weed, dandelions and rubbish heaps.

One thing I must not forget. A German baker named Wolf, in his little bakery on Fifth Street, manufactured a delectable cracker sold for years as Wolf's crackers. They are a strictly indigenous product and not found anywhere else. For at least seventy years Daytonians have eaten them with oyster soup and with cream cheese, and it is hard to imagine a substitute. The name has been changed to the *Dayton cracker* but, being made by the original formula, they taste the same. Dynasties may rise and fall and so may the Miami River and all our old landmarks may be replaced by skyscrapers but as long as we have the *Dayton cracker* we can carry on.

South of Dayton, Main Street ran out into the country soon after it passed the fairgrounds. Ludlow Street had no buildings of any account below the railroad tracks. There was indeed a schoolhouse, known as Campbell's school where a good many of the town boys went, also a stone yard to which the limestone from the quarries on the Beavertown Pike was hauled for cutting and where chisels and hammers of the workmen made a musical din on the summer air.

Then more open spaces with Irish and darkey cabins, potato patches, cow pastures and weeds, with this difference that, whereas there were commons between the ends of all the streets and the river, the Ludlow Street expanse was known as "the Commons."

My single concern with the Commons was to go there on errands for my mother relative to household help. There lived a muscular and vociferous Irish woman whose brogue resounded whenever she came to do the family washing. Her name was Shea, but we called her "She-hee," although not in derision. When she hung out the clothes it was our treasured habit to sing *No Irish Need Apply* at her, that being a popular song brought into fashion by the minstrel shows that came to Dayton.

The railroad tracks going west crossed, as they do now, the Miami River upon the last bridge of the four that connected us with the country beyond. If one had an errand on the other side, one drove up over the levee and down straight into the current which was pretty deep and swift just at that side. To me it was always a perilous adventure, the buggy seeming to swim upstream and the water not seldom sweeping through the buggy bed, forcing us to put our feet on the dashboard.

As I remember the Dayton streets of that time, my first impression, colored by the condition of our present traffic, is that of solitariness. Old pictures will bear me out. Two buggies to a block covered the traffic of 1865. Drays were a familiar feature, although they since have completely disappeared. Not even a picture of one survives. Turned, with tail to the sidewalk from which barrels were rolled up onto the sloping floor, pushed forward and held in place by stakes run through holes in the floor, they were a useful vehicle for the transportation of freight.

The streets themselves became a problem early in our city life. The underlying gravel upon which our earliest citizens prided themselves proved less of a blessing than a curse. For superimposed loads of it piled the middle of the street so much higher than the gutters that only the vehicle in the middle of the road kept an even keel. The ones on the side tilted at an uncomfortable angle.

Our limestone deposits made a sort of mortar bed when the rains came and when the winds followed, it was transformed into an alkali powder very trying to throat and nose. Pigs and cows roamed at will. Almost every family kept a cow and either used or sold the milk. At evening the cows were driven home from across the river by little boys hired for the purpose. A mother pig with her brood could nestle comfortably in a puddle on the corner of Jefferson and Fourth Streets without menace from her human neighbors. Geese squawked their way across our principal thoroughfares without molestation.

The first citizen to suggest, through the papers, that this bucolic

The carved doorway of the Daniel Mead house on West First Street.

state of things cut us off from competing with the leading cities of the nation was bitterly denounced as entirely unworthy of being listened to. Indignant letters from "Pro Bono Publico" and all his family demanded: "How can we get along if we have to shut up our livestock and go to the expense of feeding them?"

For perhaps two blocks north and south and east and west from the municipal center there were stone sidewalks, none elsewhere; of curbing and guttering there was none. An ordinance printed in an early edition of the *Centinel* forbade people driving across the sidewalks "unless absolutely necessary," but there being no traffic policeman the phrase "absolutely necessary" was left to the individual to define.

Lest I convey the impression that life in Dayton of that day was rough and primitive, let me hasten to say that there was in the decades following 1840 and 1850 a not by any means small amount of what they used to call "genteel" living. That is, there were social coteries where fine old silver and delicate china made entertaining a joy. Domestic living, if not on the precise scale of values today was still lavish and generous. Wives had so little to do outside of keeping house that they did it superlatively well.

If it be asked, "who were the moneyed men of Dayton of that day?" the mind will unconsciously travel in a different direction from that of the present. The palatial homes of Dayton are now south of the city in Oakwood and Hills and Dales, but at that time those hilly acres were nothing but a part of Montgomery County. The *Dayton Journal* for May 3, 1869 lets some light into the subject with its list of taxable incomes. It is interesting to find that the thousand dollar exemption was in force then; also all funds invested in certain classes of corporations were taxed in corporation returns and not by the individual owner. By taking these items into calculation one may ascertain the incomes of the leading men of financial standing in Dayton at that time.

Several things are to be noted: First, that fewer than seven hundred men in Montgomery County paid any income tax at all; second, these men paid a total income tax of only $62,347; and third, only fourteen men had incomes running to five figures. They ranged all the way from E. E. Barney at $10,713 to Alexander Gebhart at $30,493, subtracting, of course, the thousand dollars exemption.

The twelve remaining names on the golden list were: John C. Dunlevy, $15,004; W. K. Eckert, $11,000; Joseph Clegg, $12,688; Edward Brennan, $12,045; E. G. Beck, $19,304; Preserved Smith, $11,191; T. A.

Phillips, $11,981; D. E. McSherry, $11,914; George W. Harshman, $17,960; J. H. Peirce, $12,050; Alfred Pruden, $14,839; Adam Pritz, $12,957. So those names comprised, in 1868, "richest Dayton."

The above noted belonged to the millionaire class of that day. Other rich men were: Isaac Van Ausdal, $1,326; Eugene J. Barney, $4,369; Samuel Craighead, $3,465; William P. Callahan, $8,000; R. R. Dickey, $5,075; Charles B. Clegg, $4,265; Dennis Dwyer, $1,720; J. H. Winters, $1,283; J. A. Walters, $2,031; Ezra Bimm, $3,200; R. W. Steele, $1,873; Mary Belle Eaker, $2,673; John W. Stoddard, $6,900; John A. McMahon, $3,185; H. V. Perrine, $1,748; William P. Huffman, $6,286.

It gives one, as the French say, "abundantly to think." Here was life carried on, families brought up, social affairs conducted, charities maintained, on individual incomes that would today mean nothing less than poverty. The key to the puzzle is, of course, in the reduced purchasing power of the dollar. Money went farther in the '60s than it does in the 1930s. The Dayton of 1868 was not a meagre Dayton; it was as full of the graces and amenities of life as today, although on a different scale.

The names on this list represent the contributing forces that built up the city. The Lutheran Church, for instance, was constructed and financed largely with Gebhart money and they were not all Alexanders either. He was the richest brother but the rest did their bit nobly.

People lived well, gave big parties, set overflowing dinner tables, carpeted their parlors with gay Brussels carpets and graced windows with long lace curtains. They drove carriages with high-stepping horses and did these things on incomes which today would not keep a working man in comfort. To take single instances: Dr. Reeve, a plain medical practitioner, was never even on the fringes of Dayton rich men. Including the exemption he had a little over $3,000 a year income on which he reared four children, sending them to eastern schools or to Europe, or both, for their education; kept two, and sometimes three, horses; and lived, the six of them, comfortably and happily on such a stipend.

The John Stoddards across the river, maintained a house that even to its last day when it was demolished to make room for the Masonic Temple, was an example of carved wood, ornamented ceilings and gorgeous hangings that represented money and money and money. Down the magnificent stairway I have seen Mrs. Stoddard come, to greet her guests, in a blue velvet with a two-yard train, her white neck glittering with pearls and diamonds. The house and everything in it were proof that the Stoddards had everything that money could buy in that day and yet they had it on about eight thousand a year.

Those days are gone -- the names, the families, the big houses and the carved lintels. *Sic transit gloria Stoddard!* which may be bad Latin but allowable as sentiment.

That ogre of present-day life, the High Cost of Living, had not raised its horrible head amongst us. One could rent a pleasant house on a nice residential street for twenty dollars a month. One could boldly carry a market basket down town with only a dollar in one's pocket and get by, too. That sum would secure the Sunday roast, a week's supply of butter and eggs and vegetables enough to fill it up to the handle.

A housekeeper would be shocked at having to pay more than a dollar for the Christmas turkey. A general housework girl could be had, in 1865, for three dollars a week including the family laundry. You put ten cents into the plate at church and hoped such generosity would be counted against your transgressions. You gave a party and paid the musicians five dollars and you got a baby for the same figure.

Elihu Thompson was a well-to-do lawyer but he got along on an income of a little over a thousand dollars and, if I am not mistaken, he drove a buggy on it. Most people did, and took care of the horse themselves. Valentine Schaeffer brought up seven good Methodist children on $1,700 a year. Since a two thousand-dollar income made a man feel rich he looked and acted rich if he had it. To see Thomas Babbitt walk down Main Street (a real Main Street and a real Babbitt) was to see Rockafellerean prosperity personified. He looked like a millionaire, he walked like a millionaire and yet the assessor, Ashley Brown, has him for only about $3,500, less the exemption.

In no single way have we progressed more astonishingly since the days of which I am writing, as in health. I am not thinking of advanced surgery or antiseptics or anesthetics, but of the ordinary everyday measures which we now take to keep well but which were not even whispered in the '60s. One common ailment was sick headaches. They were recurrent. Everybody had them at intervals and always expected to.

The outraged stomach and nerves rebelled once every so often and sent the owner to bed to sleep it off and learn better if he could. Fresh air, fresh water and green vegetables were almost unknown considerations. The daily diet included meat three times a day and most of it fried. Windows were not only shut all winter but the cracks filled in with selvage from the tailors. No one ever slept out of doors, even in summer. No green vegetables were eaten until they grew in the market gardens near Dayton. Oranges were luxuries. In any family there was always one member of it collapsed with either malaria or migraine or both. The doctors did nothing but prescribe drugs, mostly violent purgatives, and quinine.

It was the popular belief that children's contagious diseases were inevitable and necessary. All children took their turn at having measles, chicken-pox and whooping-cough, and as they always would have them, "the sooner the better," said the mothers. They were even sometimes exposed to contagion so as to get it over with.

Typhoid fever and scarlet fever went the rounds of a neighborhood with tragic results. No one had yet connected a cholera epidemic with open sewers; no one saw death in an unsanitary milk supply; no one suspected that mosquitoes had anything to do with a high death rate. It was a better day for the children, and for their mothers as well, when doctors succeeded in impressing upon people that when sickness occurs it is generally some one's fault and can generally be prevented.

When a comparison with the past induces us to "count up our mercies," as the old woman did who was charmed to find that although she only had two teeth they did meet in the middle, our blessings emerge with added lustre. This brings us to the modern dentist and his works of mercy and skill. In the '60s many a vigorous man or woman of forty was as good as on the scrap heap from decayed teeth.

No one gives us more length of working days and joy in them than the dentist and he seems never to get any credit. What use are money and good clothes if you have no teeth? The art which gives to men of eighty the use of their digestion and their enunciation is a great one and insufficiently eulogized.

9

The Later F. F. D.'S

It is something to be thankful for that the F. F. D.'s could not all go into one chapter. The influence of Israel Ludlow and John Cleves Symmes, who were the first to stimulate western emigration in our directions, did not cease at their death. It was current opinion among leading and thoughtful men in the East, particularly in New Jersey, that, if a young man desired to go out into the world and try his fortunes, Dayton was the place to head for.

The character of our citizenship had been fixed by such names as Van Cleve, Phillips, Schenck, Crane, Perrine, Conover, and it was most natural that it should continue in the same strain. The exodus from Kentucky was started by the Pattersons and continued by the Steeles, the Browns and others. The whole Gebhart clan came from Somerset County, Pennsylvania, and everybody knows what they brought to Dayton.

It is pleasant to discover that most of the later F. F. D.'s marched right along in the paths marked out by their fathers. Jefferson Patterson followed his father, Robert Patterson, in the Rubicon Farm home where he raised a family of eight children, carried on both mills, went to the Ohio Legislature and, into the fourth generation, served his city.

The Phillips' sons brought with them the culture of their ancestor, the first president of Princeton University, Jonathan Dickinson. The Steele sons, Dr. James and Robert W., carried on as loyal citizens as their father did before them.

John Van Cleve, eldest child of the marriage of Benjamin Van Cleve and Mary Whitten, was a remarkable man. His impress upon the lives of Daytonians was more vital even than that of his father, for he was a graduate of Oxford, a "born scholar," inheriting not only his father's love of books and learning but an extraordinary facility as well. At the university he not only had no trouble in keeping up with his class, it was the class who could not keep up with him.

At sixteen he was teaching Latin and Greek and as for mathematics he wrote, "I consider Euclid the most pleasing study I ever undertook." Robert Steele has left the record that John Van Cleve went through Colburn's *Intellectual Arithmetic* in one day, when it first came out to Ohio. Interested in agriculture, he introduced many improvements on his farm and his beautifully kept minutes of the Montgomery County Horticultural Society testify to his love for flowers. The elder Van Cleve's methodical, industrious, and persevering habits were amplified in the son who fulfilled every expectation of his father.

John Van Cleve's life in Dayton was a solid benefit in more ways than can be told. After leaving college he studied French and German, translating a number of plays and stories from both languages. Are we telling the story of a pedant who made the most of his learning that it might set him above his fellows?

Read Mary Steele's beautiful tribute to the essential humanness of the man. He loved children and was a born teacher, he gathered the little folks around him and told them about flowers and stars and foreign countries. On free Saturdays he took them into the woods for long walks full of interest in everything in nature. Women, whom the writer only knew when they had passed the Psalmist's limit, used to be roused to an almost juvenile enthusiasm when telling of those walks with Mr. Van Cleve and gave him credit for all they knew of poetry and flowers and books.

In 1851, in contradiction to the habit of business men of today, Mr. Van Cleve retired from active work and, like a European gentleman, began to live. Study, art and music, and above all an absorbing devotion to all things that would benefit his native city, were the things that occupied Mr. Van Cleve's days. He was musician (organist at Christ Church), painter, botanist, civil engineer, engraver, geologist, collector of fossils and curios for the Dayton Library and Museum, edited for a short time the *Dayton Journal*, a correspondent with scientists and noted men of the day. His complete herbarium of plants indigenous to the Miami Valley as well as his collection of fossils have been lost sight of.

There is no need for the stately shaft of marble which, on the highest point of Woodland Cemetery, marks the resting place of John Van Cleve, for the whole cemetery is his monument. Two other cities in the United States had, at that time, beautifully laid out resting places for their dead. He determined that Dayton should be the third which, under his expert and loving guidance, it became. It was he who selected the site, high above the roofs of the city. It was he who laid it out, ran the lovely curving roads, planted the trees, often with his own hands, set out dogwoods and redbuds, maples and beeches, kept the books, and exercised all the duties of superintendent, all entirely without compensation.

He found the levee an ugly shapeless hill which encircled the town to keep the encroaching waters of the river from our streets and headed a list of subscribers for the purpose of beautifying this parkway. With his own hands he put out saplings of elm, maple and silver-leaf poplars; and a little girl who loved to work in the dirt went with him and put down in his book the date at which each tree was planted. They call it Robert Boulevard now and forget, when they walk under that noble row of branching trees, who it was that so long ago took the pains to make it the most beautiful walk in Dayton.

With the vision of making our city like the elm-embowered towns of New England, Van Cleve surrounded the courthouse with elms, and when they got to the age when the green limbs lifting to the sky framed the classic pillars in their foliage, an editor who thought that to have trees in a city made it look countrified kept at it in his paper until the elms fell victims to the municipal axe. Sad enough to forget such a man as Van Cleve but to undo his work is worse.

Van Cleve's official positions should be recorded but are not so interesting. He was one of the founders of the Dayton Library Association, promoter of many public benefits to add books to the library, he was city engineer and member of the volunteer fire brigade, he compiled a map of Dayton, helped edit the *Log Cabin* and wrote campaign songs for the Harrison rally in 1840; was an enthusiastic Whig and promoter, with James Turpin, of the Whig Glee Club.

It would be pleasant for an historian to present a portrait of this man who did so much for Dayton but there is no such thing in existence. Being somewhat over three hundred pounds in avoirdupois he was sensitive about it and never sat for his picture. It was said of him that when he went sleigh-riding in one of the little compact cutters prevalent in that day there was no room for anyone else. The lack of his portrait is a profound loss. Also, it would be gratifying for an historian to record the names of Van Cleve's descendants and to call attention to the benefits they were conferring upon the city for which their father did so much. There are no descendants, for John Van Cleve died unmarried. All there is of tangible memory is in Mary Steele's *Early Dayton*, a beautiful tribute from one who knew him well.

Jogging up through the woods from Lebanon there came to Dayton, in 1831, a young man described by those who knew him at the beginning of his career as slim, pale-faced and light-haired. This is not at all as he appeared to us who knew him fifty years later, when he was plethoric, dignified and imposing, in fact, General Robert C. Schenck.

At the time of which we write, he was on his way from the law office of Tom Corwin, "the wisest lawyer in Ohio," where he had read law for a year and from whom he carried a letter of introduction to Judge Crane. Previous to his Lebanon experience, Schenck had graduated with high honors at Oxford and, previous to that, he had come west from New Jersey with the rest of the Schencks whose name was then legion and who settled, some in Franklin and some in Lebanon. Dayton, then the largest town north of Cincinnati, was an attraction partly social, from the prominent families there residing, and partly professional from the prestige of Judge Crane's large practice.

In the saddle-bags of the traveler in search of his future was a sealed letter from the distinguished Mr. Corwin to Judge Crane, which the latter read, slowly raising his eyes from the paper to scan the features of the young man facing him. At the close, he immediately invited Robert Schenck to be his partner-in-law. The association thus formed lasted for many years and proved to be one of the most extensive and lucrative in the state.

The logical and original mind of the junior partner made its prompt impression upon the town and the state. In politics he was an ardent Whig and contributed both by money and personal prestige to the election of William Henry Harrison. It is safe to say that not a public enterprise in Dayton but felt the impact of Robert Schenck's personality. Intellectual and public-spirited, a lover of books and the fine things of life, he lent his influence to both civic and cultural enterprises in Dayton.

The documents of the time show him to have been either a founder or promoter in the hydraulic enterprise, that great power source in our first manufacturing interests; in the turnpikes which reached out from Dayton like the spokes of a wheel and brought to us all we had from the outside world; and the railroads, when they came in, owed much of their impetus to his industry.

The Mechanics Institute was his pet project, not only as manager but as actual lecturer. His free lectures -- free on his part -- were one of the sources of the finances which supported that institution. At the courthouse one evening, he aroused public opinion by his eloquence in favor of the Mad River and Lake Erie Railroad and headed the list of stockholders himself. Together with John Van Cleve and others he fostered the necessities and beauties of Woodland Cemetery.

What more natural than his emergence from these merely local interests to outside and national affairs? In 1841 Robert Schenck was called to represent his district in the Ohio Legislature. In 1843 to do the same in Congress where he remained for eight years one of the foremost workers in his party. It was during these years, Judge Crane having died, that he associated himself in partnership with Wilbur Conover, a young lawyer and graduate of Oxford. Mr. Conover took charge of the large practice of the firm which became from then on one of the commanding law firms in southern Ohio.

In 1851 Robert Schenck's attributes of statesmanship were further called upon; he represented the United States as Ambassador to Brazil where he remained for six years and rendered important service. His letters to his law partner during these years are models of wit and brilliancy, as well worth reading now as when they were penned more than seventy-five years ago. Returning to Dayton he entered into the Lincoln-Douglas campaign and was said by Lincoln himself to be the first one who ever spoke of him for the Presidency.

In 1861 came the outburst of the Civil War when Schenck made a prompt offer of his services to the government; they were accepted and rewarded with a commission as brigadier-general. That he was not a mere carpet-knight was shown by the fact that after the disastrous battle of Bull Run he was commended for "gallantry in action and coolness and discretion in retreat." Two more advances in rank made him first major-general (when no longer fit for active service), then commander of the Middle District.

However, not only his military services which were great, but his statesmanship was what endeared General Schenck to his party and his country. Elected again to Congress in 1863 he resigned his commission in the army to take his place again among the law-makers of the nation. Mary

Steele, in her *Early Dayton*, says that "a history of the career of Robert C. Schenck in the thirty-ninth and fortieth congresses would be a complete history of the military legislation of the United States through the most eventful war to its close." He had not a mere academic view of military methods and principles but a grasp born of actual personal participation in the great war.

Upon the accession of General Grant to the Presidency, one of his first acts was to appoint Robert Schenck as Ambassador from the United States to the Court of St. James. In England the recognition of his mental stamina and personal prestige won him many friends, and throughout the six years of his residence in London, he and his three daughters maintained a hospitality open alike to their own countrymen and foreigners of position and power.

Robert Schenck will be chiefly remembered in Europe as well as at home for his efforts in bringing about a peaceful settlement of the problems confronting the joint High Commission at the Geneva Conference of which he was a member. The closing years of his life were passed in Washington but he was held by Daytonians to be one of their number, our most distinguished citizen, the crowning achievement of whose life was that he used his best talents in the service of his city, his state and the nation, putting public interests always before his own. He was buried from Christ Church and carried out to the Woodland Cemetery which he had so loved.

There was another member of the Schenck family, Admiral James F. Schenck, who began as a midshipman in 1825 and ended as an admiral. Between these two phases in his life, the beginning and the end, came almost as many distinguished adventures and services as in those of his cousin, the general.

He enlisted in the navy in 1825, became a citizen of Dayton in 1836, went on frequent long cruises, rising meanwhile rapidly from rank to rank, visited the West Indies, Japan, the Mediterranean, Africa, China, Brazil, all in years crowded with active service and rich experiences. Throughout all his naval record was a fine one.

As captain of the *Congress*, in 1845, he served in the Los Angeles, the Santa Barbara and the San Pedro battles; he participated in the capture of Guyamos and Mazatlan in Mexico. In 1862 we find him in command of the frigate *St. Lawrence*, and joining the blockading squadron at Key West. In 1864, as commander of the *Powhatan*, he led a division of the squadron at the bombardment of Fort Fisher. Upon his retirement from the navy in

1869, and after his appointment as rear-admiral, Admiral Schenck came to Dayton as the pleasantest place among the pleasantest people he could find, to end his days.

There, in his home on the northwest corner of First and Wilkinson streets, he and his daughters lived and entertained their friends. The entertainment consisted not only of a famous punch brewed in the big Canton bowl known and revered by Dayton housekeepers of the old school, but by the stories told by the admiral from his long life on the sea and in foreign lands. He was a racy teller of racy anecdotes such as are not forgotten until all the hearers of them are at rest in Woodland.

My only personal recollection of the Admiral was of passing, as a schoolgirl, his side gate on Wilkinson Street and seeing him sitting in the yard under the shade of his trees telling stories to his friends. He wore white duck and a naval cap with gold lace, a costume effectively novel to us inland Daytonians. He died in 1882.

James Steele (treated in a former chapter) married Phoebe, daughter of Isaac Peirce, an officer of the Revolutionary Army, and thus allied himself with another First Family of Dayton. He died in 1841 and left two sons: Dr. James Steele, who practiced medicine for years on the corner of Third and Ludlow, and Robert Steele for whom not a chapter but a whole volume would be necessary to chronicle his services to his native town.

The merest list of his interests and activities will tell the story of loyal devotion to Dayton hardly equalled either then or now. He was founder and director of the Dayton Library Association, member for thirty-three years of the Board of Education, trustee of Miami University, one of the incorporators of Cooper Seminary, president of the Woodland Cemetery Association, member of the Ohio Board of Charities, trustee of the Montgomery Children's Home, elder in the Third Street Presbyterian Church, stockholder and promoter of nearly all the railroads entering Dayton, member and president of the Montgomery County Horticultural Society; during the Civil War on the Sanitary Commission and interested himself actively in the families of enlisted soldiers.

A lover of books and trees and flowers, it was he whom that earlier lover of books and trees and flowers, John Van Cleve, called to his bedside in the Phillips House and passed on to the younger man, as a sacred legacy, the promotion of all these things in Dayton. And they say that not long before Robert Steele passed away himself, he stood on the corner of his home at First and Ludlow and exclaiming how beautiful Dayton was,

A hitherto unpublished portrait of Henry Clay by the eminent Dayton artist Charles Soule. It was painted in Dayton when Clay was a house guest of his friend Col. John G. Lowe, but had disappeared. It was rediscovered by Houston Lowe after the 1913 flood, restored by local artist Lauira Birge. In the meantime the elder Lowes died, the younger ones knew nothing of the painting. It took the discerning eye of James M. Cox, publisher of the Dayton Daily News, former Ohio governor and 1920 presidential candidate, to recognize the picture's subject.

wished that he might come back from death in future years to see it grow more beautiful.

It is both necessary and seemly that such unsalaried public service should be kept in the minds of Dayton citizens by the building which rears its head at the end of Main Street, Steele High School. The six children of Robert Steele have long since passed away. Two grandsons, each bearing the honored name, survive: Robert Steele of Berkeley, California, and Robert Steele of Rocky Ford, Colorado.

It was Robert Steele who said of Henry L. Brown that he was "one of the best and most useful men who ever lived in Dayton," which is warrant, if it were needed, for putting the Browns among the first families of Dayton. It will be remembered that the first Henry Brown served in the War of 1812, married the brilliant Kitty Patterson and lived in the first brick house ever built in Dayton. Henry Brown 2d, lived on Ludlow Street in a large house with a large family, a large relationship and a large interest in everything pertaining to Dayton.

Those who have a personal recollection of Henry L. Brown, count it a pleasure to remember him, for he was always glad to see you. His hand grip was one of real friendship. Blue eyes, a strip of sandy hair, a slight limp from a hurt in his youth, a linen coat and his genuine cordiality made Mr. Brown a figure one did not soon forget. His real business ability had built up a flourishing stove foundry at the foot of Ludlow Street and a stove store on Main Street. But commercial affairs were not the chief end of living for Henry Brown.

Like his friend Robert Steele, he busied himself about the educational interests of Dayton, was president of the School Board for twenty-five years and all that time not a week passed but a part of it was given to the schools. He was especially active in investigating the claims of applicants for teacher positions. His knowledge of business made him valuable when there were new buildings to be erected.

Another, perhaps the first of his dear interests, was the First Presbyterian Church. For a whole long lifetime he was a pillar and a prop in all recorded ways. At one time he was superintendent of the Sunday school, at another, the teacher of a vigorous class of young men and women in the study of the Bible. During the cholera epidemic Mr. Brown was as much a hero as if he had striven on the field of battle, though he would have been the last to suspect or acknowledge it. Right into infected houses he went with food and medicine and prayers. All through that terrific summer of

1840, with the mercury at nearly a hundred, he plodded on his self-imposed errands of mercy with no thought of his own safety.

My own remembrance of Henry L. Brown was merely that of a pupil in his class and of the entertaining parties which he gave from time to time in his home -- candy-pullings in winter, watermelon parties in summer and picnics in between. He married Sarah Belle Browning and had nine children of whom none are now living.

No modern Daytonian could imagine the stately home of Miss Martha Perrine, the last of the family of that name. She had in her possession an old account book with this record: "My wife and I began housekeeping on Sunday morning, July 17, 1831." It was signed by James Perrine. The bride was Julia Darst. The Perrines were of French descent and came to America some time after the Revocation of the Edict of Nantes in 1686.

The family scattered as was usual in immigrating families and a part of them found their way to Middlesex County, New Jersey, near Freehold. In this town there is still a pew in the old church marked "Perrine" with a date early in the last century. It was the same neighborhood from which came the Schencks, the Huffmans, the Conovers, the Woodhulls and the Cranes.

John Perrine was the ancestor who came west and his four sons were James, Henry, Johnson and Garrett. The latter moved to New Carlisle, but the other three identified themselves with Dayton and became F. F. D.'s. The first business venture was a. store on the corner of Second and Jefferson, it was known as Perrine, Lytle and Shaw and maintained for many years the leading trade in dry goods in Dayton. The Perrines had daughters Sarah, Mary, Martha, Julia, and Louise. Mary became Mrs. George Shaw. Louise married Edward Barney.

James Perrine died January 22, 1864, and as a mark of respect to a man whose name had stood for strict integrity, every business house in Dayton was closed when they carried him out to Woodland. He had established high standards and served his city, Besides his business interests James Perrine was connected with several public enterprises, as president of the Dayton Bank, trustee of Woodland Cemetery and director of the first life insurance company of Dayton.

The brothers of James Perrine, Johnson and Henry, never married and survived him for many years. Henry Perrine had a retail dry goods store on Main Street in the Phillips Block (Mutual Home Building) for many years. Both brothers were socially popular and made large fortunes.

Survivors of the first Perrine, children and grandchildren living in Dayton are: Mrs. E. E. Barney, Mrs. John Bradley Greene, Julia McCoy, Mrs. H. G. Carnell and Mrs. Harry Munger.

No man's life, belonging to the plain and sturdy class of pioneers, ever deserved recording more than Thomas Brown. He was another of the New Jersey emigrants to the west, this time from Monmouth County. He was born in the first year of the century and died in Dayton in 1894.

At the age of twenty and starting from his New Jersey home Thomas Brown took a walk. He had a friend with him and they hoped to occasionally get a ride in some of the wagons that were continually on the road towards Ohio. But luck did not come their way and it had to be done by sheer pluck. On and on they kept until they reached the village of Lebanon. From there to Xenia and from there to Dayton, where the odyssey ended.

Immediately he began to be a good citizen and a leading one. He founded the S. N. Brown corporation of which he was president but he was much more than a mere business man. He was at several times a member of the State Legislature, director of the State prison at Columbus, member of the first school board organized in Dayton and one of the lessees of the public works under the law of 1861.

A devout member of Grace Methodist Church, Thomas Brown led an upright life and a long one. On one of the pages of his diary are still to be found these words: "That man is rich who has a good disposition, who is naturally kind, patient, and cheerful and has a flavor of wit in his composition." Which description accurately fitted the man who wrote it.

When a man begins his career by earning ten cents a day and ends with hundreds of thousands of dollars it makes an interesting story. In 1825, Valentine Winters worked in a brickyard in Germantown at the above mentioned salary; in 1870, he was giving birthday dinners with a check for ten thousand dollars under each plate around the table where his sons and daughters had gathered to do him honor.

His first earnings in Dayton amounted to fifty dollars a year, but five years later he was establishing the Winters National Bank, and the present Winters National Bank (Ed. Note: now Bank One) is the fruit of the seed he sowed in 1830. All the banking interests during that hundred years centered around the name of Winters.

Banking is in itself a science and rarely leaves room for activities of other natures, but Mr. Winters was an organizer of railroads and insurance companies and promoter of both in Dayton. It is told of him that he went into debt for his wedding suit and at the end of the year had paid for it and deposited thirty-eight dollars in the bank to his credit.

He was an indefatigable worker and so was his wife. Both were up early in the morning making every hour do its sixty minutes worth of work, keeping the out-go always inside of the income, he busy with ledgers and she with household affairs until, long before their golden wedding day, they landed in the big house on West Third Street.

During the Civil War, Valentine Winters loaned money to the government and gave it to support the families of soldiers at the front. He held his wealth as a stewardship and gave to any demand, either private or public, that came his way. This is the record of a rich man but rich not only in money but in friends, health, family, reputation and public confidence.

The golden wedding of Valentine Winters and Catherine Harshman was celebrated by them and their eleven children in 1879. Among the descendants of the name in Dayton are V. Winters, R. R. Dickey, Mrs. Harry Loy, Clara Winters, Mrs. Louella Winters Thomas, Mrs. J. E. Bimm, Dr. Charles McGregor, Harriet Winters Gebhart and Jonathan H. Winters.

One of the most versatile men that ever came to Dayton was a school teacher by the name of Eliam E. Barney. Just graduated from Union College he was attracted, as so many were, by the cultural demands of this small city and longed to do his share. This share was first the principalship of the old academy on the corner of Fourth and Wilkinson, and later when Cooper had given the ground for a girls' school and the citizens had subscribed the money to build Cooper Seminary, Mr. Barney was unanimously elected to be the head of that institution. One of his pupils said of his work, "He made everything so interesting one could not help learning." An inspired teacher, he began with nine pupils and ended with eighty-five.

Nothing seems to be so far from teaching as manufacturing, but after a couple of decades of this work Mr. Barney saw the demand for railroad cars and built up the Barney and Smith car works, for years the leading industry of Dayton. Manufacturing is a long way from foreign missions, but being a fervent Baptist Mr. Barney gave of his time and money to forward the work of the Gospel in other lands.

One of the founders of Denison University, he transferred to it the fervor for learning that he wielded at Cooper Seminary and built it up with money all his life. He was a passionate arboriculturist and his cultivation of the catalpa tree and introduction of it for commercial purposes was a real contribution.

The Young Men's Christian Association felt his helping hand and soul. The Cooper Hydraulic Company was conducted under his efficient presidency as was also the Second National Bank. Among his descendants now living in Dayton are: J. D. Platt and family, Mrs. Bertha Platt Thacker, and Miss Julia McCoy.

A sewer system is not a sentimental monument to a man's memory but there could hardly be a more practical one. When a city has outgrown itself and wastage becomes a menace, when city funds are low and anciently-minded members of the city council think that what was good enough for their fathers is good enough for them, then is the time for a prophet to arise that has a vision and knows how to externalize it.

Such a man was William Huffman. There were two F. F. D.'s under this name. William, the father, who came from New Jersey in 1812, and William P. who was born in 1813. William the first established a store on the corner of Jefferson and First, since occupied by the Beckel House. It is said the first meeting to form the Baptist Church was held on his porch.

He had four daughters one of whom married into the Winters family and one into the Harries family. The children of William P. Huffman were: William, Charles, Samuel (died an infant); Frank T., George P., Lizzie (Mrs. Drury); Mrs. E. J. Barney, Mrs. James R. Hedges and Anna M.

In 1889 there was a bill passed authorizing the probate judge (then Judge McKemy) to appoint three commissioners for the city of Dayton. They were William Huffman, Galen C. Wise and Dr. Hooven. It was William Huffman's work on this commission that makes citizens who know of it now raise their hats in his honor. The sewers and street paving he was determined to have, and against untold odds, of private opinion and newspaper opposition, he carried the day and Dayton was delivered from the threat to public health and the misery of mud and dust.

William P. Huffman lived for a time some miles east of town where he owned a large tract of land afterwards known as Huffman's Prairie. It was upon this level land that the Wright brothers made their first experiments in aviation. Later, Mr. Huffman moved to Dayton and built a fine residence on Huffman Hill where he lived for many years and brought up a family of ten children. He married Anna M. Tate. The living descendants of the original William Huffman include: Charles H. Simms, Colonel Frank T. Huffman, Mrs. Evelyn H. Patterson; Susannah, Geraldine, Charlotte and William P., the children of Torrence and Annie B. Huffman; and George P. Huffman.

It is difficult to imagine what the commercial side of Dayton would have been without the Gebharts. Sturdy, honest, thrifty and efficient they were; Frederick, the head of the clan, and his brothers, George and Herman, who came to Dayton in 1838. On Third Street west of Main he built a three-story building and established a general store.

Seven children he brought with him and two more were born in Dayton. They were Alexander, John, Josiah; the daughters who were Mrs. Joseph Newcomer, Mrs. Isaac Haas, Mrs. H. L. Pope, and Mrs. Cahill; and the Dayton group, Walter and Annie.

In a room in his Third Street store, Frederick Gebhart gathered a group of men who were the founders of the Lutheran Church. His two contributions to Dayton were business organization and church organization. Both prospered.

The hydraulic in its progress through the middle of town turned more wheels for the Gebharts than for any other firms. Flour mills (Simon Gebhart and Sons, East Third, 600 barrels a day); Cornice Works (W. F. Gebhart); the Gebhart White Lead Works; Gebhart Pope and Company, Linseed Oil. These were the sons and the grandsons of the Gebhart who first came out from Pennsylvania. Gebhart descendants are Mrs. Harry Turpin, Mrs. Kate Mathiot, Mrs. O. B. Brown, Mrs. Kate Haas Kennedy, Alexander Reed and family, Mrs. Isabel Reed Edgar and family, Dorothy Gebhart Carl, Miriam Mathiot Brown, Mrs. Annie Gebhart Norwood, Harry Gebhart and family, Mrs. Grace Gebhart Kinnard and Mrs. Joseph Turpin.

In the '70s and '80s, the square on East First Street between Main and Jefferson was mostly in the possession of the Harries family whose "emigrant ancestor," as the genealogists call it, was John W. Harries from Llandovery, Carmarthenshire, South Wales. He came to America in the early '30s and to Dayton not much later, bought a lot in the locality mentioned and lived there all his life.

A brewer by profession he established a brewery on Jefferson Street north of First, where he manufactured an excellent quality of real old English ale. The refuse from the brewery ran into the deep gutters where the cows, going to or coming back from the pastures across the river, were said to imbibe too freely and get fancy on their owner's hands. Back of the brewery was a shed said to have been constructed out of the timbers of the pirogue in which the first settlers came up the river to Dayton.

Mr. Harries was first and last a Briton; in his personal appearance he would have made a good cartoon for "John Bull" and in his characteristics of individuality and mastery in his own family. No modern ideas of independence ever got very far in the Harries family. His children were Thomas, William (who married Mary Huston), John, David and Ann of the original English family. His American children by a second wife were: Charles (married Lizzie Riggins), Caroline (Mrs. Young), Mary (who died at sixteen), Rosetta (Mrs. J. H. Gorman) and Emma (Mrs. William Simms).

Mr. Harries celebrated Christmas after the wholesale English custom, with a barrel of cider and a washboiler full of doughnuts to his employees and a table set with forty-two places for the family near and far. Children, grandchildren and great-grandchildren sat down to roast beef, suckling pig, roast ducks, and a dainty known as Welsh potpie.

The last member of the original family was Mrs. Rosetta Harries Gorman of beloved memory, who died not many years since and left the town poorer for want of her. For many years she lived in the home her father had built. It had been many times rebuilt, but the stairway which as a girl bride she had descended to meet her lover had remained the same through four generations.

In the Charles Harries family, who lived on the opposite side of First Street, there were seven children. They were John, Carrie (Mrs. Houston Lowe), Ella (Mrs. Harry Lowe), Charles, Harry and Emma (Mrs. Ernest Jackson). Nothing went on in Dayton that did not have a Harries in it, of one age or another.

The parties they gave and the parties they went to could not be chronicled in one chapter. The secret of it was that they were individually handsome and collectively a most attractive family, possessing much of what the French call "allure." The Harries house was the rendezvous of the gayest set in Dayton during three decades.

Owners of the name include: G. Harries Gorman, E. J. B. Gorman, Mrs. Ernest Jackson, Harry Harries, Charles H. Simms, John G. Lowe, Mrs. Robert Dun Patterson and Mrs. Caroline Patterson Bush.

In this same locality of Dayton, on the northwest corner of First and Jefferson, lived the Walters family, whose ancestors go back six generations to an Ephraim Walters who was murdered by the Indians in his Pennsylvania home and his wife and children carried into captivity. A son, Ephraim Walters, having escaped and grown up, was a captain in the Revolutionary War.

His son was the father of Dr. J. A. Walters, a graduate of Jefferson

College and well known for many years in Dayton. He lived at first in the corner house but later built one in the next lot; he married Lucetta Brooks and their children were James and Mary. For many years Dr. Walters engaged in the drug business and was all his life a member of and contributor to the Third Street Presbyterian Church. He died in 1898, greatly mourned by the community.

His son married Welthy Sheets and his daughter married Morris Woodhull. James Walters had two children, Jefferson and Edith. Edith became Mrs. George D. Harper of Cincinnati. Jefferson is known in musical circles as a beautiful musician on the violin and a composer as well. He will have further notice in a subsequent chapter. Mrs. Morris Woodhull is the only surviving child of Dr. James A. Walters, and lives in her beautiful home in Oakwood where her friends are always happy to find her.

This does not by any means include all the F. F. D.'s who have graced Dayton but it does include the most prominent who came here as early as the '30s. To go on through the later years of the last century would be to make a whole directory, so many have there been of the sons and daughters of Dayton who have worked to build up her business and social life, her factories, churches, and her place on the map of the United States.

10

Ramblings

The '60s were such charming years! Therefore I am going to take it upon myself to continue, with the excuse that it is a moral obligation to let young people of today know something about the adventures of their forebears. Historians are too apt to deal exclusively with the major facts of living and forget about the subtler undercurrents.

I have hinted at the hospitality of the '60s as exemplified in the house parties at the Patterson farm and the constant tide of visitors and parties at the Harries and Harshman homes on the Springfield Pike. It is, of course, a shining virtue, but there is no doubt that in those days it was apt to be over-done.

Hotels were not patronized to the extent they are now, even by people abundantly able to afford to do so. If you desired to visit another city and were so fortunate as to have an acquaintance living there, that made it easy. You wrote him you were coming or you just came. It was all right with him for it was what he did when he got the chance. There is no record as to what his wife said or thought.

The first intimation you were likely to have that six extra people would be your guests for dinner was when you looked out of the front window at eleven-thirty and saw them climbing out of the surrey at the horse block. *Semper non paratus* -- never unready -- had to be the motto of the housekeeper in those days. A modern hostess can meet unexpected emergencies by ordering from a well-stocked store with a delivery system. But there were no well-stocked stores and no delivery.

It was "cash and carry" right through the existence of our mothers and grandmothers. As a child I have been sent on an errand of mad emergency to scour the backyards of our neighbors or of the dwellers on "the Commons" to buy a chicken because the one we had for dinner was eaten up and another needed for unexpected company. If the chicken was found (unlikely enough) it had to be run down, decapitated, picked, drawn and cooked in *rigor mortis* for no such thing as a dressed chicken was to be had, even on market days. And any cook will agree that feathers are in the way when serving in a hurry.

The casual guests being provided with the *pièce de résistance*, other things were needed. No canned goods of any kind were to be had. Such a thing had never occurred to the mind of man or woman. Pause, oh twentieth century housekeeper and contemplate such a situation! The tinned fruits and vegetables which have made possible the conquering of the Arctic regions did not come in until thirty years later than the date of which we write.

If it was June and tomatoes were growing in the back lot, so much to the good, but if it happened to be February (and chance visitors came any old time of the year) the hostess confined her efforts to potatoes, parsnips and turnips. To buy lettuce all the year round would have seemed a pipe dream to the 1860 housekeeper.

Grocery stores were depended upon for flour, sugar and spices, the "dry ingredients" as the cook books called them, but not for fruits, meats or vegetables. I don't remember a butcher's block in a Dayton grocery previous to the '70s. The only canned fruit was what our mother put up herself, standing over a hot wood stove in the middle of summer, ladling the cooked fruit into the jars and pouring sealing wax around the edges to keep the air out. These jars were deposited in a cellar against our winter needs where they invariably exploded and decorated the ceiling.

Bread was, as a matter of course, the product of each home kitchen. If the chance guests happened to exceed the supply on hand there was a waxy product smelling of pipe-smoke to be had at the corner grocery. No desserts could be purchased. Ice cream one could indeed find by the small dish to be eaten on the premises, at Kemper's store on Main Street but it was never sent home in bulk.

Our house was large, but not large in a practical way. Much space there was to be heated and kept in order, but not much available space for visitors. As I remember, our family of six quite filled it up, yet I have seen another family of four descend upon us uninvited and stay for weeks, knowing perfectly well that "help" was next to impossible to get and that we children were "doubling up" in the other part of the house. To remember what such visitations meant to my mother fills me with hot indignation to this day and yet I never heard her complain. It was all an inevitable part of the scheme of living and had to be borne.

One case of "lending to the Lord" in the matter of giving of house and food and care will scarcely be credited in the present day. An epidemic of incendiary fires occurred with distressing regularity during the late '60s; the work, evidently, of an insane firebug. Blazes burst out nearly every night and heads of families went to bed with the expectation that the hoarse cry of "fire," so much more horrifying than a fire bell, would wake them from their beds.

Since it took some time for tired business men to rouse out of deep sleep, get on their clothes and run to the nearest engine house to man the hand pumps it will not be found surprising that every fire got a good headway before it could be checked. Dwelling after dwelling was consumed with great resulting loss and hardships.

Turner's Opera House, on the corner of First and Main, was the biggest fire in the history of Dayton, and it did not lessen the terror of citizens who did not know but their homes would be the next to go.

One night the usual alarm woke us and the glare of the flames lit up our rooms. The fire this time was in a frame dwelling on Ludlow Street called the Witherup House, midway between Third and Fourth. It was a well-kept boarding house and always full. I, with the children of the neighborhood, watched the fire with terrified fascination from the attic windows of the David Morrison house on the corner of Fourth and Ludlow.

We saw the firemen fight the flames, one of them emerged from the blazing building with a dead body in his arms and another with a body still living. This sufferer was taken, in a matter of course, into the nearest available place which was the house we were then in. What else could be done? There was no hospital or any place of any kind except a private home for hurt or sick people.

I have heard my father bemoan the fact that a man patient with a broken leg from the quarries was obliged to have as bed-fellow his own small restless son. It was fully twenty years later than the time of writing before the Sisters of the Poor of St. Francis established the small beginnings of the present St. Elizabeth's Hospital.

This unconscious and unwilling visitor from the burning house was put in a small bedroom off the dining room in the Morrison home and here he stayed, an addition to a family of ten for many weeks, helpless, suffering horribly, with no bathroom, no public nurses, the stench of burnt flesh filling the house. The sight of his marred face and the offensive dressings made the whole thing a horror to a sensitive child.

I have wondered who took care of him; the family in turn I suppose, with the neighbors to lend an occasional hand. The point to my story is, that in such a demand on human kindness nobody complained. It was accepted as all in the day's work or laid on the shoulders of Providence. A good deal has been taken off the shoulders of Providence in these days.

Casualties were not always unwelcome to children in that day, nor since. They varied the monotony of existence and made endurable the hour we had to spend in school or helping mother. Not for worlds would I have acknowledged it then but there was a distinct impression in my mind that the perennial floods with which the Miami Valley was visited were sent for the special delectation of the children. I did have, it is true, a dim impression that digging out the tacks in a reluctant carpet to get it out of the way of the inrushing water, or dragging bedding and cooking utensils from where they belonged to where they didn't, that getting tired and wet and dirty through whole days and nights, were not occupations which my parents would have preferred.

But it was a great game for us. First we hied to the river bank at the head of Main Street to see the yellow flood piling higher and higher against the bridge piers. The whole town was out, standing under umbrellas and watching the flotsam and jetsam of the current: hayricks, pigpens, logs and fences, hitting the lower edges of the bridge and being sucked under by the current. Sometimes a little house went careening by and was knocked to pieces under the bridge.

A part of the joy of flood times was that we children were held to no rules. Nobody cared whether we went to school or not, if indeed there was a school to go to. Nobody told me to wash my face or to practice. Eating a beefsteak cooked over the grate fire in the sitting room was a sort of picnic. Fun, too, to help pack a basket of food and coffee for father to take on horseback to families down on the Commons who were on lower ground than we and consequently in worse circumstances.

It was fun to watch old ladies with no seafaring experience being taken home from prayer-meeting in a skiff which tipped and bumped against the trees and made the passengers scream. All so unusual, so thrilling, so free from the monotony of other days -- we would have welcomed a flood several times a year.

And when the high water went down out of the streets it still lingered in the cellars, three or four feet deep, where in a washtub with a clothes pole to navigate with we progressed from room to room, dodging barrels and playing Robinson Crusoe on a voyage of discovery. No denying that the much vaunted Flood Prevention system, however beneficial from the point of view of property owners, has certainly put an end to most entrancing experiences which the children of today know nothing about.

All ancient Daytonians, whether they agree to it or not, will remember the old Fifth Street graveyard, the land for which had been given the city by D. C. Cooper in the childhood of our municipal years. It occupied the block bounded by Ludlow, Wilkinson, Fifth and Sixth. A solid board fence shut in the area for its entire length, broken only by a wide gate for the hearses to drive in and by a set of steps, up and over.

The graves were sunken, the gray mossy stones leaned over. It was such an utterly quiet place. Even the movement of trains at the other side of the graveyard seemed only to make the silence more intense. It occurs to me as I write how much more talk there used to be about death than there is now. And how much more devotion to lost friends. One of our neighbors used to go every single day to place flowers on her husband's grave. Summer, spring, fall and winter, it was a part of her daily duties.

One real historical fact was that one minister buried his entire congregation of forty-two in that graveyard during the summer of 1833. Cholera, of course.

There came a time when the Woodland Cemetery trustees announced that no more interments would take place in the Fifth Street graveyard. Then began the removal of bodies to the new quarters out on the hill. Ah, that was a chance for real thrills. The top of the board fence was like a crowded balcony on a benefit night. All the boys in town were there taking base advantage to get the best seats. Talking not long ago with a man who as a boy of ten assisted at that process he recalled that two heads of long hair, one black and the other red, were acquired surreptitiously from the excavators and passed around as cherished trophies.

The houses of the '60s and the '70s deserve a part of our attention. Builders of that day lacked both originality and imagination. They built solidly and well, as they hoped and thought, to last forever. Heavy oak beams and thick walls entered into all the old dwellings torn down in late years to make place for business blocks. With the exception of about a dozen big houses with halls in the middle and rooms on either side, the plan of the general run of well-to-do homes was to string the rooms along in a row without regard to convenience downstairs or privacy up.

Large double parlors with ceilings ten or twelve feet high occupied the front of the house. They were entered from a wide hall which ran the length of the front rooms and then opened on a porch running the length of the back of the house. Dining-room, sitting-room and kitchen opened onto this porch which was commonly draped with Isabella or Concord grape-vines and was a pleasant place to sit in the summer. In fact the homes of that day could not have been more delightful in the warm months.

It was in cold weather when their deficiencies became manifest. No such thing as a furnace existed in the '60s and, for many people, far into the '70s. Large air-tight stoves for burning wood or coal grates in each room furnished the heat, such as it was: torrid in front and glacial behind. Except in sickness, bedrooms were not heated.

The consequence was that, whether their names were Lowe or Stoddard or Phillips, they dressed in installments around the first fire in the house that got to going, generally that in the sitting-room. Their descendants may say they didn't, but they did. Comfort knows no concessions and when the frost makes etchings on the window-pane and when the snow creaks under foot outside one makes one's self as comfortable as circumstances will permit.

A bathroom was just as unknown as a furnace. A washstand with pitcher and basin, utensils scarcely to be found in these days, were the only means of ablutions. Other necessary adjuncts to the bath were placed at a remote distance down in the rear of the lot, where, rain or shine, frost or snow, the family repaired individually when occasion required. Their descendants may say they didn't, but they did.

The grand parlors of Dayton were lighted by gas chandeliers hung with glass prisms, the second best parlors imitated by hanging a similarly decorated coal-oil "bastard" from the ceiling at a convenient height to bump one's head. It thus happened that a faint odor of kerosene filled the air, mingled with that of oilcloth with which the floors of most halls were covered.

If a party was being held at the house of a good Methodist, instead of dancing there would be games. Supper was some diversion after which it was sometimes part of the evening's entertainment that Carrie Dudley, afterwards the famous Leslie Carter, danced the Highland Fling. She had sashes wider than any others and skirts shorter, and in spite of inevitable envy in my soul I had to confess that she did dance well. The linen covered floor, the violins, the light from the crystal chandeliers and Carrie in the middle, waving her scarf and keeping pretty feet in time with the music, is a picture quite plain after over sixty years.

There was about all these parlors of my childhood a close, dusty smell, comprehensible in winter because they were never aired. Heat, so laboriously arrived at, was too precious to waste through open windows and the gospel of fresh air was never preached. In summer it was to be accounted for by the fact that carpets were tacked down and covered the entire floor. The laying of them was such an exertion, accomplished only by Dan Bush with his kit of carpet tools, that housekeepers avoided the job as long as possible. When, in the spring, they were taken up and beaten on a line in the yard, the floor under them held a layer of fine dust that could best be dealt with by a broom and a shovel.

Blame them not, these long-ago housekeepers for shutting up their living rooms from light and air. There was another reason: flies! Nearly every family owned a horse and carriage, at least a buggy. The stable was on the back of the lot and just behind it, in the alley, the ever-growing manure pile. This arrangement was a fly factory with mass production going on all the time.

There was no city garbage disposal. Colored men who lived below the railroad used to collect it for their pigs when they did not forget. Between the neglected garbage pails and the uncovered manure piles, the flies multiplied by the million, their first duty in life being to seek out the dinner tables of the neighborhood. Fly screens not having been invented, they had free access to kitchen, bakeries and dining rooms. This necessitated the "help" of one of the children detailed for the service, standing at the head of the table swinging back and forth over the eatables a longhandled arrangement made of cut newspapers tacked onto the end of a broomstick. In more sumptuous homes it was a peacock feather duster which, for all its elegance had no more permanent effect on the flies than the humbler utensil. If the fanning stopped for a minute the flies settled back on meat platter, bread plate and pies.

Nobody seemed to mind. What was the use? There they were and there they probably would always be. Why criticize the arrangements of

Providence? No room was dark enough nor cool enough to keep the ravenous insects away. Every cake or pie that was put on the pantry shelf had to be covered with a dome-shaped screen of metal netting. It was very likely this protection which finally suggested the idea of making frames to fit in the windows. When they were first used the flies would settle on the outside, attracted by the odor of food, so as to really darken the room. It would be interesting, if possible, to ascertain what the almost entire elimination of flies has to do with the lowered death rate of the present day.

Our leading dry-goods store (no one at that day dreamed of a department store) was kept by Henry Perrine in the Phillips Building on North Main Street. In the two shallow windows opening toward the street the only temptations to passing customers were several papers of pins, some lengths of calico or barege (a thin woolen material of incredible roughness used for "best dresses") and perhaps some spools of thread, all next to invisible from the fly specks on the pane.

Inside two clerks lounged over the counters while Mr. Perrine read the paper in the back of the store. If business was really heavy he took a hand himself in measuring cloth or matching samples. One advantage of this store over those of the present day was that you could always match a piece of goods. If the dress made of it was worn out and you wanted to make it over, the same bale of material from which the dress was made was still on the shelves.

Colors were crass and unimaginative. Green was green in those days and the same tint used to paint the pump was to be found in ribbons, and no other. Muslins were incredibly heavy and close in texture. A night-gown made out of *Fruit of the Loom* was almost warm enough to go sleigh-riding in. A whole bolt of this material was used up every spring on the sewing-machine in our house because nothing whatever was to be had ready-made in Perrine's store. In fact the term "ready-made" was held for years to denote something cheap and unworthy.

Buying a "dress pattern" was an event in my mother's life and I infer in the lives of most of the ladies of that day. How many yards would be needed to make the skirt held out by voluminous "hoops" and what kind of trimming (either "gimp" or velvet ribbon) was fully discussed among the neighbors, all having different advice to give. It is recorded that merchants of that day "threw in" the "findings," i. e., the linings, whalebone, tape and buttons.

There was no woven underwear to be bought, and that which we wore was made of rough red flannel and occasioned much torment for sensitive skins. When nice old ladies came tiptoeing across the street to call on mother holding up their skirts in front to avoid the mud, I always expected to see their red flannel drawers and always did.

In the middle '70s Payne and Holden's was the leading bookstore in Dayton and there you could buy books of poetry, inkstands and paper cutters; but previous to that, what despairing searchings for the proper present to offer on Christmas morning! Lacking shopping facilities we were thrown back on our own resources, that is to say homemade presents. What horrors of decalcomania, wax flowers and wool mats we perpetrated. Everybody was either crocheting or poking a blunt needle in and out of the spaces in canvas work.

The toys of that day were limited to dolls with china heads and glossy painted curls (real hair was not thought of), tin engines that disintegrated the second time they made a trip and a monkey on a stick whose paint came off and made the baby sick. Children's books went no farther in that day than *Mother Goose* and *Robinson Crusoe*. When you had graduated from the latter there was nothing for you except grown people's books: Dickens and Scott, which perhaps was not such a privation.

Christmas trees were not as plentiful as now, never for sale and hardly ever seen in private houses. To get one for the Sunday school meant that somebody had to cut down a cedar on his lot or find a farmer who would do so. Christmas tree ornaments were also lacking, but the teachers in the Sunday school met and strung yards and yards of popcorn to loop over the branches or cranberries to give the Christmas color. Oranges were still rare enough to make desirable decorations and if a child got a sticky popcorn ball, an orange and a cornucopia full of peppermints he was happy as a king.

The joy of Christmas was not so much in the kind of gifts we got, but in the glamor surrounding the season. Once, in our neighborhood a family of children made their own tree, stripped cedar from the big trees in the yard, shaking the snow off so as not to spoil the carpet, and tied the branches of evergreen on to the branches of a dead bush pulled up for the purpose. The result left something to be desired, but we were not exacting and didn't mind if the cedar grew both ways on one branch. That tree was a joy as long as it lasted and illustrated what modern education experts are trying to teach parents, that the real pleasures of a child's life are the things he invents for his own amusement.

The paucity of purchasable articles reached far beyond luxuries like Christmas presents. Small occurrences make me recall the things we did not have in those far-off years. How would a modern mother of a family carry on without safety pins? When they were invented I have no means of ascertaining, but it is quite plain in my memory the difficulties we had making common pins do their duty.

There were no containers of any kind. Groceries were sold in bulk with no attempt to keep them clean. That we did not all die of contamination is probably due to the fact that there were not as many chimneys as now pouring out coal soot. Butter was exposed openly on market stands; oatmeal sold in bulk from open bins; spices measured out on a scale at the druggist's; meat wrapped in thick heavy brown paper that melted at a touch and had to be scraped off. Not a sign of the neat boxes that keep our eatables clean and wholesome.

It therefore happened that an empty bottle was to be put away on a shelf until somebody needed one, spare string wound on a ball and kept in a drawer, writing paper hoarded and used economically and lunches put up in shapeless packages, all for want of the results of the wisdom of modern boards of health and the cooperating manufacturers, all of whom have helped educate the public in what makes for health.

11

Other Daytonians

Not all the Daytonians of the '60s were Princeton patricians who inherited ancestral mahogany and lived on First Street. Some were quite humble folk, but if they had less of the world's goods they did not lack the compensating qualities of native wit and pungent comment. I like to think that no other town possessed such interesting people.

I would like to know where modern social classification would put Aunt Sally Davis. Would they see in her only an ignorant old woman who wore big hoops and tended her garden on the corner of Fourth.and Wilkinson. Would they see the qualities of mind and soul that we did. Would they sense the quick wit, the warm sympathy, the clever characterization of people and affairs that illumined her talk.

If she had been educated it would have spoiled her. As it was, her low-ceilinged "settin'-room," with its one little window on the side street, was a kind of "salon" where she held forth and we listened. She was never alone. But if her talk was necessarily of people because her horizons were narrow, it was not therefore ever malicious. She extracted the pith of a story and left the acrimony, if there was any, to evaporate.

Sometimes when I walk on modernized Ludlow Street I seem to see a tall ungainly ghost with a red shawl and a basket. It is Mrs. Kilworth taking home the week's wash. Wherever she takes it the children (if they have not been deceived into thinking that washerwomen are not interesting) will gather about her while she lets her arms drop down between her long grasshopper legs and will tell them, while she sways back and forth in a low chair, all about when the Indians lived on Dayton ground and how her father shot a deer on Main Street. Education had not spoiled her either, for this was before disorganizing general information began its leveling process. Ugly past belief, awkward and ungainly, Mrs. Kilworth still remains one of the figures that come out of the Dayton past to give my soul unimagined pleasure.

Uncle Tommy Morrison might qualify in the millionaire class if he lived today for he owned both sides of Ludlow Street from Third down to the railroad. Mr. Morrison was an ever-present figure in the Dayton of the '50s and '60s. His chief claim to eminence lay in the fact (attested by his relatives but unsubstantiated by data) that he, a Harrison enthusiast, had vowed if the election of 1840 was successful, to walk to Washington and hurrah for his candidate from the top of the Capitol.

He did go, on foot, and he did come back, but how he was engaged in the interim was never fully disclosed. The only contributing factor toward the truth of his adventure was that everybody knew that what Mr. Morrison said he would do he always did. There never had been any difficulties which his will could not brush away.

They say he talked very interestingly of his travels but as a child I saw in him only a white-haired, pink-faced ogre forever preaching temperance and a hell-and-damnation variety of religion much in vogue at that day and interfering as much as possible with our fun. All play and pleasure was sin in his eyes and all modern improvements the work of the devil. Continually in pursuit of some boy who had trespassed on forbidden backyards or of some girl who wore ribbons in her hair, Thomas Morrison was the self-appointed guardian of town morals of that day.

Hanging on a gate to watch Sol Puterbaugh move a family from one house to another was a favorite recreation of my own. Sol was a mastodon of a man, nearer seven than six feet tall, to whom a piano was nothing in a day's work. It was no job for him to get a heavy bureau through a doorway alone but it was some job to get himself in. After the invariable irony of circumstance he lived in the smallest house on our block. Into this tiny domicile he ducked and edged around the door frame every time he went home to dinner. Mr. Puterbaugh was as good natured as he was big and gave us rides in his express-wagon on its return empty trips.

There was a lady whose curiosity about her neighbors might partially be condoned because she watched their activities from a sickroom window. The window from which she pursued her researches belonged to an imposing stone mansion in the aristocratic row of residences on the west side of Main Street just below Fourth. Her semi-invalidism prevented activity of every sort except that of investigating to the least item all that her neighbors did, thought, hoped, bought, borrowed or built. The morning market baskets, going by under her window on their owners' arms, offered the first interest.

"A four-rib roast for Sunday dinner when they generally buy only a two-rib! That must mean the Worthingtons driving over from Chillicothe." "Raspberries? They're going to make jam. But where are the currants?" "It's early for sweet corn but they've had green beans twice this week." "Liver again! Well, it's only ten cents a pound." And so on, *ad libitum*. In this way she could visualize the dinner tables of the Lowes, the Rogers, the Lytles, the Gebharts and the Davies.

It was the latter family which unwittingly gave this lady censor her most bitter disappointment. Samuel Davies had his law office on the corner of Fourth and Main with his residence adjoining. Later he occupied a house in the middle of the block on Main Street. A moving was of interest to everybody, most of all to the housebound observer across the street. She ensconced herself at the upper window with an uninterrupted view of the household furnishings that were going to be taken out of one house and into the other. Here she would be able to discover if that table leg still waited for repairs, and if it should happen that a mirror were broken in transit she hoped it would occur between the two front gates so that she would be able to testify just how it happened.

The clock on the mantel ticked on and on and no signs of activity across the street. Could Sol Puterbaugh have had a stroke or could she have been mistaken in the day? Both equally unthinkable. What then? The fact was that the Davies found it more convenient to move by the back way, out of one alley gate and into the other. Perhaps the Gormans or the Voorhees' on Jefferson Street with their back windows looking out on the alley might see something. She couldn't. It was a blow never quite recovered from.

Fanny Stacey sewed. Every spring and fall she made the rounds of her customers. They were all the "best people" in Dayton in the '60s. She was a transplanted English woman whose misplaced H's were a source of interest to us children. She was very deaf with a face whose blankness was that of soft pale dough but with a mind behind it and a sense of humor that fairly sizzled when she opened up on the foibles and frailties of her customers. Gossip? Of course. What do you expect in a day when the papers

The seven first members of the Buz Fuz club, one of Dayton's oldest clubs. Standing, left to right, Eldredge Mead, Charles M. Wood. Seated, Charles G. Bickham, Thomas Legler, Harry Loy. George H. Wood, J. Sprigg McMahon.

lacked a personal column, when there were no movie shows, small chance to travel and few books? Fanny's talk, however, was never malicious.

Does anybody now remember what sewing meant then? I can see Fanny, sitting close to a small window shaded by a wide porch, her nearsighted eyes fixed on the seam she was hemming. It was held by a sewing-bird which was screwed to the edge of the table. This ornithological specimen had a spring in its tail which, when pressed upon, opened its beak to receive and hold the seam. There was also a receptacle for holding spools.

The needle must be set in the seam exactly back of where the thread came out of the preceding stitch, presenting when finished a row of stitches minute, exact, delicate and not so different from a seam made by a sewing-machine. In this way Fanny's needle went in and out, hour after hour, day after day, in our house and others on father's shirts, mother's petticoats and the baby's long gowns. Every garment worn had to be made in that way. Fanny's left forefinger was rasped by the needle point into a nutmeg grater surface, her eyes grew more and more nearsighted as the years went on. Fanny lived with the Lights on East Monument Avenue, then Water Street. Peace to her whimsical soul!

Any warm sunshiny day in spring would bring "Professor Brooks" out from whatever he called home south of the depot. He made it a point to appear for his annual debut on Easter Sunday. First it was his raiment that attracted the eye, as he meant it should, then his phraseology which was as gorgeous as his dress, and finally the expression of sublime self-admiration that graced his black features.

Clad sometimes in a Prince Albert coat and sometimes in dazzling white duck, with a rose or lily in his buttonhole, holding with mincing gestures a green silk fringed parasol against the rays of the sun, Professor Brooks paced the length of Ludlow Street sure of being the center of interest. The picture here painted is not complete until you had heard him acknowledge a salutation which he frequently did, for he had many acquaintances of both colors.

"How does your corporosity sagashiate this mornin'?" he would inquire solicitously of one, with a wave of his hat and a deep bow. "A lovely morning for pergrinations, madam" to another. The picture was complete. The necktie equalled the buttonhole bouquet, the bouquet equalled the parasol, and "pergrinations" bound them all together in a transcendent whole.

Never could the professor be caught napping; always was he ready with a reply. Once a loquacious and very Hibernian washerwoman met him and poured upon him a torrent of brogue. With lordly gesture he waved her aside saying "Madam, your language is too copious for my comprehension."

Why Professor Brooks played this part of a masculine Queen of Sheba no one ever knew but he remained for years a part of the entertaining street life of Dayton.

Auctions were a free source of amusement in those days. For hours before the performance the streets were patrolled by a white-haired Negro with a huge brass bell. With a voice as clamorous as the bell he advertised to the public that at a certain place would be held an auction. His official position, so to speak, was that of town bell-ringer. His brass bell and his loud voice assailed our ears whenever there was a sale of cow, horse, or house, a lost child to be recovered or anything that required prompt public attention.

On Jefferson Street, between Fifth and the railroad crossing, stood a low, dingy, frame house with various signs hanging on the outer wall. At times a gangling old man with very stooped shoulders appeared at the doorway looking out on an uncordial world. His sign said:

Dr. Rose. Discoverer Of A Positive Cure For Consumption.

If, as Moliere put it, "A beard is the biggest part of a doctor" then Dr. Rose was well equipped, for his fell down over his shirt front nearly to his waistline. This old imposter "had it in" for the medical profession and as for the doctors he was their perennial source of amusement. Handbills from the Rose dispensary scattered through the streets implored the public not to give themselves up to the tortures of the operating table or into the hands of the bloody doctors, but to consult Dr. Rose who, out of his love for mankind, had invented a mild remedy which cured every known disease from toothache to fits. One of his signs read: *No One Has Died Under My Treatment In Twenty-Five Years.*

The *chef-d'oeuvre* of them all was a hinged sign, displayed only when a funeral went by, for Jefferson Street was one of the routes to the cemetery. As the procession passed, the sign clicked and turned over. On the obverse side were the words in very black paint: ***This Is Not My Patient***.

In the days when a four-story office building made us feel metropolitan, when streetcars were innovations and getting into them an adventure complicated by mud, when buggies joggled in and out of ruts in the streets and cows were driven the length of Third Street on their way to the slaughter pens, a voice could be heard most any time of the day on most any downtown corner: "Shine! Shine! Shine!"

And now, in another century, when the courthouse is over-shadowed by skyscrapers, when the Phillips House has disappeared into the past, when traffic officers try to keep the public from destruction and when electric lights and street-paving proclaim Dayton the metropolis that it really is, the same voice is heard. It belongs, as always, to Al Shartle, as much a part of Dayton and getting as old as the courthouse.

Once, some years ago, he met a disturbed looking gentleman walking slowly along Main Street as if not quite sure of his surroundings. Shartle made his usual plea: "Shine, Sir; Shine, Mr. Conover!"

"Yes," was the pleased reply. "You may. And when you have shined them once do it over again and keep on doing it until dinner time. I have been out of Dayton for thirty years and you are the first person who has called me by name."

From which it may be rightly inferred that Al Shartle's acquaintance was a wide one and his memory for names phenomenal. For over sixtythree years this original character walked the streets of Dayton with his shine-box and greeting every customer by name. He has blacked the shoes of four Presidents of the United States: Hayes, Garfield, McKinley, and Harding; and of many governors, senators, congressmen and lesser lights. His hobby is politics of the Democratic variety and much valuable support has he given to candidates in election time.

In 1920 Al Shartle and his wife were members of the Ohio Boosters Club which went to San Francisco by special train, determined to make James M. Cox the Democratic candidate for President. While there he made a personal plea for his friend to William Jennings Bryan. Al Shartle died in 1930.

Billy Wolf walked as many miles in his day's work of carrying papers as the shoeshiner, some say from twenty-five to thirty miles a day. He carried the *Cincinnati Enquirer* from door to door, a familiar figure to all on his beat. The day began for many a business and professional man when Billy Wolf mounted the steps of the porch and handed in the morning paper. The weight of his canvas sack hanging from one shoulder gave his body a bent attitude and the heat of it on summer days marked his back with the X of crossed suspenders. He had a stentorian voice and always a pleasant word for children.

Life was not always a rosy path for Billy Wolf. Politics he loved and pursued until a fateful day when he bet a lot of money on Republican victory. The party went out of power and with it about all that Bill had saved. It made him bitter and he turned Democrat, though it is to be guessed not a very enthusiastic one, for his Republicanism was bred in the bone. Whatever his affiliation Billy was one of the best informed men in the city on local politics, knowing the factional leanings of everybody and much of the record of virtually every man in public life.

12

The Gay '70s

By 1870, Dayton was beginning to be ashamed of being small and unimportant and was developing aspirations toward cityhood. She was in that state of emergence which every community goes through on its way to cosmopolitanism.

We had left off the hoop-skirts of the past and were assuming the habiliments of sophistication. There was a gulf, however, between our ambitions and their full realization. Much building was going on. The "Commons" were closing up into streets; we were pointing with pride to one street-railway and several four-story business blocks, but the streets were still quagmires of limestone mud spattering the vehicles which lurched in and out of abrupt holes.

Men and women still in complete control of their faculties do not have to dig so far into their memories of this era to recall their annoyance when a sow with a litter of pigs was ensconced in a puddle in front of the Phillips House and had to be ejected when a bus from the depot wanted to back up to the curb. It held perhaps, passengers from the East, and it was plain they would never see a sight like that in New York City.

That was in the early '70s. By the later years of the decade public opinion had shut off live stock from the streets, but the mud persisted. It is always interesting to trace beginnings, and many things that give us pride at the present day had their inception in the '70s. In spite of the Panic of 1873, and following the period of inflation, some important new manufacturing projects were established. The Ohio Rake Company, the Barney and

Smith Car Company, the Stoddard Manufacturing Company, the Farmer's Friend Company all built large factories and put out products that were known far and wide. We had a new jail built west of the courthouse at a cost of $87,500.

West of the city, a good four miles in the country, a smaller city was beginning to rise on the brow of the hill to shelter the soldiers who helped save the Union. This was the National Asylum for Disabled Volunteer Soldiers, commonly known as the Soldiers' Home. Dayton citizens raised $20,000 towards the project and commended Mr. Gunckel, whose influence as a member of the board, guided the selection of the site.

It was a noble undertaking and nobly carried out. Buildings, drives, lawns, the view, all were a lesson in themselves as to how public beautification should be accomplished. It became our one attraction to sightseers from outside, but when they arrived the only way to reach the home was by little sawed-off street cars drawn by mangy mules on a single track the length of Third Street. Not seldom the car ran off the track and the passengers had to get out and push it back.

Every Saturday night the band played, and it was a good band as all military bands are. Dayton people ordered out their buggies, or hitched them up themselves (the best of them drove surreys or landaus), and started for the Soldiers' Home. Over the river by the dark cavernous wooden bridge, past cornfields on the way to Summit Street then up the long hill to the gates which stood open on the pike.

Round and round the band stand on the parade ground they circled, bowing to acquaintances while the old blue-coated veterans sat on iron seats at the side, and when the band played *The Star Spangled Banner* we knew it was over and we drove home until the next Saturday night. It all seemed very gay and cosmopolitan, and created the impression of London's Rotten Row or the Bois de Boulogne of Paris.

During the winters of 1869 and 1870 a wave of religious fever swept over the country. Churches organized revivals bringing many accessions to their ranks. Every summer camp meetings were held in the beautiful woods along the Miami, the woods first called Embury Park, then Idlewyld, still later Triangle Park. Tents and wooden cottages housed the worshippers who, during the month of August, met to praise and pray and sing under the oaks and elms then in their summer glory.

These meetings were both social and religious, taking the place of much that now goes on under the name of recreation. People came from all over the county and beyond. They put up tents or rented cottages and set-tled down to a month of combined picnicking and religion. The cottages faced a square in the middle of which was a platform where the preacher-exhorters and the evangelist choir-leader stood.

There might be a melodeon and there might not. At any rate the leader was equal to carrying on the whole musical program by means of his resonant voice and his religious fervor. Meetings were held day and night, but the night meetings were the most impressive.

The dark woods, the reverent people on rows of wooden benches, the foreground lit by gasoline flares nailed to tree trunks, the rising and falling waves of melody as voice by voice took it up and added to the whole, all made a scene which has forever gone out of our national reli-gious life. The Moody and Sankey hymns, bad music as they are, were good religious propaganda and brought more than one sinner to the mourn-er's bench. *Shall We Gather at the River?*, *What Shall the Harvest Be?*, *Rock of Ages*, *There is a Fountain Filled with Blood*, *Beulah Land*, *Sweet Beulah Land*, *In the Sweet By and By* woke the echoes along the river and drowned the chirp of the katydids.

As the prayers and hymns continued many were affected to tears and to action. They crowded up to the preacher's desk and knelt in the saw-dust of the ground. Those who were undecided were kept in almost silent persuasion in the rear shadows by exhorters who knew the psychic steps by which conversion was accomplished. Meanwhile the music increased in fervor, the exhortations grew in force. *Almost Persuaded* carried the weak of faith outside of themselves and straight to the mourner's bench, *When the Roll is Called up Yonder I'll be There* finished the work and the cottag-ers went to sleep that night with the happy conviction that many had been added to the fold in that one day's work.

Did it last? There are opposite opinions, but the fact remains that those fervent experiences meant for many souls a new view of life and human obligation.

It was perhaps because of this renewal of religious faith that a meet-ing which was to have far-reaching results was held one Sunday afternoon in 1870 at the Lutheran Church on Main Street. John H. Thomas presided and Francis W. Parker was secretary. The aim of the meeting was to per-petuate and determinize the unity of sentiment developed through the church revivals and turn it towards the benefit of young men. A committee with Thomas O. Lowe as chairman, was appointed to draft a constitution

The then new YMCA building, dedicated in September, 1929; home and classroom to thousands of young men.

and by-laws; the formal meeting to ratify the organization was held on March 2, 1870, and thus was the Young Men's Christian Association born.

Its history and object are well known. "To provide physical, intellectual, social and spiritual improvement for young men." The first home was on the second floor of the building on the north side of the alley near the courthouse, then occupied by the *Dayton Journal*. Later the Dunlevy residence on Fourth Street was purchased and occupied; that being replaced by what was then considered a fine building.

More expansion followed and another move made to the northwest corner of Third and Ludlow on ground presented by Miss Belle Eaker. This home lasted only thirty years and now, on the bank of the Miami, rises a noble structure whose upper floors dominate the skyline of Dayton and whose activities minister to the welfare of young men.

At first the Young Men's Christian Association activities were exclusively religious: holding meetings, establishing Sunday schools, etc. Gradually were added the attractions of a gymnasium, evening classes, a restaurant and sleeping rooms. Not their first secretary but their best, was David Sinclair of beloved memory, who, for twenty-eight years, held the post of leader and inspirer of young men. He had a calling for boys; to be in his Bible class was an education and training for life that was both a treat and a privilege. (Ed. Note: It is immortalized at this date in Sinclair Community College, named in his honor.)

The citizens most responsible for the establishment of the Young Men's Christian Association were: Robert W. Steele, E. M. Wood, G. G. Prugh, J. E. Gilbert, J. H. Winters, Josiah Gebhart, J. C. Kiefaber, J. H. Thomas, H. E. Parrott, E. T. Sweet, T. O. Lowe, W. K. Eckert, Eugene Wuichet, J. A. Shauck and G. W. Hoglen.

Inspired by the example of the Young Men's Christian Association, the women of Dayton decided to express on their part, the new birth that had come to the churches. In the fall following the organization of the men's society the wives and mothers met, planned and carried out not the first but the largest and most active association that Dayton had ever had, under the leadership of women alone, the Woman's Christian Association. Their efforts differed from the first in that they undertook no more than the relief of the poor in the most obvious ways, visiting the sick, sending supplies to the needy and offering what help they could to people in trouble. The use of rooms in the Young Men's Christian Association on Fourth Street were offered and remained for a time their only corporate home.

A more complete history of the Christian association movement in the hands of women will be found elsewhere. It is only necessary to point to the building on the corner of Third and Wilkinson to see what good will and generosity have done for the girls of Dayton.

The aims of the association have changed with its name; now Young Women's Christian Association, and according to the new ideals of human helpfulness, but the early organizers should be remembered. They were Mrs. J. H. Winters, Mrs. C. L. Hawes, Mrs. Preserved Smith, Mrs. Abia Zeller, Miss Joan Rench, Mrs. George Hoglen, Mrs. David Gebhart, Miss Ellen Brown, Mrs. E. A. Daniels, Mrs. W. D. Bickham, Mrs. John G. Doren, Mrs. E. E. Barney, Miss Carrie Brown, Mrs. Leonard Moore, Mrs. G. W. Rogers, Mrs. J. B. Thresher, and Mrs. J. A. Robert.

Still another effect of the religious awakening of the '70s was the effervescence of the temperance cause which swept over the country like a moral epidemic which, indeed, it was. The leading figure was a woman by the name of Carrie Nation who lived in Kansas but ended by becoming a nation-wide heroine. Her story was one well known to all communities and in all ages: the suffering of a wife and mother from the intemperate habits of her husband. Being a woman of grit and determination she gathered about her similar victims and led them to the source of their sorrows, the nearest saloon.

There they held a prayer-meeting on the sidewalk, kneeling on the stones and calling down the wrath of God on the proprietor. When he was sufficiently intimidated which did not take long, they marched in through the shuttered doors and taking every bottle from the shelves carried it outside and emptied it into the gutter. Barrels and kegs fared the same way and when they left, there was not enough drink left in the establishment to hurt anybody.

The news of her exploits spread, and town after town took it up. Direct action was a new thing for women who had suffered and prayed in private. It had the hurling force of a crusade and also perhaps the stimulus. Its full force was felt here in Dayton. Many a drinking place on Sixth Street began the day with an abundant stock and after a visit from the Temperance ladies was left with nothing on the shelves. The excitement had its day and faded out before other interests, but it undoubtedly had its effect on later prohibition legislation.

Speaking of the beginning of things, there was another in the '70s which meant much to Dayton. One summer afternoon in 1878 a long black vehicle drew up to the office of Dr. Reeve, then on the corner of Fourth and Ludlow, and from it descended, with the deliberation taught by their order, four Sisters of the Poor of St. Francis.

To the doctor they said, "We hear you have long wanted a hospital in Dayton. We are here to help yon." And that short parley between people who believed that serving the Lord was a practical as well as a spiritual concern, resulted in the founding of St. Elizabeth's Hospital.

In a disreputably dirty and wretched house, on Franklin Street, those devoted women established themselves. It had been a saloon and per- haps worse. It needed scrubbing and disinfecting. Both were done. And when all was immaculate and cheerful six iron beds were put up and the Sisters were ready to take care of the sick of St. Elizabeth's Hospital.

The doctors of Dayton rallied gallantly to the enterprise, giving of their professional time and skill gratis. It was not long before the demand made increased space necessary and a frame building was added on the same lot. Here forty could be accommodated and the beds were always full. No discrimination was made between the religious faiths of the patients and all who came were cared for.

The first medical staff of St. Elizabeth's Hospital consisted of Dr. Reeve, chief of staff; Dr. John Davis, Dr. Thomas L. Neal, Dr. E. Pilate, Dr. H. S. Jewett, Dr. J. D. Daugherty and Dr. W. J. Conklin. Sometime in the '80s six acres of ground was purchased on the west bank of the Miami River in what was then called Browntown and a commodious brick struc- ture erected on the old Patterson Brown farm.

It was imposing as a building and people wondered if so large a hospital were really needed in Dayton. But it has grown with the years and what was built in the '80s is now merely the small core of a vast building that stretches north and south along the river bank with a chapel and large wings extending to the western side, its comfortable wards and rooms con- taining four hundred and forty beds.

In 1873 a metropolitan police force of thirty-five men was orga- nized and an ordinance passed for the election of two constables and one or more watchmen a year. There are now (1932) two hundred and three patrolmen at work keeping Dayton in order.

In this decade of beginnings we must also list the Holly Water Works, probably the most important civic enterprise undertaken up to that time. The porous gravel sub-soil under Dayton might have been a good fil- ter when only four or five thousand people lived over it but when the population doubled and trebled the number of cesspools in juxtaposition with the wells became a disturbing thought to dwell upon. A pump in the backyard was the best water-works our ancestors boasted in the '50s and '60s.

In the spring election of 1869 the question was put up to the people of a complete system known as the Holly system. It was started in 1870 with a very few miles of service supply but has increased with every year of the extension of the boundaries of Dayton until it now has reached the extent of over three hundred and eighty miles of water mains. A full account of the system will be found elsewhere in this history.

Whoever invented the expression, "The Gay 'Nineties" was too young to know how gay the '70s were. We were gay but we were sentimental. Oh, how sentimental we were! If we had our photographs taken, we posed leaning on the back of a chair in an attitude of contemplative despair with finger to forehead and downcast eyes indicating the recent loss of our only remaining relative by a violent death.

If we sang songs, they were always about death, particularly of the young. *Darling I Am Growing Old, Oh My Darling Nelly Gray, Where Are the Songs that We Once Used to Sing? Long, long ago, Long ago.* They dealt with graves and tears and weeping willows.

We always sang at picnics or around the piano at one of the homes. Saturday afternoons on a canal boat or perhaps in a leaky skiff, anything that was available to take us beyond the city limits. In buggies up the Covington Pike to Lovers Lane which crossed Stillwater River in an old covered bridge, a grove down the River Road, the Glen at Yellow Springs, all resounded on moonlight nights to our chorused voices.

We're Tenting Tonight on the Old Camp Ground, Way Down Upon the Suwanee River, Old Black Joe -- lugubrious and mournful but punctuated by sudden bursts of laughter that belied our sombre sentiments, and impressed the fact that we were eighteen and not eighty. The very titles of the old songs carry with them memories of the blessed decade.

Sweet and Low brings back a straw ride out to a farmhouse on the Salem Pike, now well within the city limits; *Maryland, My Maryland* of the Soldiers' Home when it was the fashionable resort for horseback people every Saturday night. Sometimes we came back by the Germantown Pike or by the Cincinnati Pike, singing *Dixie* or *My Old Kentucky Home*, the horses' steps on the hard road putting queer stops in the music.

We were not trained singers, except as Mr. Turpin and high school morning singing made us, but it was music -- let one dare to deny it! It puts "canned music" to shame for it thrilled with thoughts that a phonograph never gives: youth, and hope and foolish yearnings. There is more to music than mere figures on a staff.

It will be put down, I have no doubt, to the usual delusions of age when I say I know that young people in the '70s had gayer times than those in the 1930s. For one thing the winter sports have quite disappeared, due to what unscientific people think is a change in seasons. Meteorologists claim that they have not changed; it is we who think they have.

I bow to the dictum but maintain my points, and they are several: First, that every horse-owning family in Dayton had its sleigh, either the trim little cutter for the fast trotters, or the big family sleigh to hold a crowd. These sleighs had their place in the barn along with the buggies, surreys or family carriage, just as necessary for getting around in the winter and more so, than wheeled vehicles.

Second, that from the first of November on, every hardware merchant had a string of shiny steel skates hanging outside his door, sign positive that the river might freeze up any day, when the rush demand would come. The school pupils watched the ice, reporting on it every day; that it was "freezing smooth" or "not quite thick enough yet to bear." If snow came and spoiled the skating, it only offered another joy, that of sleighing. An icy storm that coated the streets was welcomed because it made a "good bottom" for the sleighs. Two hours of good business-like snowing and one began to hear the bells on the streets, a rapturous jingle of which no child or man now knows the charm.

The Miami River for the major part of the year was a great nuisance, breaking over the levees, drowning out farms, messing up our streets and filling our cellars with refuse. But when the mercury went down to zero it mended its ways and became the greatest playplace in the world. When word came that the ice would bear, with every boy's cap and every girl's coat on the hall racks in the schoolhouse hung a pair of skates, ready to grab and run for the river when the bell rang at the close of school.

Woe to him who had not scanned his Cicero correctly or to her who lacked one necessary problem in geometry! For, making up lessons after school was an iron rule and apt to cut playtime short in the skating season. Those who did get there promptly found the river frozen from bank to bank and from bridge to bridge. In exceptional weather one could skate from the mouth of Mad River almost to the mouth of Wolf Creek -- one glassy shining sheet of ice.

Main Street, north from Third, showing the old and new courthouses. The "new" one was demolished to make way for the Arcade plaza.

Everybody seemed to be there; young and old, girls and boys, for in those days everybody, except the paralytic, knew how to skate; they had plenty of chance to practice. The good skaters kept to the middle of the river, the beginners hugged the shore to keep out of the way of the long lines, who, with interlocked hands, swept up the river with swift graceful strokes. When we got skilful enough to join one of those groups what ecstasy it was to get into motion!

Holding fast to hands on each side, starting with a good purchase on the outer edge of the skate-runner we swept grandly to the right as far as our combined impetus would carry us, then to the left, each new departure getting more and more momentum from the weight of our combined bodies until, in gradually increasing curves, we covered nearly the width of the river in each rhythmical oscillation.

There were show skaters whom we learned to look for every winter, keeping a place free from the crowd to exhibit their skill. Such a one was Jesse Booher, a carpenter, always on hand at the first freeze and always surrounded by admirers. He wore, not the new-fashioned club skates, but old flat wooden ones with the runners turning up over his feet in front, and on these pre-historic utensils what glories did he not perform! Fancy outlines, "figure eights," circles, back-strokes with crossed feet; every movement graceful, though he was a heavy man and an old one.

If the river failed us, we went to Bimm's Park out by the water works on Keowee Street, where the ice could be kept free from snow and freeze without interference of wind or currents. We walked that long distance from the center of town every Saturday morning, we skated all day, we walked back at night, tired but ecstatic, every nerve tingling with the exercise in the cold, ready for a supper of sausage and sweet potatoes, and for lessons, some music of the family orchestra and then to bed. Movies say you? Motor rides? Take them all away. We prefer the '70s.

In the '70s we knew everybody who drove a horse and buggy or wore a sealskin coat. The term "society" was beginning to be used to designate the frosting on the social layer cake. This was the day when Billy Franz led the cotillions and Stowe Forgy was the handsomest bachelor, when McLain Smith, John Patterson, the Crane brothers and R. I. Cummin organized the assemblies, held in the third floor of the building on the southwest corner of Jefferson and Second. Never, I am sure, were the girls so pretty and so imposing in their long trains and big coiffures or the men so striking in their "Burnsides" and dress coats.

How fashionable we were in those days of bustles and trains! How we laughed (politely and surreptitiously I mean) at the sequestered old ladies here and there, who still wore hoops. Our outline was so very different, and of course different meant better. No girl ever wore her own hair but piled on switches, puffs and braids, the whole gathered into an immense "chignon" on the back of the head.

The outline, which with hoops had been that of a bell, now resembled that of a pouter pigeon, for with bust-improvers in front and a bustle behind, each girl was a fair reproduction of that pompous bird. And what a marvel of dressmaking was the gown of the period! Twelve to fourteen yards of silk went into it. There was the tight-fitting "basque" with darts catching all the fullness below the bust and whale-bones to keep it smooth.

A skirt, long enough behind to drag six or seven inches on the floor, (or sidewalk) trimmed with rows on rows of "knife-pleating," an overskirt trimmed with the same and looped upon the sides, the whole tied back underneath to further emphasize the pouter-pigeon effect! Underneath were skirts on skirts, all of them long, some of silk to rustle against the lining of the dress or starched to do the same for summer dresses.

This mass of heavy material was dragged behind every woman who walked on the streets of Dayton. If she were cleanly and hated to sweep with her "train" the dirty sidewalks she held it up with her right hand into a huge bunch which much impeded her walking but was accepted as are the rulings of Providence and the dress-makers. One's dancing man, if he were clever, learned to grasp from his fair partner this unmanageable mass of substance and hold its weight himself while the two negotiated the ball-room floor and tried to keep out of the way of other couples similarly burdened.

The bustle itself was a sort of bird-cage affair to tie on under the dress behind and hold the train to its proper place. Sometimes it was known to work a little on to the side, when the appearance of the wearer could only be described as an awful warning.

A modern girl might well inquire how, with clothes of this volume and description, we traveled. The question is pertinent and the answer to it is, the Saratoga trunk. It had to be "Saratoga" because Saratoga Springs was the mecca of the fashionables in the '70s, and if you went anywhere it was good to create the impression that you were going there. The so-called trunks were created to hold the dresses. Standing, the largest of them, thirty inches high, long and wide in proportion, each was a job for a baggage man. Hence the term "baggage smasher." To treat those trunks rigorously was their sole retaliation to the vanities of the female sex. Each one held from four to six trays and each tray held not more than one dress, the puffings and loopings held out with tissue paper. With four or five such trunks to accommodate the party dresses of a debutante, traveling was traveling, indeed.

It was in this sort of a costume that we went calling every afternoon. That is, we either went calling or stayed home to be called upon. There was nothing else to do with our time. We tied our tall hats on over our chignons, donned very tight gloves, seized our bunch of skirts valiantly from behind and with a silver or pearl card case started on our rounds. Since it was a purely empty gesture it was not a heart-breaking disappointment to find the ladies out. We could then leave a card with the maid, mark out the name from the list and go on to the next. Or, we dressed in our best and sat in the front parlor from two o'clock until five waiting for the bell to ring and usher the visitors to our plush chairs.

Speaking of calling is a reminder of the habit of New Year's calling, at its height in the '70s and a pretty custom while it lasted. It had been for many years the custom for gentlemen to make the rounds of their lady friends on January first, to wish them a Happy New Year but in the '70s it became a formal holiday observance.

The men in groups of four engaged a "hack" from the livery stable for the afternoon. Arrayed in silk top-hats (called stovepipes by the irreverent), Prince Albert coats, white vests and lemon-colored "kids" these resplendent creatures made their rounds. Beginning at the extreme east of the residence section with the Andersons, the Harries, the Walters and Kitty Parmely, they progressed from doorstep to doorstep the length of First and Second and Monument Avenue (then Water Street).

Just ten minutes was the extent of time offered on the altar of society, unless we may add, things were very good in the dining room, when the call might be somewhat prolonged. The girls put on their best and gathered, also in assemblages of from four to ten, in the parlor of one of the number. There, from behind the inside shutters they watched for the carriages or the sleighs of their guests. Sometimes several equipages arrived at the same time and when this happened it was proof positive that the affair was going as it should.

As the callers arrived they were invited to the dining-room where, on a table spread the length of its capacity, were laid everything in the nature of things to eat that ambitious hostesses and clever cooks could provide. At one end a large block of hollowed-out ice held the raw oysters; at the other a vast cake lifted its frosted ornaments toward the ceiling, in the center a confection made of macaroons and candy, and dotted in between these *pièces de resistance* were moulds of jelly, bunches of celery, plates of sandwiches, cold meats and biscuits.

A centerpiece of flowers in January would have been unthought of, the florists not having as yet learned to raise the flowers or promote the demand. What quantities of coffee were drunk, what piles of sandwiches disappeared! What numberless little cakes and chocolate drops were consumed, it would never do to tell at this late day. Once in a while there were rumors that a beverage stronger than coffee was offered and accepted, but this did not happen often and made a scandal when it did. Wine or no wine, the occasion was an intemperate one in its way for all concerned ate more than they should and had indigestion afterwards.

There was rivalry on both sides. The men tried to see how many calls they could get in from noon until midnight and the girls hoped when the visiting cards were counted theirs would be seen to be the most popular group. Besides, finding it so easy to gain entrance into the best houses, men who were quite strangers to all of social Dayton, hired a hack and went the rounds, sure that every door would open to them to swell the total of calls. It was not long before hostesses, comparing card lists, discovered the imposture and it was this, more than the change of fashion which eventually drove New Year's calling into the social discard.

The men who were the most industrious in New Year's calling could also be counted on for serenades. A visiting girl was an excuse for the swains with good voices to gather, about one o'clock, moonlight preferred, on the front lawn of her hostess' father's house and sing with a shrill tenor and a booming bass, *Drink to Me Only With Thine Eyes*, *When You and I Were Young Maggie*, *The Old Oaken Bucket*, I *Dreamt That I Dwelt in Marble Halls*.

Let the modern reader laugh, but girls nowadays don't know the thrill of being wakened by four good voices in the quiet night, getting out of bed, pulling down the shade and lighting the gas, a sign to those outside and below that the music was appreciated. To carry the affair to its logical (and hoped for) conclusion was to have the father get up and dress and invite the singers inside to have something from the sideboard. But fathers seldom rose to such heights of hospitality.

Late in the '60s and early in the '70s spiritualism had its greatest vogue. Neighborhood parties gathered in one home or another for amateur seances when they were supposed to hold converse with their dead friends. There was much talk of table-tipping and mysterious rappings all of which rather frightened the younger members of the family. I remember one old couple frequently at our house, who thought of nothing, talked of nothing, but their wonderful experiences. The fervor spread until every evening was given up to it.

Then as suddenly it died down and the world turned to planchette. This, not being so gruesome appealed to the younger people, who at every small gathering sat around a table with their hands on planchette while the varnished board wrote laborious screeds or galloped wildly over the paper. Queer, how that inanimate thing seemed to be acquainted with so many of our jokes and could even make witticisms of its own. Planchette in turn has gone into the limbo of forgotten and discarded interests, but there is no lack of successors and they appear with every new generation.

No chronicle of the '70s would be complete without a story of the First Street racing when snow covered the ground. It was not an era of sports, so-called (how could it be when girls' skirts reached the ground?) but winter brought its own recreations, and of these sleigh riding and skating were first.

When, because of the snow-covered river the crowds of sightseers found nothing to watch from the bridges, they betook themselves to First Street which, from Main to the levee, was the scene of the sleighing carnival of each winter. It was wider than the other east and west thoroughfares and less high in the middle so it made a straight and smooth roadway for about eight blocks.

On each side the curb was crowded with on-lookers watching for their favorite drivers and the fastest horses. There were not a few of both in Dayton at the time. John S. Lytle, among the fourteen horses in his stable on South Main Street, had a pair of blacks that could do a mile in three minutes. His was a familiar figure in the sleighing season. So was his son, H. V. Lytle, who had a gray mare, a good saddle horse, and fast pacer named *Trinket*.

Charles Harries was a lover of good horse-flesh and drove *Alice* triumphantly to the plaudits of the sidewalk observers on First Street. J. D. Platt's *Busy Boy* was always heralded as one of the best trotters in Dayton; so was *Daisy*, owned by Charles L. Phillips. Charles Freeman was a fre-

The Loretto Guild, Catholic equivalent of the YWCA, stood for many
years on West First Street.

quent driver but he owned no leading horse of his own. He generally was to be seen behind a gray pacer belonging to Mike Nipgen, a horse that eventually took honors at State and county fairs.

Another professional driver was Rube Myers a familiar figure about all the stables in town and the track at the fairgrounds as well. He owned very fast horses which he paraded on the First Street track. Andy Makely, another of the same persuasion, had a flyer that passed many another on the long stretch toward the river.

These were the leading fast trotters in Dayton but there were others, not perhaps blue-ribbon horses, but which added much to the gayety of bells, flying feet and glistening snow. Mrs. Edward Rowe was there and made a good time. The historic Patterson sleigh, the property of four succeeding generations, built in 1810, painted black with yellow rings, was always looked for and cheered as a part of our pioneers days. Perhaps in the back seat could be seen the venerable Mrs. Jefferson Patterson, enjoying the scene as much as if she were forty years younger.

Some of the large family sleighs were very handsome, graceful in outline, beautifully painted and with curving dashboards to keep the flying snow from the driver, the back seat hung with expensive fur robes. But First Street will never see that gay pageant again. It belongs to the vanished '70s.

Domestic architecture and household decoration, it was thought, took great strides in the '70s. We began to be ashamed of the old fashioned houses and had not yet learned how really beautiful they were. People who lived in dignified brick homes talked of "remodeling," and people who were just building put up atrocities called "Queen Anne" cottages, where futile turrets, bay windows and sawed fretwork porches called the public's attention to the taste of their owners.

Inside the houses was also revolution. The whatnots went into the attic; oil lamps on fringed mats followed. A gas drop-light with a long pipe gave illumination to evening readers. Most everybody was putting in furnaces and bathrooms. The advertisements mentioned hardwood floors and hot and cold running water as unusual attractions in their real estate bargains. We did not "do decalcomania" any more, but we learned to make macrame lace and hung it around the marble mantels, varied sometimes by a felt lambrequin with cut edges and appliqued horrors. We pinned Japanese fans onto the wall and hung Japanese umbrellas under the chandelier.

The piano was ornamented with a plush "throw" and the mantel held vases holding gilded cat-tails. Lessons in china-painting, wood-carving and Kensington wool-work were the vogue; everything that was gildable we gilded: shovels, bread-bowls and cake-spoons, nothing was sacred.

It is not surprising that, with such aberrations on the part of consumers, producers would show no imagination for beauty. In every article of use or for wear the manufacturers did their utmost for the uglification of life. I cannot remember, in our part of the country at least, that the decade from 1870 to 1880 produced one simple, original or pleasing design. There were neither artists nor craftsmen, there were only mechanics at a turning-wheel or a fretsaw.

Furniture was heavy, over-ornamented and highly varnished. The beautiful old designs of the colonial mahogany were abandoned in favor of gimcrack scrolls and ornaments without meaning. Towering headboards to beds bore machine-turned melons, peaches, rosettes and curlicues and stood on carpets of brussels roses and lilies.

Jewelry was ornate; common silverware was crass, cheap and ordinary. The stimulus given by the Centennial Exposition at Philadelphia in 1876 was potent in its influence but was a long while in getting universalized. We had not yet learned the charm of genuineness. It was an unblushing era of pretense, of false-fronts on stores and on dowagers, of artificial protuberances of the female figure, of mannerisms and affection of speech. Only our recreations were simple and natural.

Oh, the '70s! The gay sentimental '70s! the pretentious affected '70s! the romantic, ugly, self-conscious '70s! The '70s when we hung chromos on our walls and read *Lucile* and Ouida and Laura Jean Libby! The forever-vanished '70s, how far away they seem -- and are!

13

Fin de Siècle

The 1880s were notable for several, if not ornamental, then excessively imperative, municipal improvements. In the preceding decade the Holly Company had supplied us with a most satisfactory system of waterworks, still functioning acceptably But for anything beyond that Dayton was a mud-be-spattered, garbage-ridden, rubbish-littered little town.

The situation became at last so irritating to all concerned that in the years between 1880 and 1890 we achieved sewers, paved streets, electric lighting and a telephone system. It was high time for all four.

The first suggestion of the advantages of the telephone appeared in a local paper some time during 1878, but it was advanced more as a curiosity than as a practical possibility applicable to Dayton. Alexander Graham Bell, in an attic in Boston, had made his first audible communication with a person at a distance.

George L. Phillips, a young business man of Dayton, read of it, was interested and investigated. He went to Boston, was struck with the enormous potentialities of the invention and came home to set the business world on fire. It was not easy. Everyone admitted the advantages, providing they could be put into application, but buying stock was a different matter.

By another year the papers were roused to deadly earnest as they depicted the necessity of getting the doctor or the fire department in a hurry and with no means of communication better than a horse and buggy or a firebell. They declared editorially that if people only grasped the convenience, to say nothing of the saving of time and labor, of conversing with their friends so easily the new contrivance would be quickly available. That it was, is due to the faith, industry and optimism of George L. Phillips. He talked of nothing, thought of nothing, occupied himself with nothing but the Bell telephone in Dayton, and in a second visit to Boston contracted for the necessary equipment and had it sent on.

The first telephone exchange was installed over the business house of Keifabers Brothers, at 118 East Third Street, with the Keifabers themselves as first subscribers. The earliest directory consisted of a single sheet headed: "Dayton Bell Telephone Company" and held the names of ten subscribers: the Keifabers, three Phillips: T. A., George L., and Charles A., the American Express Company, the Beckel House, George F. Rohr, J. K. McIntire, William Sander and J. W. Johnston.

Business in the new office did not exactly boom. Not more than a dozen calls went through the exchange in a day and they not by number but by name. Ten office employees carried all the traffic. The first woman operator was Lily Althoff (Mrs. Arnold Gwinner); the first chief operator, Minnie Glaser (Mrs. Nanendorf). By the fall of 1879 quite a list of subscribers had come in and the telephone system began to look like an enterprise to be reckoned with.

The equipment was primitive. In order to allow entrance and egress for service wires in this first exchange, augur holes had been bored in a wooden shutter. When the number of subscribers mounted up to sixty, the attention of Mr. Phillips was called to the fact of the lack of more space. His answer was to ask if there was not another shutter, right there, in which could be bored another sixty holes and when that was used up would be time enough to worry.

The widest imagination could not, at that time, picture the possibility of a hundred and twenty subscribers in Dayton. At the present writing (1930) there are fifty thousand. Small hints here and there, in the papers of that day reveal the difference between then and now. It was some time in 1880 that we read that the telephone exchange would be closed on Thanksgiving afternoon from two until four, to enable the employees to eat "A fine Thanksgiving dinner."

Of course, the telephone system grew. It could do no less when once started. Soon the fire-engine houses were connected, then the police stations, the newspaper offices, the banks, the Soldiers' Home, mercantile houses and finally private homes. In 1881 telephone connection was established between Dayton and West Milton, Piqua, Xenia and Miamisburg. The first long-distance call from Indianapolis was taken and answered one October day in 1881 from the T. A. Phillips home, 24 West Fourth Street, in the room that is now the tea room of the Young Women's League.

The telephone has become such an hourly necessity that it takes one's breath away to read the objections against it, especially from those approached to become stockholders. It was "only an experiment after all;" their money was "safer in the bank than with the telephone company." "Dayton would never be large enough to make it a really paying investment." Boys raised a great outcry because the wire interfered with their kiteflying. People were afraid to have wires installed on account of danger during thunderstorms. All of which is the inevitable experience of every new invention.

It was in 1882 the great servant of mankind (especially of his wife), electricity, came to Dayton. Up to that time our streets were lighted by dim and flickering gas lamps. Little boys with a ladder over their shoulders and a torch in their hands ran from one corner post to another, hooking the ladder on to a crosspiece in order to reach the gas cock, pushing the torch under, turning on the gas and running on to the next.

In our homes we still scratched the immemorial match (on the box if we were well brought up, on the wall if we weren't) and scorched our fingers in the process. The resulting illumination was weak, uncertain and malodorous.

Dayton had heard that other cities were using electricity; it seemed possible, but needed demonstration. On the "Commons" below the railroad some enterprising engineer erected two dynamos with power obtained from the engines of an obliging sawmill near by, and for the first time these unsightly wastes were brilliantly illuminated. The city fathers came and saw and were convinced.

A company incorporated with a capital stock of one hundred thousand dollars soon followed and received orders for a few arc lamps. Merchants saw at once the advantage to their customers of well-lighted stores. Like the telephone, electricity grew under pressure of its own selling power. From small beginnings in 1882 electric power and light has developed into the present twenty-million dollar public utility, embracing seventeen private and municipal plants, serving some fifty thousand customers in eleven counties in southern Ohio.

The present power house stands on the river bank two miles and a half south of the center of the city where the C. C. C. and St. L. railway crosses the Miami and from which the power for all these stations is generated. (Ed. Note: Built in 1916-1918, it was demolished in 1988-1990.)

The domestic necessities for the "juice" increased with the magnifying imaginations of the manufacturers of accessories. Percolators, sweepers, cooking ranges, irons, fans, heaters, hair-curlers, and dish-washers all testify that life could hardly go on without electricity in the home.

That it did go on in the '80s meant unremitting labor for the housekeeper augmented by the entire absence of any public eating places except the hotels. If the cook left, as cooks had a habit of doing in other times besides our own, the head of the family and the empty-stomached school children appeared with rigorous punctuality at meal time and had to be fed. Schools never imagined the noon lunch hour. The word "cafeteria" had not yet been coined. Tea rooms were unknown. The railroad station, the Phillips and the Beckel House and the free lunch at saloons were the only refuges for the business man.

Hence, "Woman's place was in the home" became an iron truth in those days. She was expected to and did employ the arts of a dozen or so trades and professions in her housekeeping but no one thought her capable of selling stockings or using a typewriter. Therefore she was only beginning to penetrate into the business world. In 1880 just six offices had girl stenographers and it is recorded that the head of one of them was seriously argued with by his fellow lawyers for having yielded to the threatening tide that would surely end in disaster.

It seems incredible that in view of the earlier descriptions of mud in Dayton streets, we should leave had to wait until 1889 for paving. The theory supporting us was our confidence in the filtering powers of the underlying bed of gravel through which the river swept at certain intervals. It was indeed a godsend in the beginning but in time the natural question arose: "Why put faith in gravel after eighty-eight thousand people have come to live over it?"

The City Council was immovable, as councils were apt to be in those *laissez faire* days. It was criticized in the papers, petitioned, importuned and threatened. Twice, committees were appointed, but never a report offered or even, it is said, a meeting held. Quoting from the minutes of an organization of citizens we find this summing up of the city management of that day: "It is a political football, kicked hither and thither at every municipal election. The winning side is inevitably made the beneficiary of the victory, until another election changes the political complexion, But not the character of the government. The Council, the Board of Education, Fire Board and Infirmary trustees are all under the control of the successful political leader designated and the 'boss'."

Patience under such conditions became a vice. At a meeting of exasperated citizens called by A. C. Marshall on November 11, 1889, A. A. Winters presided, H. E. Mead acted as secretary and A. C. Marshall made the opening remarks. A committee was appointed consisting of the following ten persons: A. C. Marshall, E. N. Thresher, Jacob Linxweiler, Jr., J. K. McIntire, Walter Worman, W. P. Callahan, W. D. McKemy, O. I. Gunckel, Jacob Decker and Samuel W. Davies. This preliminary committee sent out a call to other citizens from whom in turn was formed the Committee of One Hundred with A. C. Marshall as permanent chairman. Six (sic!) sub-committees followed with chairmen: Executive, E. M. Thresher; city government, G. N. Bierce; legislation, W. D. McKemy; sewers, J. W. Stoddard; street improvement, D. E. Mead; parks and levees, Jacob Linxweiler, Jr.; finance, A. Bauman.

The necessary legislation for accomplishment was secured by Hon. George W. Houk, Colonel D. B. Corwin and James Turner. How the work was accomplished by installing sewers, paving the streets and beautifying the parks is too long a story to tell here. Suffice it to say, that these unsalaried private citizens gave their valuable time, held innumerable meetings and used their professional and business influence for the benefit of Dayton and as far as is known, there is not a public monument erected to any of them. As for the elected public officials, they sat in the City Hall and industriously drew their salaries.

The first results of the Committee of One Hundred was that when people drove out to East Fifth Street they found, between Wayne Avenue and McReynolds Street, a stretch of good, solid, smooth wood-block pavement. It seemed too good to be true. But that was indeed the beginning of what spread (in spite of complaints that it would impoverish property owners) to the year 1930, when there are in Dayton over three hundred miles of paved streets (and a few less alleys) and more coming all the time. Mud, dust, chuck-holes and hog-wallows are all but forgotten.

But it must be remembered that we, the citizens of Dayton, might still be wading ankle deep in limestone soup if it had not been for the labors of the Committee of One Hundred. The next result was that in 1890 a complete system of sewers was begun in the center of town and from year to year carried out to the extreme limits of the city, delivering us at once from private property cesspools and of consequent sickness and pestilence. By 1909 there were one hundred and fifty miles of sanitary sewers in Dayton and ninety miles of storm sewers. Today (1930) there are two hundred and sixty-eight miles of sanitary sewers and 143 miles of storm sewers.

The 1880s saw Dayton embellished by a number of notable public buildings among them the Public Library erected in Cooper Park, from plans by Peters and Burns. The architectural style is a free treatment of the southern French Gothic or Romanesque; the construction is of Dayton limestone with trimmings of Marquette red sandstone. Frederick Poole, the prominent Boston librarian, was consulted, and advised many of the details of the inside arrangement. For fifty years it has stood among the elms in Cooper Park, a handsome and sufficient building in which to house and from which to distribute books to the public.

In 1881 the so-called "new" courthouse was perpetrated, that anomaly of architecture labelled *Justiciae Dedicata*. This building is said to have cost Montgomery County $174,945 and it has been jocosely intimated that this sum was $174,940 more than it was worth.

In July, 1880, Myron T. Herrick, afterwards Governor of Ohio and later Ambassador to France, came to Dayton and carried off as his bride, Miss Kitty Parmely from her home on East First Street.

In the middle '80s a great addition to the western edge of town was constructed, then known as "Robert Fill." Not many people, when they walk along that tree embowered parkway named Robert Boulevard, know to whom Dayton owes it. Named for its promoter it has become his noblest monument. Beyond the levee between it and the river, there stretched in 1880 an area of pasture land on which the family cows of ancient Dayton were nourished; then an expanse of gravel, then the river, at most seasons of the year a thin and harmless stream, at others a raging torrent.

Therefore it happened that the levee, supposed to be a promenade on the river bank, was so far from the water as to be a misnomer. This condition existed from Monument Avenue Bridge to Third Street Bridge. The arched elms overhead, the contribution of John Van Cleve, who converted the bare embankment into a much-prized thoroughfare.

The first to see the advantage of adding those wasted areas to the rapidly growing city was Mr. James A. Robert. He met at first the most violent and outspoken opposition, the public seeing only in the double plan of deepening the channel and adding available building sites, more danger than ever from floods. But Mr. Robert knew what he was about. He got his brother, a practical engineer, to come from the east and look over the situation. The two together worked out the plan but it was James Robert who accomplished the details. A steam-shovel was put in, excavating the gravel from the bed of the river and piling it on to the land, gradually bringing the level of the fill up to the top of the levee.

Thus the whole area now known as Robert Boulevard and Sunset Avenue, together with the homes upon them, came into existence from the fertile brain of James A. Robert. At first glance it looked like a marvelous money-making scheme, for real estate values were going up. It should have been, but James Robert "was not ten cents richer for all his labors of four long years." The investment he put in he got out and that was all, plus the personal satisfaction of seeing a much-needed improvement realize itself.

On July 30 and 31, 1884 there occurred in Dayton the third of the four biggest crowds in her history. The first was the Harrison campaign in 1840; the second when Goldsmith-Maid ran in 1860; the Wright celebration is yet to be told. The third occasion, of which we are now concerned, was the reunion of the national Grand Army of the Republic and the dedication of the soldiers' monument which still stands guard at the head of Main Street (Ed. Note: Returned to its rightful spot in 1994 after years of exile across the river from downtown.)

Since the intention was to bring to Dayton as many people from outside as possible, the preparations consumed not only weeks but months. A list of the citizens instrumental in making the arrangements and heading the committees sounds like a roster of the social and business life of those Dayton years: Major W. D. Bickham, M. P. Nolan, A. A. Simonds, Harry Lowe, Hon. Samuel Craighead, A. J. Williougby, Hon. George W. Houk, Col. E. A. Parrott, Hon. John G. Lowe, General Gates Thruston, Captain E. Morgan Wood, Col. W. J. White, General S. B. Smith, A. D. Wilt, E. Stowe Forgy, J. K. McIntire, Hon. J. A. McMahon, Charles E. Pease, Captain S. W. Davies, L. D. Reynolds, A. Newsalt, O. B. Brown and A. C. Marshall.

These were the leaders and there were hundreds of helpers. To most of them, survivors of the Civil War, this celebration was a vital and a personal matter. It began at daybreak of the 30th with reveille and an artillery salute. First in order of the day was an inspection of the Soldiers' Home by the visiting guests with Governor Brown and Chaplain Earnshaw as hosts.

In the afternoon a parade formed on Main Street composed of sur-

The Soldiers' Monument, the unveiling on July 30, 1884 snagged as thousands, including ex-president and Mrs. R. B. Hayes, watched.

vivors of the war, on foot and in carriages, military companies in uniform, posts of the Grand Army of the Republic, children from the Soldiers' and Sailors' Orphans Home at Xenia, veterans from the National Home and the Old Guard Post. To the head of Main Street they marched amid the huzzas from a hundred thousand throats, past the grandstand where stood ex-President Hayes and Mrs. Hayes, General Joseph G. Hawley, General Rosecrans, Senator Sherman, General R. P. Kennedy with prominent Daytonians, and came to a halt where the veiled monument awaited its share in the ceremony.

Following the usual flowery oratory suitable to the occasion, Hon. George W. Houk presented the monument to the city of Dayton, Governor Hoadly accepted in appropriate terms. Then something went wrong. The monument seemed to not care to cooperate. It would not be presented, accepted nor unveiled. The ropes to release the enveloping sheet were pulled and nothing happened. They were pulled again and yet again, with no perceivable effect.

The shrouded figure stood immovable on top of its pillar, careless of the agonizing emotions in the breasts of the Grand Army of the Republic and just as careless of the rain which took that opportunity to come down with such whole-souled vigor as rain can only do on occasions of public rejoicing. The crowds were packed so tight nobody could get away and there was no shelter to go to if they had. For one long-drawn-out hour, during which a chimney cleaner was sent for, "shinned" up the pillar, released the sheet and clambered down (to the quite genuine applause of the crowd) that rain continued.

It even kept up while the massed choirs sang the anthem and then, having done all the harm possible to uniforms, feathers and patriotism, it ceased and the sun came out bright and warm. The anthem was written by Mrs. John Hancock, the music composed by W. L. Blumenschein, *Peace to their ashes; their graves are our pride*.

In the evening the scene of interest changed from the crowded streets to the equally crowded banks of the river. The thousands that had filled Main Street earlier in the day from curb to curb spread themselves along the north and south banks from the Main Street to the Dayton View Bridge and massed themselves on each. In the rear of the stately homes then fronting on Monument Avenue, the sloping lawns made a sort of dress circle for the honored guests, they being divided between the Bickham and the E. M. Thresher premises.

As the sun sank towards the West in the haze of that summer after-noon the spectators saw, majestically rounding the current of the river, what the papers announced as "The United States Fleet." It consisted of two Mississippi River iron-clads, led by the flagship *Union* under com-mand of (Admiral) E. B. Lyon. Historical accuracy demands the admission that the gunboats were cleverly constructed out of boards, painted black and propelled by side-wheel paddles worked by man-power at a crank on each side.

These formidable vessels were each mounted with two field pieces and two mortars. Just below Main Street Bridge there opened up on the fleet a deadly fire from a rebel battery (two small brass cannon hidden in the fringe of tall sycamores that even then remained along the north bank). The fleet came to anchor and fired a broadside in return. Then the troops poured ashore, led by Captain A. D. Knecht. The rebel yell resounded on the air answered by the cheers of the brave Yankee boys.

The crowds on the bridges encouraged the Union troops with answering cheers amid which the rebel stronghold was taken. It was an occasion to thrill even the most hard-boiled of observers. The boom of the cannon, the black smoke belching from the stacks of the gunboats, the cheers of the attacking troops made a never-to-be-forgotten scene. As for the flagship the records tell nothing of its ultimate end. Perhaps it did not hold together long enough to be described.

As the dusk fell and the stars came out, the crowds still lingered for was there not a superb display of fireworks announced? And who wants to miss anything like that? Memory tells us it was all the reporters said about it. The set pieces were sent for at large expense and set up on the very edge of the river so that each, as it came into blazing prominence was repeated in the glassy surface of the water.

The Coat-of-Arms of the United States was the first to elicit the loyal cheers of the populace. Then came *On Guard* (a soldier on duty), *Aladdin's Jeweled Trees, The Flowering Aloe Tree, The Star of America*; in addition there were forty-eight rockets with parachutes; aerial bouquets, showering golden rain and colored streamers and twelve pyrotechnic bombs, while all up and down the river on both banks were set off at inter-vals colored magnesium lights so that throughout the long evening's pro-gram there was not a single moment of darkness.

A *Journal* reporter, carried out of himself by the splendor of the spectacle wrote that the "grand Stoddard mansion on the hill, partially revealed by the glow of the rockets, was a fine embellishment of this novel nocturnal spectacle."

No Stoddard home any more! No Bickham and Thresher lawns sloping to the river's edge. Big buildings of the new Dayton have pushed the old homes into the past, and of the Daytonians who worked so hard to celebrate in 1884 how few there are left.

Booth Tarkington it was, if I am not mistaken, who first called the last decade of the century "The Gay Nineties." Richard Le Gallienne called them "The Romantic 'Nineties" and Mencken the "Electric 'Nineties." All three were more or less right.

The '90s were gay, they were romantic and they were electric. But most of all the '90s were sophisticated, with a sophistication that passes all description. All expression (never to be questioned since it was French) came into the vocabulary of those palpitating years. It was *Fin de Siècle* (called by the ignorant and ribald "Finn de Sickel"). It was used to characterize our clothes, books, manners, opinions, fashions, emotions. Everything was *Fin de Siècle*. It carried a sense of things having gotten to a state of perfection hitherto unknown. Some of it I suspect was due to the impact of new impressions brought in by the Chicago World's Fair in 1893.

At any rate, the seriousness with which we took ourselves was not to be questioned. We felt that of all the other past and gone civilizations, we alone, and our new cultivation had now definitely "arrived." We knew so much. We thought so deeply. Our taste was so unquestioned. It did not seem possible that there could be much ahead of us to learn. Prohibition and suffrage were just jokes. Nobody believed they would ever become realities.

Art was just beginning to be spelled with a capital letter. We imagined that our taste in pictures could not be doubted, but if a present-day housekeeper should inherit the cherished parlor ornaments of the '90s she would order each one deposited where the ash man could carry it into oblivion.

We were devoted to Howells, Mrs. Humphrey Ward and Bellamy's *Looking Backward*. Trilby entranced us with its flavor of foreign life. A part of the *Fin de Siècle* atmosphere was to introduce French phrases into conversation, *de rigueur*, *savoir faire* and *au revoir*. We put *P. P. C.* on our visiting cards and *R. S. V. P.* on our invitations with but a nebulous idea of what it all meant. Artemus Ward as a comic satirist had long ago been

191

Women's Bicycle Club parading in the 1890s (above). A "tally-ho" party of the same era prepares to set off for the Soldiers' Home. Included, left to right, are John H. Patterson, Mrs. Angus Dunn, Miss Temple, Anne Patterson Woodhull, Miss Leslie Temple, Harry Stoddard, Julia Patterson Moorhead, Mrs. J. H. Crane, Mrs. J. H. Patterson, Mrs. Charles Mead, Billy Franz, S. J. Patterson, Jefferson Crane, R. D. Patterson, Mrs. George Ewing, Ed Bunstine, Mrs. Tappan, Mrs. Charles Smith (below).

pushed into a back place on the bookshelves, but Mr. Dooley was coming into his own with his daily comment on Congress.

A sign of social prestige in those days was an iron stag to stand on the lawn under the trees. If we didn't have a lawn and couldn't afford the stag there was a substitute almost as good. It was an iron horsejockey to stand at the curb with up-stretched hand to hold the hitching strap of the next visitor who came with a horse and buggy.

The 1890s were the days of stiff shirtwaists for ladies and little sailor hats perched high upon their coiffures. The days also when at dinner parties the gentlemen guests looked wistfully out from a V-shaped opening formed by the immense sleeves on either side of him.

It was during these years that bicycling came in, and what a craze it was! The first machine to appear had one large wheel in front on which perched the acrobat rider, and a small one at the back. To fall off of one of these contraptions was equivalent to an Alpine disaster. Sensible manufacturers, foreseeing the invasion of women into this recreation, invented the "Safety" in which the two wheels were nearer of a size and then everybody took to it.

A wheel for each member of the family became the rule. Dignified matrons, mothers of grown children (and long before the fad of "reducing" came in) went pedaling solemnly along country roads and wiping their brows in the hot sun. The Soldiers' Home was still a weekly resort, and on Saturday evenings the Pike, from edge to edge, was filled with bicyclers of all ages and conditions. Wheeling became the absorbing topic of conversation. Dressmakers were in a panic because there was no more dressing for dinner. Ladies came to the table in their circular bicycle skirts and what was to become of the trade?

These wheeling skirts were the first intimation that women were entitled to the use of their legs and, I believe, the beginning of their emancipation in the matter of clothes. A double skirt, each cut on the circular, gave ease to pedaling, and the fullness was such that the bifurcation was not apparent. But its baleful influence could be felt and thundered at in all the citadels of "female" purity and decorum.

The very word "divided skirt" was known to throw some ministers and editors into spasms of outraged virtue. The lowering of standards of "womanly behavior," the "smothering of decency," the "decline of the home" and the collapse of the universe were some of the things predicted by the *Dayton Journal* if these awful garments became universal.

Freer dressing gave an impetus to sports for women. That it came far short of what is known today as freedom may be seen if Charles Dana Gibson's drawings of the '90s should be disinterred from back numbers of illustrated magazines, drawings depicting girls playing tennis in "gored" skirts four yards in circumference, touching the ground at every point, and lined with a heavy crinoline "dust ruffle." The sleeves fit with skin tightness on the lower arm where the muscles want free play and stuck out a third of a yard on either side of the wearer's shoulders.

And the hats of the period. Ah, who shall do them justice? It was as if the milliners had designed them while suffering under an attack of delirium tremens. They mounted to undreamed-of altitudes, sat high upon the head with a brim that dipped and soared, the crown topped with a veritable jungle of verdure and blossoms all united with cascades of lace, curling ostrich feathers and flamboyant ribbon bows.

Fashion never could have conquered the hat of the period but the automobile did. When two decades later no amount of skillful pinning or veiling would keep it anchored to its place while whipped with the wind of rapid transit, the small close hat came into its own.

One of the results of our new birth, so to speak, was the rise of a new community self-consciousness. If it were true that we had "arrived" it was well to know what we had arrived from. Our local historian, Mary Davies Steele, reminded us that it was in the spring of 1796 that occurred the stirring events that led to the settlement of Dayton. From her sick bed she wrote articles for the papers telling again how the first settlers came from Cincinnati by river and by land, how they disembarked at the head of Main Street, how they built homes, planted corn, shot game, endured malaria and the rest of it.

Now the calendar said 1896 and time by the clock for a centennial birthday party. Some well-oiled memory disclosed the fact that the shabby old grocery on the corner of Main and Monument Avenue was the original Newcom Tavern, the first real house built in Dayton. Through the generosity of citizens led by John H. Patterson and the impetus of the newly organized Historical Society under Hon. C. W. Dustin, this building was rescued just in time from the hands of the wreckers, who were making place for an apartment house.

Underneath the weather-beaten clapboards the original logs were found intact as well as much of the interior floors and finish. What better peg upon which to hang an historical celebration? A new place was found for the old resident on the edge of the river in Van Cleve Park where, stripped of its unsightly outer garment and restored with roof and chimney, it took on a new air of dignity and interest.

Public-spirited citizens here and there in Montgomery County discovered that their attics held antiques, some of them the actual former furnishings of the cabin, and these they brought with outstretched hands, eager to restore the old building as near as possible to its original condition. The whole spring was a culminating apotheosis of the "old."

Spinning wheels were contributed by old ladies who used them during the three days of the celebration. Beds and cradles, Dutch ovens, candle molds, hominy mills, pewter candlesticks, cider presses were some of the mementoes of the housekeeping of a hundred years ago, which may still be seen, mute testimonials of the daily life of our pioneer ancestors. No other city, we believe, possesses such an historical relic, a museum in itself and our most dearly prized possess ion. (Ed. Note: Now a prized exhibit in Carillon Park.)

Not a citizen of any age or sex but had some part in the celebration of our birthday anniversary. Every school in the city held appropriate exercises. They "spoke pieces," sang songs and told again the settlement story. A procession that started at the Newcom Cabin and came back to it, included floats bearing school children (ten thousand of them), Indians, pioneers in the garb of the early century, Dayton industries to serve as contrast, the fire department, with banners and bands and cheers and flag-waving and pleasant hysteria of all kinds.

Across the southern side of the courthouse was hung a row of locomotive bells with groups of ringers working in relays so that not a minute, day or night, should lack its contribution of ear-splitting clamor. What with the procession, the crowds, the bells and guns and the shrieks of joy from the throats of thousands of small exuberant boys there was nobody, surely in the Dayton of those three days, but knew what our centennial meant.

The outstanding part of the celebration came in the evening with the performance of *Daytonia*, a pageant depicting a hundred years of community life in our city and given in the Grand Opera House under the personal direction of Harry E. Feight. Quoting from the pages of the *Daytonia* program we find a veritable orgy of melodrama.

Act One: Newcom Tavern as it was first built, at the mouth of Mad River, and surrounded with thick woods. Arrival of visiting settlers in Conestoga wagon; attack by Indians (here a deviation from history, since the

Main Street bridge and Steele High School, now a parking garage (above)

The ultra-modern, campus-like NCR factory, an industrial wonder then.

worst the Indians ever did in Dayton was to get drunk and yell); arrival of soldiers; skirmish; repulse of savages. Moonlight scene showed a vision of the future Dayton, with trolley cars passing the new Steele High School. (Although this date was only four years before the appearance of the first "horseless carriage," nobody on the staff of managers foresaw the automobile.)

Act Second: Dayton in 1841; Third and Main streets looking north (the setting being copied from an old water color by John Van Cleve, and loaned by Miss Martha Holt). There were one hundred and fifty players in this act, and they presented a May Day celebration in Steele's Wood (in 1840, the popular place for picnics being the hill behind the present Art Museum). A colonial minuet in Eighteenth Century costumes was danced, and a double quartet of singers finished the act.

Act Three brought the spectators to the opening days of the Civil War, and here a great chance for pathos and capital letters: *The Interior of a Dayton home in 1861*; *Breaking Home Ties*; *Drilling of the Awkward Squad on Main Street*; *Off for the War!*; *Troops Passing the Old Court House*. (Of this scene the souvenir program declared it "the most thrilling and realistic stage effect ever presented.") Apparently five thousand troops, including infantry, cavalry, artillery, together with numerous bands and drum corps passed in view of the spellbound audience.

Act Four depicted Chickamauga at sunset; "where hundreds of our Dayton boys fought in defense of their country's flag." *Realistic and Sanguinary Battlefield*; *Exalted Bravery*; *The Hero's Death*; *Visions of Mother*; *The Attack*; *Lincoln*; *Emancipation*; *Peace!*

Act Five consisted of four allegorical transformations: (1) the Landing, April 1, 1796; (2) Dayton in 1829, showing arrival of first canal boat from Cincinnati; (3) Dayton in 1865; (4) Dayton Today -- The Gem City Of America! All finishing in a burst of patriotic glory under the direction of the Dayton Guards, and such eminent civilians as Charles Wuichet, R. P. Burkhart, Harry Weidner, B. F. Hargrave, Alfred A. Thresher, Charles Harries Simms, Abe S. Bickham, John R. Tomlinson, Edward B. Grimes, Dan E. Kumler, Frank Conover, Chas. G. Bickham, Harvey C. Phelps, A. F. Thiele, Charles J. Geyer, Chas. F. Knecht, Wood Patton, Wm. B. Sullivan, Albert J. Dwyer, Edward G. Pease, Chas. W. Beiser, Joseph W. Mead, Wm. H. Simms, Moses Wolf, P. A. McGowan, Daniel C. Larkin, B. B. Thresher, Chas. M. Wood, H. C. Graves.

The ladies who lent their efforts to the enterprise included Mes-

Two views of Dayton, Ludlow Street looking north from Fifth (above), Third Street looking east; the former YMCA building is now City Hall.

dames S. H. Carr, J. D. Platt, O. B. Brown, Wm. Craighead, W. F. Gebhart, Jos. H. Crane, Phillip Rotterman, F. J. Ach, Robert C. Schenck, J. B. Thresher, and others.

Among the actors were Clement Herchelrode, J. Howard Davies, Harvey Conover, Thomas B. Herman, Dr. Fred C. Weaver, C. G. L. Breene, E. W. Hanley, Edward Pease, Perry Weidner, Harrie Pease Clegg, Carl Loy, Fred T. Darst, Louise Howard, Mary P. Davies and others.

The singers were Mrs. H. H. Bimm, Mrs. Fred C. Weaver, Mrs. Herbert B. Brown, Miss Maud Reber, H. H. Bimm, Frank A. Palmer, Harry L. Munger and Harry B. Turpin.

We cannot, even with the added wisdom of thirty-five years, look back with superiority upon the melodramatic extravaganzas of *Daytonia*. In the first place it was well done. Harry Feight saw to that and this was not his first dramatic experience. Then, whether they knew it or not, there was in the efforts of the promoters of Dayton a deeper purpose involved.

What this purpose was may be seen by an analysis of the foregoing list of names. To one who knows Dayton those name represented all religions, all organizations, all affiliations. Catholics worked side by side with Protestants; Jews with Gentiles. In all other interests they were divided and separate. Here it was not a question of any one concern, but of a single common loyalty to Dayton. During this celebration one practical lesson was learned by those who took part in it, a lesson that was to serve them well on a future occasion of which not one of them dreamed: how to work together for the sake of the city.

Captain Sam. W. Davies, being asked to write a page for the souvenir program on "Dayton of the Present" (that is, 1896), thus delivered himself:

The Dayton of today is beautiful, rich, powerful and prosperous. We invite the stranger and sojourner to cast in his lot with us. We will help him if he is good, furnish him with a fine bed in a splendid hospital if he is sick, put him in the new stationhouse if he is bad, and if he dies we will bury him in the most beautiful cemetery in the country. What reasonable man, alive or dead, could ask more?

Thirty-five years later, Dayton with outstretched hands still says the same to the stranger within her gates.

University of Dayton, from humble beginning to one of the best private universities in the nation.

14

Transportation

"Transportation," said Senator De Armond at a meeting of the Miami and Erie Super-Highway Association in 1928, "is a never-ending evolution. It is never finished."

The truth of the assertion is plain when we look at the history of transportation as a local whole. The program of a hundred and thirty years would read something like this: (i) Flatboats on the river, oxcarts through the woods; (2) Conestoga wagons on the corduroy roads; (3) Stagecoaches on the turnpikes; (4) Freight and passenger boats on the canal; (5) Railroads; (6) Automobiles on the super-highways; (7) Interurban cars; (8) Gasoline bus connections; (9) Airplane.

So, if a historian were meticulous and exact he would begin the story of transportation in Dayton by describing the hewing and laying down of the huge logs across the middle of Main Street to prevent teams from sinking in the mire and dragging their wagons with them.

Then, and up to the present, transportation has been the perennial question before the people. In the first decades of the last century it was how to get in to the Ohio wilderness and now, in 1931, how to make a quick movement of our products out to the purchasing world. Ours is the easier task for we have learned one important lesson: that it is not travel which brings transportation but transportation which brings travel. Our pioneer ancestors were always waiting for enough people to go somewhere to begin to build a railroad there.

The Van Cleves, Newcoms, Thompsons and Harmars had no

sooner settled down in their mud-surrounded cabins along the river bank than the question of transportation bobbed up. Unless they could make it possible for other settlers to get in, Dayton could not be a metropolis. The earlier roads were not the result of scientific survey but were the natural growths of necessity.

The very first penetrators of the wilderness followed either the Indian trails or the buffalo trails. The first were not more than eighteen inches wide, the beaten path of lines of savages in single file; the second were wider and well-trodden and, what was of great importance, they invariably led to water. If one wandered off either of these trails he was likely to get mired in a swamp or buried in the undergrowth.

In the case of the Cincinnati Pike, our earliest highway, it followed logically the windings of the Miami River. Main Street was its upper end in the Miami Valley. The first attempts to increase transportation facilities in and around Dayton were to drain the swampy places and lay down logs, making the corduroy roads so execrated by our ancestors; the next to fill up the holes with gravel of which, as we already know, there was an unending supply.

The main difficulty in getting in Dayton was that the little settlement was embraced by an elbow of the river which had to be forded, a difficult thing during spring and fall freshets. Therefore ferries were a necessary adjunct to improved roads. They were rough hand-over-hand-on-a-rope affairs dragging a clumsy raft from shore to shore at the call of a whistle or a shout from passengers on the far bank. The first were at the head of Main Street, on Salem Avenue and First Street and at Fifth or Washington Street. (The present names misleading as at each place there was then nothing but dense woods.)

It was the War of 1812 which impressed upon this part of Ohio the necessity of military roads to supplant the rough highways of the pioneers. In 1809 Dayton was connected by improved (though we would not call them passable) roads with Cincinnati, Franklin and Hamilton on the south, Springfield, Urbana and Piqua on the north and Xenia on the east. This was the pioneer good-roads movement and it went on until by 1830 one could drive in fourteen different directions without having to be pried out of the mud.

A familiar sign in our country drives, even as late as the '70s, was the well-sweep pole of a tollgate across the road, a sign to dive into one's pocket for some small change before the pole would be lifted and allow the horse free passage. Highways like these, kept up by toll charges radiated in every direction from Dayton like the spokes of a wheel. When the term "toll-pikes" was used it meant that the roads were kept up by levying a small amount on all passers-by, repairs being kept up by super-imposed layers of gravel, the work being done by farmers on off-seasons.

That historic highway, the old National Road, was extended into Ohio in 1825, reached Springfield in 1837, and although it did not pass through Dayton, it did pass through Brant, Tadmor and Vandalia and connected the northern section of the Miami Valley with the eastern states. Third Street, Dayton, was a loop of the National Road, as old excavated milestones prove, connecting Richmond, Springfield and Dayton. It was the first and only east and west artery for wagon travel and was considered such a boon that travelers would come from as far as Kentucky and Tennessee to reach its comfortable roadway before turning east or west. It was the first example of the use of Federal funds for local construction.

Family carriages carrying girls of the '30s to school in the East always went by the National Road. Improved roads soon meant public stage transportation. It was in 1818 that the first stagecoach service was established between Dayton and Cincinnati. Up to that time Daytonians who wanted to go to Cincinnati were fortunate if they had a private carriage. Those who did not, walked or went on horseback.

It was hard to convince the public that enough people would ever want to go so far away from home to make a weekly stage profitable. The expense was, indeed, great but in time it paid for itself, and the weekly service had to be doubled. By 1828 twenty coaches were making daily trips in both directions.

A trip to Cincinnati in the '20s began at five in the morning from where the stages started, on the south side of the courthouse on Third Street. Not the old courthouse, which was not built until 1850, but the older courthouse on the same site, a frame building flush with the sidewalk. The journey ended at Cincinnati on the afternoon of the second day, the intervening night being spent at Hamilton.

The fare charged was eight cents a mile and fourteen pounds of baggage were allowed each passenger. Twelve persons were accommodated in such a vehicle, three on the back seat, three on the front, three on smaller seats between and two beside the driver. Four horses drew the stage and they were changed every half hour, sometimes more frequently if the roads were very bad.

A canal boat comes up to the Dayton port (above).

High school class of 1898 starting for a picnic at the Bluffs; public library, Cooper Park, in background.

The founders of our Dayton were men of vision and action. They meant that Dayton should excel commercially. The promise was here; it was theirs to actualize it. We have seen in a former chapter how the great project of the Miami Erie Canal was instigated and promoted. The Dayton branch at first only connected with Cincinnati and all freight from the north was wagon-hauled to the mouth of Mad River and there embarked on the huge freight boats for the south.

Our section of the canal began near the mouth of Mad River, descended the Miami Valley through the villages of Miamisburg, Franklin and Hamilton, then followed the course of Mill Creek to Cincinnati; length when completed sixty-seven miles. In 1837 it was extended as far as Piqua, later to Toledo. The section between Dayton and Cincinnati cost nearly a million dollars. The canal in Ohio, as in other sections of the United States, was the actual and visible means of freight transportation and much passenger traffic for a period of thirty years and more.

Railroads were being spoken of, it is true, but casually and apologetically as of something that sounded well but would never materialize. The Miami Erie Canal was always prosperous, its peak year being 1851 when tolls amounted to $350,000. A canal boat carried eighty tons, just what one freight car does today. In the 1820 and 1830s, all the stock carried in Dayton stores came from New York by the Erie Canal to Buffalo, by lake to Cleveland, thence by Ohio and Erie Canal to the Dayton Miami Canal and up to Dayton, a distance of twelve hundred and forty miles.

Later when our canal was linked up with the whole system freight came much more direct. After 1861 the railroads took an increasingly larger share of the traffic but the canal continued to function as an important part of our state-wide transportation system until the '70s, when the first talk of definite abandonment was heard.

The social-recreational side of canal travel is told in many personal narratives of the last century. Old Dayton letters mention visits made to friends in Cincinnati, how parties of church people engaged a boat and spent the Fourth of July picnicking in the woods either south or north of town.

That this was not the only aspect of canal travel is witnessed by some of the tourists who came among us; Harriet Martineau, Harriet Beecher Stowe, President John Quincy Adams, William Dean Howells. The latter probably was the only one who came through Dayton, the others went from New York to Cleveland by the Erie Canal where the accommodations were approximately the same as between here and Cincinnati. Harriet Beecher Stowe wrote in *Godeys Ladies' Book* in 1841 that passing a night in a cabin of a canal boat, whose dimensions were ten by six and six feet high in the company of thirty ladies and children, was a horror. We suspect her figures were somewhat less than accurate but we accept her conclusions.

The Duke of Saxe-Weimar-Eisenach (what were dukes doing in the middle west then?) complained of the insects. Fanny Kemble did, too. The *Travelers Guide*, that early *Baedeker*, advertised that a certain boat had accommodation for a hundred and fifty people, in which case the thin husk mattresses with which the passengers were provided were laid closely side by side on the cabin floor, those under the tables being considered the most fortunate since they at least could not be trodden on.

It is worth while re-reading Dickens' *American Notes* for his racy description of canal travel in 1842. How when night came he found suspended on either side of the cabin three long tiers of hanging bookshelves designed apparently for volumes of small octavo size. "Wondering to find such literary preparations in such a place I discovered on each shelf a sort of microscopic sheet and blanket; then I began dimly to comprehend that these were our sleeping accommodations for the night."

By the '80s the canal had deteriorated. Boats still wound their way around the bluffs and up toward Dayton. The horses were no longer be-ribboned, and they were not horses, but mules. From the stable accommodations at the end of the boat the extra mules gazed pensively out of a window on the passing landscape which we presume they liked better than going along the towpath with the towing-rope dragging at their flanks. A stovepipe sticking up through the deck and the odors of fried onions spoke the domestic joys of the mariner in charge and his frowsy family.

Thus are the mighty fallen! It was John H. Patterson in his tiny office as toll-collector for the canal on Third Street, who first spoke his mind on the gradually lessening receipts of this mode of transportation and its inevitable disappearance. The tolls had shrunk from $350,000 to $24,000. His business acumen told him of the impossibility of the canal competing with the railroads and for years he worked for its abandonment.

The first spadeful of earth for the building of our Dayton Canal was dug at Middletown with appropriate ceremonies, in July, 1825. The first boat arrived on our shores in May, 1827. The curtain drops. One hundred years are supposed to elapse, and do. Another ceremony at Middletown;

this time (1927) they dedicate a monument to the men who built the canal and celebrate its final abandonment. But this story belongs to a later narrative. The next act of the transportation drama belongs to the railroads.

Patterson Boulevard is constructed on the canal's former bed. Charles Smythe of Brown Street, in recalling the changes in that part of Dayton, writes in the *News*:

All these things are today changed and buried under the march of modern things. The canal with its mud and slime, its turtles and frogs, its snakes and bullheads, its sluggish waters, its swill and unspeakable filth, is filled in, covered up and forgotten. The leather-faced, leather-lunged, hard-drinking mule-driver with his cruel bull-whip, the three-span mule teams, the creaking, straining tow-rope, the stub-nosed canal-boat with its crew and its captain with the walrus mustache, are all today hardly a memory. Somewhere they are each and all reduced to unrecognizable dust.

In studying the history of the railroad transportation that has affected Dayton in the past hundred years we find ourselves in a maze. When the railroad fever really came in it must have taken investors by storm. They went at it passionately. It was assumed that any place connected with any other place by railroad was sure to become a metropolis. We infer this because the records reveal road after road legislated about, contracted for, constructed, lapsed into bankruptcy through lack of capital or patronage, bought in by some more prosperous road, amalgamated and absorbed.

Some of these abortive concerns were the *Dayton and Western*; *Dayton and Union*; *Dayton, Columbus and Xenia*; *Dayton, Greenville and Miami*; *Dayton and Southwestern*; *Dayton, Cleveland and Toledo*; *Dayton and Ironton*; *Dayton, Fort Wayne and Chicago*.

The vast trunk lines now stretching from coast to coast were undreamed of in 1850. What roads there were came from local enterprise, connecting short distances and detached from each other. Few roads ran north and south, so the unfortunate traveler who wanted to travel up or down the state was forced to change two or three times between here and Cleveland. "Making connections" was a terror, especially at night.

Take the evolution of the Big Four. It began in 1832 when the Ohio Legislature passed an act incorporating the *Mad River and Lake Erie Railroad Company* to run from Dayton to Springfield, Urbana, Bellefontaine,

Tiffin and Sandusky. The contract for construction was let in 1848 and that part of the road completed between Dayton and Springfield in 1857. Later the upper part of the road was abandoned in favor of another route that had been laid out by the *Sandusky City and Indiana Railway Company* who were willing to lease the road to the *Mad River and Lake Erie* for ninety-nine years.

In 1854 another lease and a change of name to the *Sandusky, Dayton and Cincinnati Railroad Company*. In 1865 it went into the hands of a receiver, and was reorganized as the *Sandusky and Cincinnati Railroad*. After more leases and more changes of name it eventually was absorbed into *Cleveland, Columbus, Cincinnati and Indianapolis*, the *C. C. C. and I.*, or as we know it, the Big Four, a part of the New York Central System.

The railroad seeming to be most largely a Dayton concern was that chartered in 1846 and known as the *Cincinnati and Dayton*, later as the *C. H. and D.*. The Dayton end was contracted for in 1850 and the first excursion train ran on September 13, 1851. Since then its trains have taken us down to Cincinnati for much more than half a century. The former *Dayton and Michigan* road has been incorporated with it making better north and south continuous passage.

When the *Erie* road reached Dayton it was not yet the *Erie* but the *Atlantic and Great Western*, otherwise the "Broad-gauge." It was a road that had nothing to do with Dayton except that it ran through it on its way from the East to Cincinnati. In those days there were three gauges for track construction: broad, narrow and standard. From Cincinnati to Dayton the eastern road had only the *C. H. and D.* right of way to use. It could do this only by straddling the standard tracks by its own broad-gauged tracks. This made four rails to a railroad track instead of two.

When these double rails crossed in switches or crossings the resulting "frog" extended many feet and the cars running over them made a regular devil's tattoo of clatter. Although the whole length of the *Erie* road was over eight hundred miles it was only on this sixty-mile stretch that this peculiar phase developed. Because of the "straddling" the trains on this stretch were mixed, that is, some of the cars traveled on the outer set of rails and some on the inner and in this heterogeneous way the train finally reached its destination at Cincinnati. This state of things lasted for thirty-three years after the *Erie* road was built.

In time this double trackage was abandoned. How then could the Broad-gauge get to Cincinnati? This way: a hoist was established at the extreme end of East First Street, Dayton, and there the body of each car from the Erie was raised, its bogie trucks replaced by those of standard width and then lowered, the whole performance occupying only a few moments. Of course the inconvenience of an odd gauge grew as transportation demands grew and about the year 1878 it was decided to change to standard gauge.

After all preparations were made the whole eight hundred and thirty miles of *Erie* trackage from New York to Dayton were changed in width during one night, trains running as usual the next day. So passed the last broad-gauge from the railroads of this continent.

It was not until 1895 that the system was called the *Erie*. Its whole career is tied up with the financial history of this country and the railroad wars which were a part of it, recalling such names as Gould, Fiske, Vanderbilt and Daniel Drew. Our interest in it concerns only the fact that for so many years it was the only one of the great traffic lines to the east and our only way of getting directly to New York.

The *Americana* vouches for the fact that the *Erie* was the first railroad to run trains by telegraph, the first to use printed time tables, the first to run Sunday trains (thereby it is to be supposed, making useless those puritanical big doors that closed the Dayton Union Depot from Saturday night until Monday morning), the first to make special service for the city milk supply and the Sunday papers. It was the first to run excursion trains, the first to install parlor cars and, before dining-cars were dreamed of, to establish eating-rooms along its route. The signal cord now running through the cars for the use of the conductor was an innovation of the *Erie* road; so was the building of spur tracks to foster local industries.

There was abundant room for all these improvements. The sanitary arrangements of the early railroad cars can only be expressed by a large round cipher. People ate lunches and threw the paper on the floor. There were no toilets. At intervals the brakeman went through the train with an ice-water can, painted a grained yellow, held in a metal frame as were also the six tin cups intended to assuage the thirst of a whole train load of passengers in hot weather.

The soot from the engine was unspeakable. Not only on the *Erie* but on all railroads, the construction was flimsy. In place of the hundred pound steel rails of the present day, oak stringers were used covered with five-eighths of an inch strap iron. The first engines weighed only ten tons including fuel and water, as against the modern locomotive of two hundred and eighty tons with tank capacity for seven thousand gallons of water and ten tons of coal. The early passenger coaches were a sort of amplification of the stagecoach which seemed to be their only conception of a carrying vehicle. The average speed of such a train was ten miles an hour and even this was considered by the ultra-pious as flying in the face of a Providence who never meant that people should travel faster than a horse could go.

Following the Panic of 1873 came a period of narrow-gauge building and much capital was invested in the belief that the lower cost of construction and equipment would make such roads formidable rivals of the older roads. Such an enterprise was the *Dayton and Ironton Road*, locally known as the "Narrow-gauge." The future of Dayton and Xenia were to be saved by direct connection with the coal fields of Ohio. For economy's sake it was built as a narrow-gauge and as it was supposed to be for everybody's benefit everybody was to help pay for it.

Nearly everybody did, by buying stock, but it never was a success. Into the hands of manipulators who held up construction and limited its completion in every way (perhaps in the hope of being bought out at a good figure as so many roads had been), the *Dayton and Ironton* remained for years nothing but "a streak of rust on the landscape." After all these disastrous experiments both extra width tracks have been abandoned and there remains only the standard gauge.

Another example of imbecile enterprise was the *Dayton, Xenia and Belpre* road (later the *Little Miami*). If the reader begins at Xenia and with a pencil runs a line directly east on the map, he will hit Belpre, a little obscure village on the Ohio River opposite Parkersburg. This was supposed to be the future metropolis which the *Dayton, Xenia and Belpre* road was to bring into existence. This queer, unscientific, hind-side-before construction of railroads was the way all the big trunk lines came into existence. The traveler had to use any number of small sections of track before the consolidation took place which resulted in the through routes.

For years everybody who wanted to go east on the Pennsylvania had to drive to Xenia on the pike in a buggy, arrange for the buggy to be driven back to Dayton and take the train for New York. Then, for more years we had, when coming west on the Pennsylvania to change at Xenia and take a small dirty local the remaining fourteen miles back to Dayton.

Now what changes, what improvements! Dayton lies on four big trunk lines, the *Big Four*, the *Erie*, the *Baltimore and Ohio* and the *Pennsylvania*. On these several lines fifteen trains leave Dayton for the East every twenty-four hours and as many arrive. The traveler eats his filet mignon, his ice cream and tropical fruits as casually while crossing the mountains of Pennsylvania as he does in his own home. Starting from the Union Station at Dayton he emerges in the Grand Central or the Pennsylvania at New York after a not at all fatiguing trip of sixteen hours.

As far as freight facilities go Dayton is in a strategic position for shipping to all parts of the United States. Few points within a hundred miles offer equal advantages. These four major roads carry heavy shipments of through freight. The city is well equipped with industrial sidings-many of the larger industries have their own. There is universal reciprocity in switching arrangements. Package car service is varied and prompt and is available to many points with good connections at important transfer cities.

There came a time in Dayton, as it does to all cities, when travel by steam was too inelastic for ordinary conditions, when the need arose for hourly communication between the cities of the Miami Valley. It was about 1895 when arose the development of the inter-urban electric railroad which promised to revolutionize not only the passenger but the freight and express transportation as well. As the name indicated it proposed to furnish transit between cities by means of high speed electric cars operating directly into the business centers of the cities through which it passed.

Right here we meet the same story as that of the railroads-syndicates, passionate promoters, stock-sellers with gilt-edged promises, over-capitalization, receiverships, forced sales, consolidations. More money was lost than made. It was found that none of the existing laws which had been drawn for steam railroads and street railways covered this new character of public enterprise, so its development proceeded without much, if any, public control.

One would think that the builders of the interurban would have learned something from the experience of the steam railroads in the varying gauges of tracks. But no. The gauge of street-car tracks in Cincinnati was six inches broader than "standard" so the interurbans of standard gauge could not use the tracks for terminal purposes but were compelled to discharge their passengers outside of the city limits.

The first road in the southern part of the valley was the *Cincinnati and Hamilton*, later lengthened to the *C. H. and D.* So that now those familiar letters mean not the old steam railway, but the new interurban. It acquired an interurban property that had been in the hands of a receiver for ten years. Seventy-two miles of trackage on a grass grown, rickety, right of way; cars from fifteen to thirty years old, uncomfortable and costly to maintain; power supply inadequate, shops small and crude. After the expenditure of nearly a million and a half, the road boasted new tracks, ten de-luxe cars, old ones burnt up, large steel and concrete shop buildings with necessary machinery, track improved, new electric switches, service equipment purchased and another hundred and eighty thousand dollars expenditure contemplated. There is a double track connection with the enormous new Delco-Frigidaire Plant of General Motors at Moraine City at a cost of $37,000. Both freight and passenger service on the improved road show gratifying increase.

The *Dayton and Xenia Traction Line* was organized in 1900. There is a branch to Spring Valley. Dayton and Troy are connected by interurban which goes through to Lima, Toledo and Fort Wayne.

The *Ohio Electric* operates under five districts: Southern, Western, Central, Eastern and Northern. And so it has come about that on almost any corner of the street at any hour of the day-or the half hour-a car will come along taking passengers to towns east, north, south or west, picking up freight at small villages off the main railroad and offering a daily and hourly convenience to people who want to go somewhere in a hurry.

But the interurbans, convenient as they are, are having their own particular Waterloo which, as may easily be guessed is the ubiquitous ever-present automobile. If stockholders need a reason why they do not get the dividends that were promised them they have only to drive out in either direction from Dayton, and these cogent "reasons" will pass them at the rate of about one every two minutes. How can the interurban survive when it is out-classed, out-run, out-grown by the privately owned Ford car? It can only proceed from place to place on its own tracks; the automobiles can run up its owner's private lane.

Farmers take their products to market on their own wheels and by their own power; simpler, easier, quicker and in the long run more economical. The electric train makes its plea for freight, and lo! "Ship by truck" becomes the slogan and families can move from the house in one city directly to the new home in another with no crating or hauling of goods. How long the interurban will last is on the knees of the gods. Transportation is, indeed, a "Never-ending evolution."

And if the automobile and the motor-driven truck make their own particular competition, how about the motor buses? These long, rapid vehicles are seen more and more on the roads in this state and every other, carrying thousands of passengers from town to town and even connecting up the two coasts of the United States. They are eating into the profits of both steam and interurban roads.

In Dayton, within the last few years the following bus lines have come into operation; *Dayton and Xenia*; *Lebanon, Cincinnati and Germantown*; *Dayton-Farmersville*; *Dayton-Lewisburg*; *Greyhound Lines*; *Dayton-Osborne-Fairfield*; *Miami Valley Transit* (Belmont-Beavertown; Troy-Piqua-Sidney); *King Bros.* (Lebanon-Cincinnati-Germantown); *Dayton-Columbus-Springfield*; *Greenville-Dayton*; *Dayton-Northern*; *Inter-Cities* (Troy-Piqua-Sidney). Marvelous! that from the corner of Fourth and Wilkinson, where so many of us used to go to the old Central High School, one may take a bus to Los Angeles!

We are not forgetting includes transportation within the limits of Dayton, meaning of course street railways. It is interesting to note that in the minds of the first promoters the idea was rather to open up for the real-estate market large farms lying within a mile or so of Dayton rather than making money out of streetcars. The first enterprise of this kind was called the *Dayton Street Railway*, chartered in 1869 on $75,000 capital stock, and was to run from east to west on Third Street.

The location of the Soldiers' Home beyond the western corporation line was a hopeful feeder for transportation. The promoters of this venture were influential men of financial standing: William P. Huffman (president); Harbart S. Williams, George W. Rogers, Charles B. Clegg, John W. Stoddard, E. J. Barney, W. H. Simms, and C. J. Ferneding. In 1884 the capital stock was increased to $300,000.

As soon as it became understood that a way of reaching the Soldiers' Home was assured, excursions became the great source of revenue for the street cars. Hardly a day in the year but train loads of people arrived at the Union Depot, poured up Wilkinson Street to Third and embarked on the cars.

Encouraged by the success of the Third Street railway and hoping to do something for the outlying districts to the north and south of the city, a company was organized to establish the *Dayton View* line. Its first directors were J. A. Jordan, J. W. Stoddard, William M. Mills, J. O. Arnold, George W. Lion and William A. Barnett. It was capitalized at $35,000. Charles B. Clegg was president of this line for many years.

The route ran first from Union Depot along Main and Monument across the river, out Salem Avenue to the corporation line which was then

The earliest streetcars were horse-drawn (above).

Five ways to get to Dayton: Miami River, electric traction, automobile, canal boat and steam train in use at the same time.

at Plymouth Avenue. Later by absorption and reorganization with S. B. Smith, president; E. E. Barney, secretary and G. B. Harmon, treasurer, it became the *Oakwood Street Railway* and now extends from below the southern corporation limits to Catalpa Drive in Upper Dayton View. Both Oakwood and Dayton View were virtually created and maintained by this transportation service.

The next street railway was the *Wayne and Fifth*, chartered in 1871, capitalized at $100,000, administered by S. D. Edgar (president); M. Ohmer (vice-president). Since then the men concerned in its maintenance have been Ezra Bimm, S. N. Brown, J. J. Bradford, Joseph Kratochwell, Eugene Wuichet and H. H. Bimm. Its route first connected Alaska Street in North Dayton with the Dayton State Hospital at the head of the Wayne Street hill. It has since been extended to near the corporation line on the Shakertown Pike.

The *White Line*, now known as the *People's Railway*, was the first to install electric motors. It was built to connect the Soldiers' Home with North Main Street in Riverdale, opening up Germantown Street and giving access to St. Elizabeth's Hospital on the south side of the city. Its incorporators (1887) were J. A. McMahon, M. A. Nipgen, J. E. Lowes, C. D. Iddings and W. B. Iddings. Capital stock, $200,000.

As the northern, southern, eastern and western parts of the city answered to the stimulus of convenient transportation, its effect was soon felt in the localities between the points of the compass, and the outlying districts northeast, northwest, southeast and southwest began to call for easy access to the business center.

Then we have the *Dayton Street Line* touching the Xenia Pike at one end and Catalpa Drive at the other, making a diagonal stretch through the city and the *Leo Street* doing the same from the southwestern limits at Cincinnati Street to the northeastern at Leo Street in North Dayton.

And so the needs grow and the supply follows. One by one the outstanding portions of the city are brought by car or bus lines to contact with the sources of supply: the markets and the department stores.

Is the transportation story finished? Not as long as the thousand factories of Dayton bring their operatives here, who must have homes. Every year the city reaches out street by street, each lined by little dwellings whose families must go to work or to school or to the shops. Soon the car service follows and one can hardly tell whether the demand or the supply comes first. It is the beneficent circle building Dayton into a metropolis.

But again we ask, is the transportation story finished with the steam cars, the interurbans, the buses and the street cars?

Hark! The answer comes from the sky above our heads. There, like a speck in the blue, soars a droning craft the like of which our fathers never dreamed in their wildest flights of imagination. It connects the east coast with the west; it carries passengers and mail, it may before long carry freight. In spite of storms and cold or heat, its pilots keep at their heavy task that the world may have more rapid transit.

THE AIRPLANE! Is it the last word in transportation?

15

Dayton Writers

The most cherished archives of the Dayton Public Library contain a thin volume of some sixty pages bound in yellow marbleized paper -- or was, before the congenital weakness due to eighty years of service had made a new cover necessary. On the stained title page may be read *A Sketch of the History of Dayton*, by Maskell E. Curwen, Thomas Odell, Publisher.

This was the first book written in Dayton and should not be overlooked by future historians. Indeed all those in the past have consulted it and it may be said to be the basic material for all we know of our beginnings. It was published after Dayton had passed the half century mark and the writer felt that nothing could be more important than to record its remarkable progress.

Curwen wrote from actual cognizance and has left a book which is a medley of Indian history, personal anecdotes of the first settlers, a description of the first town plat, the incorporation of Dayton, the first newspaper, the War of 1812, the great flood of 1847, together with good moral observations and quotations from the poets. It is to be hoped that the little book will last another eighty years to be consulted by many more readers and authors, for it is a well-told story, more and more interesting as time goes on.

Dayton has been noted for its commercial rather than for its literary attainments. Nevertheless when the tale is fully told there will be found quite a number of writers whose fame has extended beyond our locality.

John Van Cleve, perhaps the first real scholar among us, has already had biographical mention in an earlier chapter. In 1828 he was owner and proprietor of the *Dayton Journal*, contributing editorials and literary articles and finding time among his multitudinous duties to translate Schiller's *Robbers* and to do some charming sketches, fairy tales and plays. His best work was done on the *Log Cabin*, that satirical sheet that had such influence during the Harrison campaign in 1840. His political skits were accompanied by caricatures drawn and engraved by himself.

It is to Mary Steele that we owe most of the information we have of this remarkable man, which brings us to the Steeles, father and daughter, who both meant so much to Dayton. Robert W. Steele's memory has been enshrined in the high school named for him and is a well-earned honor for his taste for books, his interest in the schools and all that was intellectual and cultural among us.

An article by Mary Davies Steele appeared in the *Atlantic Monthly*. It was entitled "A Learned Lady of Gournay" and was the picturesque narrative of an early intellectual woman of French birth at a time when few women anywhere in the world knew as much as how to spell. We were accustomed to seeing articles by Robert Steele, mostly in the local papers, and now here was his daughter, a semi-invalid and recluse, coming forward out of the twilight of a sick room to contribute an article to the leading American monthly.

Encouraged by the cordial reception of her first essay Mary Steele wrote *Early Dayton*. Based primarily on Curwen's book, there was an interesting accumulation of local history in the added thirty years and no one better qualified than she to put it down. Belonging to the old families, she could write from personal knowledge and experience of things and people in the Miami Valley. It still remains a much-read and often consulted book.

The Speeches of Thomas Corwin, compiled when Corwin was at the height of his reputation by Isaac Strohm, a Daytonian, were published by the veteran newspaper man W. F. Comly. In this volume you will find Corwin's great speech on the Mexican War in the Senate, 1847.

The Houks, George W. and his wife, Eliza Thruston Houk, were both writers. George Houk was literary, not by profession but because he couldn't help it. Everything he wrote had the tang of originality, spice and grace, even when he was writing obituaries for which he was much in demand. A deep student of the English classics, Mr. Houk's writing reflected their source. Eliza P. Thruston Houk was the daughter of Robert Thruston, a brilliant member of the Dayton bar, and Marianna Phillips Thruston, afterwards Mrs. John G. Lowe. An 1851 graduate of Cooper Seminary, she developed a taste for books and reading which became the basis for her own literary work.

Several published books remain to Mrs. Houk's credit. The first is a long poem entitled *Puritan*, contains two hundred and forty-five stanzas in Spenserian verse. Another long unpublished poem of Mrs. Houk's celebrates the accomplishments of Virginians as the first book does those of the Puritans, is called *Virginius*. A published essay of a purely scientific nature was read at Portland, Maine, before a meeting of the American Association for the Advancement of Science at its annual meeting in 1873. She also published the 1905 *Memorials of Gates Thruston*.

Dr. J. C. Reeve, during his life was called "the best medical reviewer in the country," his contributions in this line being found most often in the *Journal of Medical Sciences*, Philadelphia. His most notable published work is a translation from the French of *History of the Discovery of the Circulation of the Blood*, by Flourens, secretary of the Academy of Medical Science, Paris, 1851. He also wrote papers on medical and surgical subjects. In the *Ohio State Historical and Archaeological Quarterly* is an article on Henri Bouquet, the French explorer in North America.

Major William D. Bickham was a clever and caustic writer and called the best paragrapher in the newspaper world of his day, and one of the leading war correspondents of the Civil War. His major work, written when he was volunteer aide-de-camp to General Rosecrans, was *Rosecrans' Campaign with the Fourteenth Army Corps*. His letters to the press give a vivid picture of men and battles, different phases of army life, and are a valuable contribution to the literature of the Civil War.

Sidney A. Reeve, youngest son of Dr. J. C. Reeve, might also be included among Dayton writers, although he has lived many years in New York. He was professor of gas and engineering at Worcester Polytechnic Institute for many years, lecturer at Harvard and at Annapolis, and a consulting engineer in New York. His first book, *The Cost of Competition*, was reviewed widely in periodicals on both sides of the ocean.

Loyal Dayton historians are prone to include William Dean Howells among our writers, but it is an unsubstantial claim. Howells did live here for a short time when his father owned and edited the *Dayton Transcript* and the son set type and otherwise supported the dying sheet. About the only record the great novelist gives of his association with Dayton is that when they could not make the paper go they went down to the Miami River and went swimming, which is what a good many Dayton boys have done between that time and this.

Charlotte Reeve Conover is the author of several works of historical or biographical interest. *Concerning the Forefathers* is a volume dealing with the fortunes of two pioneer families, the Pattersons and the Johnstons, both being forebears of the late John H. Patterson. *The Story of Dayton* is a small book written especially for children in the grade schools in order to interest them in the town in which they lived. It was a result of the renaissance of local patriotism following the flood of 1913.

For three years Mrs. Conover conducted a department known as "The Secret Society of Mothers" in the *Ladies Home Journal* from which she became widely known throughout the women readers of that magazine. For a period of twenty years or more her articles appeared with regularity in one or the other of the Dayton papers.

As time went on Dayton writers increased in number and prestige. Of late years there has been a surprising harvest and they have ceased to be merely local. Leading all these is Anne O'Hare McCormick. Her work has been crowned by the *New York Times* in its weekly magazine whose pages seem never to be so interesting as when they include an article from her typewriter. She excels as a political correspondent and during the last presidential election her weekly papers on the promise of the campaign were widely read and incessantly quoted.

She seems to be able to be in all places at once and to secure interviews with the most exalted personages who have denied themselves to lesser scribblers. And because the books are written hot off the brain they are vital and gripping. It was foreordained that her letters to the *Times* on Russia, achieved at the price of a long and arduous journey, should go into book form, which they did, under the title of *The Hammer and the Scythe*, (Alfred A. Knopf), acknowledged to be the authoritative book on Russia.

It is but natural that Dayton, being the center of aviation interests, and aviation itself such a soul-stirring occupation, that knights of the pen should turn up and illuminate the subject. *This Aviation Business* by Lieutenant Ernest W. Dichman is an attempt by a former field officer to supply a plain chronicle of aviation.

Another book, written especially for boys, is by Marguerite Jacobs Heron, a member of the department of technical data of Wright Field and she calls it *Knights of the Wing*. To say that this book is a best seller is to say it all. Boys from one end of the United States to the other pore over *Knights of the Wing*. Miss Jacobs has the rare skill of handling technical details without letting them interfere with the charm of the narrative, and is accurate into the bargain.

A kindred subject is on the title page of another work by an aviation pioneer, Lieutenant Lester J. Maitland, who made the historic flight across the Pacific and is now in the Air Corps at Washington. But he wrote his book in Dayton and called it *Knights of the Air*. Maitland adds to his own experiences that of the great flyers of history, the Wright brothers, and will be held as the completest record yet out of the heroes of aviation.

The one really nationally known poet that we have ever had is Paul Laurence Dunbar. Born of a mother who had been a slave, reared in humble circumstances, educated in the Dayton public schools, what promise could there have been for the gift that set him apart from his fellows and gave him both rapture and grief?

When Richard Watson Girder, editor of *Century Magazine*, published that charming lyric *When Malindy Sings*, he had no idea that his contributor was a black man. The poem was beautiful, what difference the color of the writer's skin ? It was through Gilder that Dunbar met William Dean Howells, Joel Chandler Harris, James A. Hearne, Ruth McEnery Stuart, George W. Cable and the other eminent writers of the time, and in turn through them he had his New York experiences and afterwards went to London where he read before Queen Victoria at Buckingham Palace and was received by the best in England.

This is not the place for a long critique of Dunbar's poems. But the best of them, those that will live, are *When Sleep Comes Down to Close the Weary Eyes, When the Co'n Pone's Hot, In the Morning, A Drowsy Day, The Poet and his Song, When Angelina Johnson Comes Swinging Down the Lane, Jump Back, Honey, Jump Back, Behind the Arras.*

His first poems appeared in small volumes: *Oak and Ivy, Majors and Minors, Lyrics of Lowly Life, Lyrics of the Hearthside, Lyrics of Love and Laughter, Lyrics of Sunshine and Shadow.* All of these have been gathered within one binding and with a biographical sketch by Lida Keck Wiggins and with an introduction by William Dean Howells. The poet began life as an elevator boy and ended it a voice of the century and the prophet of his people. He lies in Woodland Cemetery.

When a book by a Dayton author finds its way to the desks of Con-

The beautiful old public library in Cooper Park on East Third Street, built in 1887, was torn down in 1962 and replaced by the present library.

gressmen, who reach for it to consult on a matter that is holding the attention of most of the United States, it is something for which his townsmen may justly feel gratification. This is what happened to Lewis F. Carr's late volume *America Challenged.*

Horace Lytle was born a lover of dogs. His favorite prepossession has resulted in a number of books that will be enjoyed by those who hunt, those who hike, and those who love to sit by the fire and read about the great open spaces. The titles are: *Breaking a Bird Dog*, *Bird Dog Days*, *Sandy*, *No Hunting* and *The Story of Jack*, considered one of the best dog stories ever written, and *How to Train Your Bird Dog.*

Mr. Lytle also wrote the chapter on "Pointers and Setters" in the de luxe volume *Upland Game Bird Shooting in America*, published by the Derrydale Press, New York, and has contributed articles and fiction to the *Saturday Evening Post* and other national magazines. He is Gun Dog editor of *Field and Stream* and writes an article for them each month.

Joseph N. Sharts, a local attorney, is the author of quite a number of works of fiction which show a certain insight and power of characterization. The titles are *Ezra Caine*, *Hills of Freedom*, *The Romance of a Rogue*, *Vintage.*

We have at least one Dayton writer whose work falls behind the constant demand of her publisher and that is Helen Joan Hultman. A teacher by profession, Miss Hultman excels at writing clever detective stories. Her ingenuity is marvelous. The reader never knows where the plot is taking him and not until the last page are all the murders cleared up and all the malefactors brought to judgment. She has chosen for her best title *Find the Woman.*

Miles H. Krumbine, when he was pastor of the First Lutheran Church, contributed to the *Century Magazine* two essays, and together with two sermons preached in Leon Mandel Hall at the University of Cincinnati, and other Sunday utterances they were gathered into a volume entitled *The Way to the Best* and published by the Doran Company. The twelve sermons make a book of unusual spiritual appeal.

Dr. J. Morton Howell (LL. D. Otterbein) was a practicing physician for a number of years and still maintains his nominal residence in Dayton. He has written several professional books, and in 1922 Dr. Howell was appointed Minister from the United States to Egypt. During his sojourn there he had unusual opportunities to record matters of political interest, the result of which was a comprehensive book on that country.

Henry Preserved Smith, now deceased but formerly of Dayton, has been professor of Biblical history and interpretation in Amherst College, also Davenport professor of Hebrew and the Cognate languages in the Union Theological Seminary. He is the author of *Essays in Biblical Interpretation* and *Old Testament History.*

How Men Make Markets is a book for juniors on the place commercialism takes in the development of the world. It is a compilation of the various talks on Commercial Geography given to his classes in Steele High School by the beloved and revered professor, William B. Werthner. Macmillan is the publisher.

Edwin L. Shuey, for years identified with educational and social service work in Dayton, published *Factory People and Their Employers.* It is a practical handbook on factory conditions, the relations between capitalists and their workers, the inspiration for which Mr. Shuey gained while in the employ of Lowe Brothers and the National Cash Register Company, both of which are laboratories for social study.

Edward W. Keever is the author of *Shorty of the Tank Corps*, a story of the great war. (Ed. Note: Shorty Keever was "Letters to the Editor" editor when the publisher arrived in Dayton in 1946 as a reporter for the old *Dayton Journal.*)

Charles Wuichet, in his collection called *The Sunny Side of a Busy Life*, proves how much cheer he added to social life in Dayton when he was alive. These are papers which were read at the Present Day Club, the Woman's Literary Club, the Alumni Association of Central High School and on divers other occasions. There is much Dayton history in them.

August F. Foerste is our indigenous authority on geology as Mr. Werthner was on botany. The two collaborated, one in the text and the other in illustrations, in a fine large volume entitled *Geology of the Vicinity of Dayton with Special Reference to Hills and Dales and Moraine Park.* The whole region of this valley gives abundant material for such a work .

Another teacher of beloved memory, Grace Greene, for many years head of the Normal School, and whose name the lately built Normal School bears, compiled a collection of her favorite poems used in the teaching of her literature class work. The book is called *The Golden Treasury* and is much prized by those who were the fortunate recipients of her inspiration.

John F. Edgar wrote a book, which he eminently could do, about the old families of Dayton. If one is after biographical or genealogical details, consult *Pioneer Life in Dayton and Vicinity.*

James L. Vallandigham has written the *Life of Clement L. Valland-igham*, his distinguished brother, member of Congress from this district, and has also compiled his speeches on "Abolition," the "Union and the Civil War" included in a volume *The Record of C. L. Vallandigham.*

Alfred Addison Thomas always wielded a pregnant pen although he did it more rarely than his friends wished. His compilation of his father's (Rev. Thomas E. Thomas) letters, his anti-slavery correspondence, are good reading and give incidentally not a little inside Dayton history. *To My Son* (Thomas Head Thomas) is so parentally human that it should be better known. While he was general counsel for the National Cash Register Company Mr. Thomas made a compilation from various sources and called it *The Temptations of Employes who Handle Money* (N. C. R.1910).

Helen Rickey Albee lived in Dayton in her girlhood although her later life has been spent in New England or Washington. Her father, James Rickey, was the leading bookseller in Dayton and had a store on Main Street near Second, where the book lovers of the little city used to congregate and where his daughter probably got her first inclination toward authorship.

Among the technical writers of Dayton none stands higher than Charles Howard Paul, engineer, United States Reclamation Service; construction engineer Lower Yellowstone project; constructor Arrowrock Dam, Boise, Idaho; with Miami Conservancy District (for design and construction); ex-member Dayton City Commission, Chamber of Commerce, American Society of Civil Engineers. One of his papers in 1922 was awarded the Norman medal (for best contributions to engineering science) by the American Society of Civil Engineers, the oldest of the engineering societies.

My Progress Book in English for the Second Grade Children is the title of a book written by Miss Ida Odelle Rudy and Miss Gretchen Smalley, principal of Harmon Avenue Elementary School in Oakwood, which has just been issued by the American Education Press at Columbus. It is designed to help the children to gain language expression through life activities familiar and interesting to young minds.

Harry Aubrey Toulmin, not an original Daytonian but a lawyer-author who has contributed largely to the literature of business and invention, has put out a number of valuable volumes of information and reference. They are *The City Manager, a New Profession, How to Keep Invention Records, Bothering Business, Trade Mark Profits and Protec-*

tion, *Air Service of the A. E. F., Patent Law for Inventors and Executives* and *Millions in Mergers*.

The latest Dayton author is Philip McKee, whose book *Big Town* is published by the John Day Book Company. It is a biting satire on the customary American town. If it sounds like the author's home town it is because in some of its aspects Dayton is just that kind of a place. It shares with its contemporary communities the elements of buffoonery, exaggeration, bragging, boosterism, the lost cause of the "noble experiment" and the taint of graft running through it all. Nothing escapes: churches, schools, the "Y," the Rotary and the women's clubs. All are exposed. Perhaps it is good for Dayton (and the other Daytons) to have their weaknesses laid open to view. The foreword is by Sherwood Anderson.

Merab Eberle is a young woman whose verse has just begun to appear in some of the best magazines. The *North American Review*, the *Christian Science Monitor*, *Christian Century* and the *Christian Endeavor World* are some whose pages have carried her work.

Another young poet of note is Sylvia Margolis.

16

Development of Art

The paucity of art aims and art interests in Dayton sixty or seventy years ago need not trouble us now. Dayton has always been a commercial center and its community life a part of the great business world. We began in a small way, but we have fitly grown.

The first painter who was a real painter to come to Dayton was Charles Soule. His canvases, those of them that fortune spared from the havoc of the flood, still ornament the walls of Dayton homes. His marked ability was along the line of portrait painting, and his touch was so sure and his feeling so deep that his work was much more than locally known and he became the teacher of artists who really stood higher in art circles.

His daughter, Clara Soule Medlar, was also an artist, but a teacher as well. Mr. Soule painted the generals and admirals, the judges and doctors, the beautiful young matrons and the charming girls. Miss Soule painted babies and roses and landscapes with lovely feeling. There was another daughter, Mrs. Octavia Soule Gottschall, who exhibited much ability in water colors, and was active in organizing art clubs and classes among the women of Dayton.

Two other portrait painters deserve to be remembered, John Insco Williams and Edmond Edmondson, the former also noted for his studies in still life -- fruit pieces -- and the latter for several panoramic canvases.

It was in the late 1870s and early 1880s that Dayton came to life from the point of view of picture painting and picture loving. Mary Forrer Pierce was teaching painting in the old Cooper Seminary, Miss Sophie

Loury, whose work in miniature was exhibited with the Art League of New York, and Miss Laura Birge, a pupil first of Clara Soule and later a student in Munich, Paris and London were the leaders.

In 1880 several amateur organizations devoted to art work sprang into existence. There was the Amateur Sketch Club and the Decorative Art Society under the direction of Professor Broome, having a pottery and ovens for firing, and devoting much enthusiasm to china painting. Otto Beck, a student in Italy and Munich, was a Dayton boy who ended by occupying a position of responsibility in Pratt Institute, and whose pictures hang in Brooklyn and Washington. His friend, Victor Shinn, was also a promising artist who soon left Dayton for the Technical High School in Brooklyn.

All these personalities and efforts were inconspicuous, but they were genuine and provocative of interest among Dayton people. For we were, in those years, lamentably undeveloped. We had no pictures; we saw no pictures; we seldom traveled and knew little of what there was to see in the great world of art.

But slowly things happened. Here and there were souls who knew what was beautiful. If they could, they purchased; some, like Professor Robert, bought photographs and gathering a group of friends talked well and interestingly. The Threshers as a family have always contributed to public education in matters of art.

The first definite movement towards art organization developed in 1902 was the Dayton Society of Arts and Crafts, with Mr. B. B. Thresher as president; Mrs. J. B. Thresher, vice-president; Mrs. Margaret Stoddard, Mrs. Chas. U. Raymond and Mr. Houston Lowe as directors. Classes were held in a business block on the site of Rike's store, and Mr. Mann, of Grand Rapids conducted them. Instruction was limited to wood carving, jewelry, and other craft work and perhaps for the reason that its scope was limited interest waned and the organization died a natural death.

But other promoters were not idle. If I have said that Dayton was uncultured in the beginning, I mean what is called "the man on the street." But there has always been in Dayton a vision-seeking, stubborn minority who kept always in their hearts what Dayton might see and do if she were taught. They, in time, did the teaching.

Among these agencies the Dayton Public Library and Museum did notable work. It collected mounted reproductions of works of art, developed a library within a library of books devoted to art and from time to time tempted the public by modest exhibits in the Museum.

In 1912 Miss Linda Clatworthy, then Dayton librarian, having returned to Dayton from an extended trip to Europe, was filled with enthusiasms for making Dayton an art center. On her daily way to the library through the park she was in the habit of meeting Mr. Houston Lowe on his way to his office, and the two devotees discussed at length their hopes and ambitions. (Just a hundred years before, Daniel C. Cooper, the first benefactor and promoter of beauty in Dayton, gave that park to be, as his will expressed it, "a pleasant walk forever." Under its spreading elms and oaks these plans were talked out by two worthy descendants of his same public spirit)

Miss Clatworthy's first aim was to have Dayton join the newly organized American Federation of Arts. Having made a trip to Washington on this behalf, Miss Clatworthy returned with a comprehensive program for the stimulation of art interest in and the beautification of the city. It was a broad conception, comprising industrial art, school art, art for the community and beauty for the city.

With this nucleus of effort there came into existence in 1912 the Montgomery County Art Association, whose object was to foster an interest in art, through lectures, exhibits and loans of pictures. The first president was Mrs. Henry Stoddard, whose glowing and contagious enthusiasm proved to be epidemic in the end. She loved, thought, dreamed and talked pictures. She could see beauty in everything and had discriminating taste.

The second presiding officer of the Art Association was Mr. Houston Lowe under whose devoted leadership the organization made many strides forward. Another ardent supporter was Miss Annie Campbell, for years a teacher of art in Steele High School and painter in oil and water colors. Mrs. Henry Loy gave generously of her time and cultivated taste. She and Mrs. Stoddard were the moving spirits in organizing exhibitions of paintings and trying to induce a rather tepid public to attend.

In 1917 the name of the organization was changed to the Dayton Art Association. From that time on its activities enlarged and increased. The Dayton papers were supplied with publicity on pictures and artists, it filed records relative to the current items of art history in Dayton; it enlisted in the fight against a proposed increase in the tariff on art objects; it secured a fine collection of oil paintings through the American Federation of Arts, which was exhibited for two weeks.

In 1916 a series of lectures of popular interest on art subjects were arranged by the association, to be given by members of the local group, and with this plan came a slowly developing understanding on the part of the public that Dayton had at last a real nucleus of art-loving and art-promoting citizens who, if were allowed and encouraged, which they were, would lift their native city to a place in the culture of the nation. When the audiences for these lectures reached the five-hundred mark it was felt that the good work was underway.

The association in its infancy suffered principally from the lack of a center of its own. The lectures had to be given in borrowed halls, the exhibitions likewise; and although the Board of Education was generous in its granting of the Steele auditorium, something it was felt should be done towards a permanent home.

All this came about through the generosity of a group of private citizens who purchased a substantial old residence on the corner of Monument and St. Clair, formerly the home of the Kemper family and, with extended additions and remodelling converted it into Dayton's first Art Museum. The garden, under the generosity of Mrs. Harrie G. Carnell, became a replica of the lovely colonial grounds of one of the earlier governors of Ohio, Thomas Worthington.

It was high time. No stronger argument for a special building was offered than the flood of 1913. That calamity was responsible for some good things, as well as many bad ones. This time it emphasized the necessity for concentration and protection for works of art. It happened that at the time of the inundation there was a collection of water colors on exhibition in Memorial Hall, another of the projects of the enthusiasm of Mrs. Stoddard, Mrs. Loy and Miss Campbell. The premises were under water, and the pictures ruined, but as they were fully insured the artists were reimbursed.

The Art Association (under the incorporated term of the "Dayton Museum of Art") found itself thus happily ensconced in a building with a hall giving space for pictures and lectures, where a library of art subjects could be accommodated and where classes under competent instructors studied drawing, painting in oils and water colors, commercial art, costume design, elements of composition and design. When ninety young people took immediate advantage of this privilege, and the Art School became a hive of industry and enthusiasm, the acme of the hopes of the promoters seems to have arrived.

All this was a good many years ago, and what has happened since needs many a page to record, but those who worked so hard for its accomplishment should be held in happy remembrance. Their names were: Houston Lowe, James M. Cox, P. B. Thresher, Mrs. H. G. Carnell, Orville Wright, Robert Patterson, Mrs. Robert Patterson, H. A. McMillan, Mrs. Henry Stoddard, Mrs. Henry Loy, Valentine Winters, Mrs. Lee Warren James, Electra Doren, F. J.. McCormick and Mrs. McCormick, E. A. Deeds and Mrs. Deeds, Mrs. G. Harries Gorman, Mr. Louis Lott, Miss Martha K. Schauer, John B. Hayward, Miss Virginia Blakeney, Miss Annie Campbell, Mrs. George G. Shaw, Mrs. Scott Pierce, Mrs. Walter Kidder, F. H. Rike, E. L. Shuey, A. D. Wilt, William B. Werthner, Adam Schantz, H. E. Talbott. Some of these served on committees, some were trustees, but all gave of their talents to push forward this admirable effort to bring to as high water mark as possible the rising tide of the love of art in Dayton.

It seems too good to be true how soon that first Art Museum was outgrown. It was in the beginning such an ambitious undertaking, and now, suddenly, it was found inadequate for its uses. The commercially minded, art-ignorant, apathetic people of Dayton, the street car riding, shopping, movie-going people had looked with indifference upon the enterprise. Art, they thought, if they thought of it at all, was not for the general public; it was a fad of certain rich people.

Drawn by the merest curiosity in the first place, they entered the doors; had the pictures explained to them, read about it in the papers, listened to some lectures, were gripped with the universal appeal of beauty, found a glimmering of the delights it held, went again, sent their children, sometimes contributed of their own small resources and finally crowded the walls to their utmost. Young people discovered that the classes offered in poster designing and craft work pointed a practical way to make a living. The classes were crowded, the exhibits were crowded, and at last it came to be an accepted fact that there would have to be larger quarters.

Here it is that Mrs. Harrie G. Carnell comes definitely into the story. As a girl, Julia Shaw had traveled extensively in Europe and brought back many impressions. Few young travelers of that day saw as much and retained as deep enthusiasms. Of all she saw, Italy impressed her the most; she loved its cool galleries of ancient canvases; she thrilled at the convents, chapels, churches and palaces with their murals and windows and statuary; she began to sense the characteristics of the different schools of painting.

At that time she guessed no more than any one else that her love for the beautiful and her local patriotism for the city of her birth would unite into one ambition which had its final efflorescence in the lovely warm-

Mrs. Harrie Gardner Carnell, donor of the Dayton Art Institute museum.

hued structure which now curves so gracefully around the edge of the hill above the river.

Mrs. Carnell had been the moving spirit and the chief contributor to the old art museum on St. Clair Street. She had enlarged rooms, laid brick walks, built sparkling fountains and planted beds of flowers. If the museum was outgrown as a school and an exhibit it was certainly outgrown as a field for Mrs. Carnell's generosity. She wanted more room to be generous in, and therefore announced that rather than help expand the old quarters further she would offer a new art building to Dayton.

It was just at that juncture that an ideal site for such a structure came on the market -- the high lift of ground at the junction of Forest and Riverdale avenues, formerly owned by the Hawes family and always a dominating point on the bank of the Miami River. "Just the place for an art museum," explained many a lover of art and lover of Dayton. But a contractor for an apartment house had the inner side of the bargain and it was considered a hopeless proposition.

To minds like Mrs. Carnell, however, nothing is hopeless. She wanted that site and, to make a long story short, she got it; or rather Dayton did, and now a fifteenth century Italian Renaissance palace, with graceful curving stairways and arcaded inner courts rises proudly above the city. Its inception is an interesting story. Forty miles north of Rome is the little town of Viterbo. In it is a five-sided villa built on a rise of ground and approached by graceful steps. Cardinal Alexander Farnese was the owner and sometimes resident there during the Renaissance period.

It was this villa which suggested the present building, although whereas the original had five sides this has or will have eight. The octagonal front of the facade lends itself with charming appropriateness to the curve of the brow of the hill. The yellow sandstone of the walls was brought from quarries near Cleveland. Mr. Edward B. Green of Buffalo, New York, was the architect.

A peculiarly happy thought it was to build with the possibility in mind of future expansion. If the art spirit and the art culture in Dayton grows in the future in the same proportion as it has in the past, the original plan of an octagonal building will afford ample space. *The building was built with only five sides; the remaining three wings will finally be built in the upcoming 1996-1997 renovation/expansion.*

---

* 1995 material in italic thanks to Sara C. Weber, Public Relations Director, DAI

Three pairs of bronze doors open into the foyer, with its flooring of red Italian tiling and its information desk adapted from old Gothic storage bins. Facing the main entrance the eye is impressed by a staircase of Indiana limestone leading to the sculpture court and passing on the way a landing which gives place to a replica of the Virgin and St. Elizabeth by Andrea della Robbia. Here, too, at the mezzanine level is an ample lecture hall whose coffered ceiling by Joseph F. Stridy, of Chicago, shows four corner panels representing the arts of Sculpture, Painting, Music and Literature. *The foyer now is called the Lower Court and the sculpture court has been renamed the Great Hall. A portrait of Mrs. Julia Shaw Carnell by John Christian Johansen now hangs where the della Robbia reproduction stood.*

The enclosure made by the structure is divided by the music room, into two cloisters which were Mrs. Carnell's own idea. Once to the architect she remarked jocosely, "No cloisters, no building." So cloisters there are, a north cloister and a south, each with vine-draped arches, groups of sculpture, twisted columns, with acanthus-leaved capitals and brick pavement. *The north, or Gothic, cloister and the south, or Italian cloister, are separated by the Renaissance Auditorium.*

The Art Institute cannot be seen casually or in a hurry. Many a stroll must be taken through the halls and courts before the whole of its beauty is revealed. The architect kept one thing constantly in mind, that of ease and relaxation on the part of the visitor. On one side the building gives on the river and the city; the other on to the greensward of the cloisters, each only a few steps from the other. Comfortable chairs offer themselves on every side. The result is that the much dreaded modern distemper classed as "museum fatigue" has no place in the Dayton Institute,

To the interesting furnishings and adjuncts of the museum there is no end, and all from the generous heart of Mrs. Carnell. There are "peepshows," Chinese temples, fountains, beautiful door linters, a miniature reproduction of the Baptistry doors at Florence, carved chests, pottery urns, a Chinese garden enclosing a pool with Chinese fish and oriental aquarium plants. *The peep-shows and the pool are no longer here.*

Most fascinating are the chapels opening into the cloisters. The Gothic chapel has an exquisite stained glass door of such rare beauty that it was held over in Buffalo for a special exhibit before being sent to Dayton. The south cloister is developed in Italian Renaissance character with marble columns from the fourteenth, fifteenth and sixteenth centuries surrounding a lovely stone fountain containing a bronze statue, "The Joy of the Waters" by Harriet Frishmuth. *The statue no longer stands in the cloister.*

But it will be impossible to go into all the beauties of the Art Institute. They are increasing all the time. Always in her trips abroad Mrs. Carnell has the museum in mind. As she said in her speech of dedication when she presented it to Dayton: "I feel as if I were giving into your hands a child of my own. Be good to it."

Moreover, the Museum has been a family affair with the Carnells, Mr. Carnell giving time and sympathy and advice every step of the way, and Jefferson Patterson seconding his mother's efforts by purchasing beautiful additions to the collection during his wide and varied travels. *He gave many pieces included in the Asian Wing, which is now named after him.*

The human activities going on under its roof include exhibits and the Art Institute School. Five hundred young men and women take daily advantage of day or night classes, going all the year round under such competent instructors as Siegfried R. Weng, Director; Martha K. Schauer, Director of Saturday School; Margaret Beck; Frank M. Betz; Howard Breidenback; Edward R. Burroughs; Bernice E. Buyer; Margaret Chatterton; Roy Cheesman; Ruth Boes Herr; Irene Hoffman; John M. King; Robert Koepnick; W. P. Lloyd; Louis Lott; Leroy D. Sauer; Ellasson R. Smith; Mrs. E. M. Thacker; Grace Valentine; Seth M. Velsey; Don Wallace; E. Paul Wilhelm; and John Zwinak.

The school closed in the 1970s and now only studio classes for children and adults are offered three times a year. Educational programs, serving more than 50,000 persons each year, include the classes, tours, lectures and gallery talks.

The Saturday school for children under the direction of Miss Martha Schauer is one of the most valuable services of the Institute. Who knows how many artists and craftsmen have been lost to the community through having had no means to cultivate their powers? Here, the men and women of tomorrow are given the fundamental principles of art and aesthetics which, whether they become machinists, mayors or millionaires they will carry with them through their lives. Miss Susan Odlin has been active in promoting the love of art among children by entertainments, and talks on art every Saturday morning. Over thirteen thousand children availed themselves of this privilege during the past year.

Beauty belongs in every occupation of life. From the lack of a sense of it more cities than Dayton have suffered. The next generation will not,

The Solitude of the Soul by eminent sculpter Lorado Taft of Cincinnati, one of the museum's early treasures.

we hope, endure the monstrosities perpetrated in the past in the way of monuments, buildings and bridges, but will insist upon good taste and true art in public things.

The Dayton museum entails only the climbing of a flight of steps so near to the center of the city that everyone can enter. Instead of a fixed collection there are rotating exhibits. Instead of dim galleries, a formidable atmosphere and weary miles to pass over, the Dayton museum is bright, hospitable, friendly and educational.

No further proof of the wisdom of the founder and the trustees is needed than to see the men, women, and children mounting the steps from Riverview Avenue on a Sunday afternoon. No other proof than what they see and hear when they have entered the doors. For the twin art of painting-music, has its due share in the feast of soul which the Museum offers. The programs of the Sunday afternoon concerts have included the best amateur and professional talent in Dayton. Organ concerts, choruses, violin and piano soloists, under the auspices of the Dayton Federated Clubs, have given joy to many otherwise deprived hearts.

It took the brain of Mr. B. B. Thresher to borrow the modern library idea and apply it to pictures. It was he who instituted "Circulating Gallery of Portable Pictures." Unique in the beginning it has since been copied in other cities. Through the cooperation of a large number of the prominent artists of the country the Dayton Art Institute put into circulation, under the same rules and regulations under which the public library issues books, a circulating gallery of pictures.

The plan works out happily both ways. It enables the man of moderate means to enjoy upon his own walls, for a limited time, the work of a fine artist; it results, in not a few cases, in the artists selling the picture because the temporary borrower finds he cannot do without it. Most of all it results in a constantly widening appreciation of art through the only means known, that of intimate and daily association with pictures. On the back of each picture are printed the main facts of the artist's life and his successes and a few lines of appreciative criticism that may serve as an avenue of approach to its evaluation. The selling price is marked on the picture, and the fact that it may, if desired, be purchased on the installment plan. *Although this practice has long since been discontinued it is still true that the Art Institute inspires local collecting. In fact, patrons are encouraged to collect and guidance is often offered. This helps with the museum's main source of art acquisition: donations from local artists and collectors.*

Virgin and St. Elizabeth by Andrea della Robbia, from the collection of the Dayton Art Institute museum. This plaster reproduction is no longer on view.

In the space of three years no less than seventy important canvases have been sold in Dayton, where previously no interest whatever in good art existed. In some instances the children in a schoolroom saved their pennies and bought a canvas as a permanent possession of their school. From the wide endorsement that this plan has had from artists all over America and the favorable comments made in both this country and in England, it is plain that a new epoch in the promotion of the love of art has been successfully inaugurated. It is known as "The Dayton Plan." The collection includes original paintings in oil, original water-colors by eminent living American artists, reproductions of Old Masters and block prints and etchings and bronzes.

It is not mere local self-satisfaction which gives high rank to the Dayton Art Institute. It is being known about, inquired about and its best features copied by other art associations far and wide. The impetus it has given to Dayton connoisseurs is incalculable. It has promoted collection buying on the part of Daytonians, some of which are housed in the homes of the owners, some deposited as provisional loans or downright gifts, in the Museum itself. Mr. Frederick Beck Patterson, has cultivated and indulged a taste for English portraiture and owns a number of notable works of this type. Mrs. R. R. Dickey's famous collection of fans, and Mrs. R. D. Patterson's laces both exist in the museum as indefinite loans.

The museum has some good outside friends, like Mr. Leo Flesh of Piqua and Mr. William Cullen of Springboro Pike, who have loaned from time to time their own collections. Mrs. Evelyn Huffman Patterson, has loaned her collection of English portraits. A Metcalfe landscape, now very rare and valued at $15,000, has been presented the museum by, Mr. John B. Hayward. A Flanders tapestry of the Louis Quatorze period is the gift of John G. Lowe.

Lorado Taft, the master sculptor, has been very generous to the Dayton Institute, having presented it with his group "Solitude of the Soul" also a bust of Hamlin Garland and a cast of St. George, by Donatello. He also made possible the purchase of the peep-shows in the lower hall, those idealistic presentations of art in Florence in the fifteenth century. They were made in his own studio and the prices reduced so as to place them within reach of the museum. Mrs. Carnell purchased one and the Kettering Foundation the other. Mrs. Carnell also presented a superb tapestry by Oudenard of 1600 A. D.

The supporting membership of the Art Institute is composed of:

Founders, Benefactors, Fellows, Life Members and Active Members. The total membership up to April 1, 1931, was one thousand three hundred and twenty-three. Of these names some are donors of large sums of money; some have loaned or presented gifts; some have been presidents or served on the board of trustees; some have given lectures or taught classes, or served on committees or sponsored social activities, or written interpretative articles for the papers. In short they have one and all, each in his or her own way, made Mrs. Carnell's gift a practical reality. *As of January 1, 1995 there were 5,200 members in various membership levels from Individual up to the Jefferson Patterson Society, a circle of higher level donors. In addition, corporate and individual donors, have contributed money, art works and gifts of service.*

The list of Founders, as they appear upon a bronze tablet set in the wall of the loggia are: Frederick P. Beaver, Edward A. Deeds, Mary P. Davidson, Charles F. Kettering, Elizabeth Hill-Smith, George H. Mead, Henrietta C. L. Patterson, Jefferson Patterson, Katherine H. Talbott, John B. Hayward, Harrie G. Carnell, Edith W. Deeds, Anna B. B.Gorman, Olive W. Kettering, John G. Lowe, Elsie T. Mead, Frederick B. Patterson, Robert Patterson, Orville Wright and Lillie Gebhart Mayer.

If distinction could be made there would be five names which stand out as the chief supporters of the plan. They are John G. Lowe, Robert Patterson, B. B. Thresher, John B. Hayward, and Robert G. Corwin. From the first they have been warm and generous promoters of the Art Institute. All would deprecate personal particulars; suffice it to say that one of them has acted in his professional role of legal adviser, one contributed the qualities of a business man; one has given of his supreme selective taste in choosing exhibits; one has devoted time, material and spiritual gifts to the cause, and one has not once, but several times, without solicitation and with the utmost caution, pressed into the not unwilling hands of the treasurer, a check for ten thousand dollars. *More recent museum benefactors include Mrs. Virginia W. Kettering; the late Elmer R. Webster and his collecting partner the late Robert Titsch, who bequeathed their entire 870-piece collection of American decorative art; and Donald and Sue Dugan of Oakwood, who donated their entire Oceanic Art collection of more than 900 pieces.*

Of directors and supervisors Dayton has enjoyed the services of some outstanding men. The first was Herman Sachs, who came in 1921 after twelve years in Europe at the head of an art school and as a leader of the modern movement. His work both there and here included portraits, ceramics, tapestry and craft work. He was an artist of original and superlative quality and a pioneer in introducing designs for inlaid marble.

Theodore Hanford Pond was born in Beirut and his childhood spent in Europe and the Holy Land. At nineteen he came to America, studied at Pratt Institute and afterwards taught designing wall paper, carpets, stained glass, furniture and jewelry. Pond came to Dayton and took up work in the old art museum on St. Clair Street where not only his work in silver and textiles created much admiration, but his personality as evinced in his teaching and lectures aroused the creative enthusiasm of all who came in contact with him. Now director of the Art Institute at Akron, his influence in Dayton can never be fully measured.

The current head of the Dayton Art Institute is Seigfried Weng, whose youth and zest, whose fine technical training and inbred love of art fully qualify him for the position. Born in Oshkosh, Wisconsin, he studied at the State Teachers College, took his bachelor's and master's degrees at the University of Chicago. A year with the Art Institute and postgraduate work at Harvard completed Mr. Weng's formal education. His informal training consisted of a loyal and joyous association as docent in the studio of the great sculptor, Lorado Taft. During that five years he made two trips to Europe as assistant to Mr. Taft, an inestimable privilege. As an artist Mr. Weng's best work is in block printing, but his interest lies primarily in sculpture. *Mr. Weng served as director from 1929 to 1950 and was followed by Dr. Esther I. Seaver (1950-1956); Mrs. Alvin Raffel (1956-1957); Thomas C. Colt, Jr. (1957-1975); Bruce H. Evans (1975-1990); John W. Herbert, interim (1991-1992) and since 1992 Alexander Lee Nyerges.*

In summing up the achievements of Dayton artists the name of Hugo B. Froelich, whose untimely death a few years ago was a distinct loss to art, comes instantly to mind. He was a Dayton boy, educated at the old Central High School, and became connected with Pratt Institute and also with the Prang Company in designing. He also conducted the Froelich-Snow Summer Art School in Chicago. Mr. Froelich was a much quoted authority on art matters and the author of a number of textbooks on art.

Miss Anne Campbell has built for herself an enduring monument in the hearts of high school pupils whose budding love for art she has fostered through many years. Long study when a girl with Miss Laura Birge, then with Otto Beck, after that with Arthur W. Dow, a year at Teachers College, two summers abroad, study in the National Gallery, Louvre and Rycks

Two studies by Jane Reece, Dayton's most famous photographer: the Dayton View bridge (above) and the Main Street bridge in snow and rising water. Many of her photographs are in the museum's collection.

Museum; most of all, continued devotion to her work have brought Miss Campbell to the place of honor among the artists of Dayton.

Mercy Crowell Brett, although not now in Dayton, deserves to be counted in, because she is a gifted natural artist and still remembered here for her studies in water colors and crafts work. Her present home is in California, where she made her immediate mark among the artists of that state and is now in charge of the drawing classes of the Palo Alto High School.

Another absent though not forgotten Dayton artist is Ernest Blumenschein, who began as a violinist, went to Paris to study, got shifted into art and whose illustrations frequently meet the eye in the current magazines. While living in Paris his home was a rendezvous for the American artist colony, and his pictures exhibited in the Salon. *He was a founder of the Taos Society of Artists in New Mexico. The Dayton Art Institute will feature a major retrospective of his work in April 1997.*

Although in the meaning of the word art, as accepted in the distant past, Miss Jane Reece is not an artist, she is one of the foremost who have raised the pursuit of photography into its due rank among the fine arts. Through her unerring sense of values in light and shade, in composition and design, she has acquired the distinction of being a "pictorialist."

A practiced searcher after beauty and, with her camera, in long walks afield and during her trips abroad she has found and recorded it in unexpected places. Her works are exhibited in the collections at the Carnegie Institute in Pittsburgh, in Cleveland, New York, Buffalo, Detroit, and Omaha. Her photographic skill is well known in Europe, and exhibits are in constant demand. They will be found in Vienna, Salzburg, Austria, in Copenhagen and in Saragossa, Spain.

Her portrait of Lorado Taft seated at the base of one of his statues has been hailed as outstanding A new invention of hers in which color plays an important part is said to be about to revolutionize pictorial art.

Honors for Miss Reece have been many. Her medals include one from Hamburg, five from Canada, one from France, one from Italy, one from Edinburgh. She lives in a transformed engine house on Riverview Avenue, where she receives her friends, pursues her art and from time to time gathers about her by exhibitions, art of all kinds, her own included.

Over her career Miss Reece developed an important relationship with the DIA, where she promoted photography as a fine art and often exhibited her prints. In 1952 her donation of several hundred "Salon Prints" formed the core the Jane Reece Collections and Archives. Follow-

ing her death in 1961 the entire contents of her studio, including her Salon catalogs and reference books, her important issues of Camera Work, *her camera, hundreds of her photographs and several thousand negatives all were bequeathed to the Art Institute. In 1978 the negatives were placed on deposit with the Wright State University Archives for cataloging and storage. The Dayton Art Institute continues to care for her photographs and is planning an important exhibition of 250 of her best-known and most representative works for the spring of 1997.*

Other photographers whose work has earned high praise include Mr. John Kabel and Mr. Frank M. Betz, two of whose pictures are reproduced in this volume.

In Miss Martha K. Schauer, whose flower studies of rampant color are a joy, we find not only a producer but an interpreter of art. An industrious and loving transcriber of beauty she has exhibited water color renderings at the Brooklyn Museum of Art, the Ohio Water Color Society, the Ohio Modern Painters Society and the Dayton Art Institute. Many have been purchased and hang on Dayton walls.

She became director of that happy hive of creating children, the Saturday school at the Institute in 1926, and in 1927 organized the first Summer School and directed it until it was absorbed into the regular Art School. She organized the first "art week" and served as chairman of the Art Committee of the Chamber of Commerce; is now a member of the Board of Trustees of the Institute.

Her weekly articles in the local papers have taught many people what to look for at the Institute and why. In one of her articles Miss Schauer says: "Dayton has always had beauty as a dominant objective," in support of which she cites the wide streets laid out by Daniel C. Cooper, the elms planted by John Van Cleve and the dignified classic courthouse.

Robert Whitmore is a Dayton boy, although now in connection with Antioch College and living at Yellow Springs. His work is full of feeling, and more people besides his own fellow-citizens have learned to look for it in exhibits of paintings and etchings. Three of his works were accepted for the exhibit of the Chicago Society of Etching. His work in color has also received wide notice and sincere admiration.

Walter W. Pfeiffer, a graduate of the Maryland Institute of Art is instructor in the Dayton school, and carries on class work in pottery, silversmithing, jewelry, engraving, wood carving. His work has been shown in important exhibits in Boston and Minneapolis, and many points between.

Of Mr. Brainers Bliss Thresher's work as a craftsman it is difficult to speak with proper appraisement. His artistic instincts are *sui generis*. Scarcely known in Dayton, his work is on permanent exhibit at the Grand Central galleries in New York and frequently sold. His inlaid screens, radio cabinets, triptychs, lamps, are to be found in some of the most exclusive and artistic homes in America.

For his foundations he uses cypress wood of beautiful graining and by a process known only to himself (and which he says "comes by prayer and fasting") he eliminates the substance between the lines of the grain of the wood, leaving nature's pattern in relief and qualified by color or gold. Upon this foundation and in designs always different and striking he superimposes silver or gold, ivory or shell, horn or copper, as his taste dictates. His studio contains materials which he has gathered in travels far and wide from Mexico to the Orient, and which he uses in amazing designs and intriguing patterns.

Always interested in fine craftsmanship, Mr. Thresher began while in college to work in wrought iron, in a hired forge of the village blacksmith. This occupation proving too boisterous for home consumption he turned his attention to quieter media. It was pioneer work in those days and gained great acclaim. The Boston Museum of Art, the Art Institute of Chicago, the National Arts Club, New York, the Detroit Society of Arts and Crafts have all carried from time to time Mr. Thresher's beautiful work. An international exhibition of Applied Arts in Turin, Italy, also contained specimens. His bas-reliefed ivory sculpture, where the background is cut away and gold substituted, has been compared to the work of Cellini.

With all this well-earned acclaim Mr. Thresher remains a prophet in his own country and has never had his picture in the Dayton papers.

There is a group of ambitious and conscientious women painters in Dayton who are gradually making their mark in the local art world, and beyond. Miss Rosalie Lowrey devotes herself to portraiture with gratifying results. Her first study was under Robert M. Oliver at the Dayton Art Institute, later at the Art Students' League of New York. She has painted a number of Dayton women, the most outstanding being Jane Reece.

Mrs. Juliet Burdoin has a studio in Dayton and one at Gloucester, Massachusetts, where she paints busily all summer and exhibits in the fall. Many of her most beautiful pieces are painted from her own window in Gloucester of fishing boats in the harbor. Mrs. Burdoin uses both oils and water colors and chooses as her subjects landscapes, flowers and portraits.

Mrs. Abby Lytle Wuichet contributes to the Dayton summary some well dealt with examples of flowers and landscapes and Mrs. Jess Brown Aull is another of the women artists of abundant promise and charming achievement. Her studies in Brittany give one a real glimpse of medieval Europe.

Mrs. Howell Howard not only has the outstanding modern collection in Dayton, but is herself actively engaged in painting. Her water colors and oils have been shown in the exhibition of Independent Artists in New York, and in Cincinnati.

Paul E. Wilhelm, a young sculptor, has had his pieces in exhibit of Independent Artists and in the Legion of Honor gallery at San Francisco. His work claims more and more attention from connoisseurs. Albert Loos, Alvin Raffel, Stephen Gilinan, Robert J. Smith are all doing good work as painters; Phillis Kumler Thacker, Seth M. Delsey, Robert Koepnick and Eliza Talbott Thayer (of Newton Square, Pennsylvania, but formerly of Dayton) as sculptors.

Louis Lott is our veteran architect, landscape planner, lover of art, lecturer and promoter of public interest and upholder of the Dayton Art Institute. He studied in Cologne, Munich, at the Ecole des Beaux Arts, Paris and has spent many years on the Continent and in England.

In summing up the activities and community service of the Dayton Art Institute the writer meets the insuperable difficulty of limitation of space. To enumerate the exhibits would require not a chapter but a bulky catalogue. Not a day in the week nor a week in the year but sees something vital and educational offered to the public and the public begins to understand. Nearly fourteen thousand people entered those doors during the year of 1930. All will come again. *During 1994, more than 250,000 visitors attended the museum and its programs.*

The glow of the sunset touches the ancient stone columns under whose arches people sit listening. They are people who, most of them, have never been to Europe, have had no training in appreciation and have spent all their lives in Dayton. Yet here they are, drinking in the beauty of art which they feel belongs to them, and treading the paths of culture open heretofore only to the sophisticated and the rich. There are children, too, not noisy and romping but quiet and receptive, learning their lesson, too, that man does not live by bread alone.

It is the triumph of democracy in art.

17

Music and Musicians

Limited space exists for a very long story. For the beginnings of it we must go back 1823. In the small, insignificant Dayton of that day we find the sproutings of community music in a group who met and sang under the leadership of the versatile John Van Cleve, organist and choirmaster of Christ Church.

They called themselves the Pleyel Society and rehearsals were held in the jury room of the older-than-old courthouse which stood on the site of the present "Old Court House."

When Van Cleve passed away there seems to have been for a while no one to replace him. Toward the 1840s we find Louis Huesman, pianist-organist and teacher of both, organizing choirs and giving concerts. In the 1860s and 1870s two names stand out: Charles Rex, a short, blond German, and Adolphe Carpe, a tall, blond German, who between them divided the music pupils that the census of Dayton then afforded.

Our musical efforts as pupils were mere amateurish gropings. Every house had a piano. Without it the parlor was not furnished. Every girl took music lessons. She had to. The polite role for a visitor was to ask the daughter of the house to play. He had to. After much urging and many apologies for being out of practice and many explanations that the piano needed tuning, she whirled the stool up and whirled it down, then, having gotten the audience into a highly expectant state, she obliged by a rendition of *The Mocking Bird, with Variations*, or *The Monastery Bells*. This they called in those days "performing" on the piano.

Until we grew up into a more sensitive and sincere appreciation of music, what agonies the poor teachers must have endured I

My own very earliest musical memories go back to sometime in the 1860s when James Turpin, then our leading musician, directed a cantata entitled *The Haymakers*. The soloists were Ella James (Mrs. Kneisley), Ella Green, John Worman and Will Lowe. This *magnum opus* was staged in the only place in Dayton where the rich and the great did congregate to see and hear whatever histrionic or musical art had to offer -- Huston Hall. It was in reality a barn-like structure with flat ceiling, whitewashed walls, wooden floors and high windows looking out on Jefferson Street. Along the walls were niches for busts, marked "Weber," "Lizst," "Beethoven."

The Haymakers was a bucolic composition dealing with milkmaids, hayfields, farmers, and sunsets. Fresh faces and young clear throats need no apologies and Mr. Turpin was a good conductor. The girls wore large hoops called "tilters," wide-brimmed be-ribboned hats, neat little heelless slippers with elastic crossed on the instep and other things appropriate to the haying field. The funny man, supposed to be from the city, and the butt of ridicule, was named Snipkins. Every time he made a stage entrance he fell over the wheelbarrow, eliciting ecstatic applause.

Following the flood of 1913, flames devoured the walls of Huston Hall and many of the musical and dramatic memories of the older people of Dayton went up in smoke. For here was where Ole Bull played, where the abolitionists, led by Wendell Phillips, thundered against slavery, where the great temperance advocate, John B. Gough, lectured, where General Tom Thumb, Mrs. Thumb, Commodore Nutt, and Minnie Warren delighted young and old, where Bayard Taylor in *Views Afoot*, gave some people the first desire to see Europe.

Here we saw *Ten Nights in a Barroom*, Maggie Mitchell in *Fanchon the Cricket* and Bill Cody's *Wild West*. Emerson spoke there, so did Horace Greeley (for whom the society folk prepared a complimentary banquet only to find he ate nothing but bread and milk. Lesser attractions also occupied Huston Hall. A painted canvas panorama, rolled at each end on wooden cylinders which revolved when worked by a handle behind the scenes, gave us our first impressions of the Arctic regions. Thus were displayed marvels of imposing icebergs, roseate aurora borealis and life-like polar bears. Meanwhile the lecturer out in front told his story.

During the Civil War, when the Sanitary Commission (the ancient equivalent for the Red Cross) needed funds, Mr. Turpin and the singers again came to the rescue and put on another cantata, *Queen Esther, the Beautiful* by Bradbury. Once more Ella James (by this time the recognized leading soprano) sang the title role. In royal purple velveteen with near-ermine bands, a golden crown and her long hair in braids, she was a vision. Will anyone who has ever known Mrs. Kneisley deny that she was surpassingly beautiful or that she sang divinely?

It was not until the fall of 1874 that the vocalists of Dayton found themselves, so to speak, in an organization known as the Philharmonic Society. On August 25th of that year a group of musically-minded men met in the directors room of the Dayton National Bank; among them H. V. Lytle, James A. Martin, John N. Burkitt, W. A. Phelps, Samuel Phelps, J. A. Brenneman, William Gebhart, Walter W. Smith and W. C. Herron.

From this nucleus grew the Philharmonic Society. They had at hand as director a most remarkable musician, Leon Jasciewiescz, a Russian whose company of charming singers went around on the inhospitable soil of America because nobody appreciated them. To hear Mr. Jasciewiescz conduct was a revelation of the capacity and cultivation of the human ear.

After quite a few minutes of singing and the chorus had dropped, as choruses will, a tap on the music rack, a pause in the voices, a hummed note from the leader, and we suddenly knew how far we had wandered from the correct pitch. No other director that I ever knew could hold the correct fragment of tone where it belonged against the united voices of the choir.

Rehearsals in the dusty upper room of the (then) *Journal* office (across the alley just north of the courthouse) where with Mr. Jasciewiescz leading were the faces and voices of the musical world of Dayton: Mrs. Kneisley, Agnes Stout, John Bell, John Burkitt, John Shauck, Fanny Favorite, Ella Butz, Charles Snyder and the Dickson sisters. Or, when Otto Singer came up from Cincinnati to direct for our part in the Cincinnati May Musical Festival! To see Mr. Singer with raised baton for what he called an "al-lay-gro-wee-wa-che" movement was to taste all the ecstasy that a cat may feel for a king.

The compositions given by the Philharmonic Society from its inception in 1874 until its abandonment some years since would include many of the great musical masterpieces of the time. The mere mention of the Philharmonic Society inevitably brings to mind the name of W. L. Blumenschein, for so many years its patient and painstaking director. Organist and choirmaster of distinction, teacher by the love of it, composer of no mean capacity, Mr. Blumenschein deserves the everlasting memory of his fellow-citizens. He led not only the Dayton society but the Ohio Saenger-fests (Dayton and Springfield), the Indianapolis Lyra Society and the Springfield Orpheus. He directed the Cincinnati May Musical Festival in the spring of 1891.

Mr. James A. Robert's influence on music in Dayton must not be forgotten. He played in the Baptist Church; he lectured on Palestrina and Bach. During his principalship of Cooper Seminary, in the 1880s and 1890s, he attracted to his orbit musicians of the piano and strings who played to appreciative people the best of the great composers' works. He should have due credit for promoting musical taste in Dayton through three decades.

It was in 1888 that, stimulated by the enthusiasm of Mr. Robert and inspired by the example of musical clubs in the East, two friends and music lovers, Mrs. O. F. Davisson and Mrs. Harvey King, decided to put in motion the plan for a club in Dayton. An organization meeting called on October 15, at the home of Mrs. E. Morgan Wood, resulted in the Mozart Club, with Mrs. Wood as president, and thirty-five active, thirty-five associate and fifteen honorary members. All were serious musicians.

The Mozart Club was not narrowly musical, since it exacted from its associate members the reading of essays on the lives of composers or subjects calculated to explain and clarify the musical parts of the program. In the 1890s a signal honor was conferred upon the club in the form of a bronze medal signed by Theodore Thomas and awarded by the World's Fair Committee to the representative of Ohio in concert at the World's Fair: Mrs. Ella J. Kneisley; already hailed as one of the finest interpreters of sacred music in the country.

Of the teachers much should be said since they laid the foundations for not only good playing but good listening in Dayton: Hermann Marsteller on the violin, from whose hands came most of those who now belong to orchestras and do solo work.

Miss Amy Kofler, with her talented faculty, Miss Parks and Miss Schwill, drew together in her studio recitals in the McIntire Building, frequent groups of appreciative listeners. Jefferson Walters, a violinist of remarkable power, who delighted audiences with his finished and sympathetic playing, is also a composer whose pieces are sometimes heard in concert.

Charles Waldemar Sprague has been for many years and still is one of Dayton's finest pianists and most inspiring teachers. Miss Idelette Andrews, with her flaming eyes, auburn hair and musical enthusiasm, gave much to Dayton while she lived; when she died she left to the Dayton Public Library her extremely varied and valuable musical library.

Charles Holstein, a violinist of splendid talent, carried on for years, in addition to his teaching, a string quartet of undisputed artistic rank in which he played first violin, Jeanette Freeman Davis, second violin, Albert C. Fischman, viola and Ira Leslie Davis, double bass.

Henry Ditzel is what might be called a self-made musician, having worked under such disadvantages to secure his position as organist and teacher. Bookkeeping in the daytime, lessons from Mr. Blumenschein and practicing at night, was the long road he triumphantly pursued to his goal. Germany called him and he went -- worked, studied, came home -- took the First Lutheran organ and stands in the front ranks of Dayton musicians.

There are whole families who have collectively ministered to our musical prestige. The Schencks, for instance: Joseph for years organist and choirmaster at Emmanuel Church; Nora, also a finished organist; Robert, a violinist, now with the New York Symphony Orchestra.

The Funkhouser family is all delightfully musical, the grafted members as well as the original clan. Mrs. Charles Funkhouser is an accomplished organist and choir leader, and Mrs. Jessie Landis Funkhouser possesses a sweet and true alto voice. Mrs. Ethel Martin Funkhouser inherited from her father, James Martin, her absorption in music, and from her mother accuracy and feeling in piano work. She ranks easily as the foremost accompanist in the city.

The Turpins were, as a family, leaders par excellence in musical Dayton. James Turpin was teacher of private pupils in piano and voice all through the 1860s and 1870s and director of singing in the public schools. For years he played and conducted in the Third Street Presbyterian Church choir. His daughter, Jeanette, was a conscientious teacher and musician of taste. Harry Brown Turpin, during a lifetime of singing and teaching, discovered and developed two voices that have meant much to Dayton, Mrs. Clara Turpin Grimes, who for years ranked as our leading concert soprano, and Cecil Fanning, a baritone. Mr. Turpin discovered the latter, encouraged him, taught him, brought him out, took him on concert tours, ending with a levee and dinner at Buckingham Palace in London, where he sang before the king and queen.

We are in debt to the Lytles for good music. Sixty years ago both John S. and his wife, Mary Voorhees Lytle, were lovers of music and sang in the old Third Street Presbyterian choir. Harry V. Lytle was first a pupil of Dennewitz and then of Marsteller on the violin. He played the cello in the old Central High School Orchestra and while there Mr. Turpin prompted him to sing. For sixty years he has kept busy singing and organizing. The first vested choir in the city (Christ Church) was due to him when he was choirmaster; the Philharmonic Society hails him as charter member. For forty years he has given continual service as singer in the Masonic Temple. Mrs. Lizzie Lytle King sends out each season new piano players trained by her, while John Lytle is known to every Daytonian from his place as organizer and leader of the Lytle Band.

The Becker family should not be forgotten, the first one being Louis B., a German-Swiss, who came from Lorraine to Dayton in 1842. Pianist and director at sixteen, he was known here chiefly for his manuscript transcriptions at a time when there were few printing presses for music. His death, in 1914, left a musical progeny: Louis C. Becker, violinist, teacher and leader; Henry C. Becker, director of the Municipal Concert Band; Christian M. Becker, cornetist; John W. Becker, artist of reed instruments; Alice Becker Miller, pianist, successful teacher and director of the Alice Becker School of Music. Her daughter, Florence Miller Underwood, inherits the family tradition and uses it with her dramatic soprano voice. The Beckers are proud of the fact that one of their ancestors, a friend and collaborator of Schumann, made possible the publication of the works of Sebastian Bach.

Dayton has many German citizens who brought their music from the fatherland with them. The outstanding Liederkranz in Dayton is the Harmonia Society under the leadership of Carl A. Schlaefflin. It entertained the National Saengerbund most successfully, as recorded in a Detroit paper dated 1853. It would be interesting to know where four hundred singers could assemble in the Dayton of that day and include an audience. Our Harmonia is a member of the Nord Amerikanerische Saenger-Bund which once in three years gathers in a certain city and gives forth its five thousand voice chorus. For precision, shading, tone volume, and beauty of rendition these German societies are preeminent.

In the 1880s and 1890s the Mendelssohn Quartet gave us beautiful music and was much in demand at public functions. The personnel included the leading men's voices of that day: H. V. Lytle, first bass; John

N. Burkitt, second bass; Samuel F. Phelps, first tenor; and John N. Bell, second tenor. So long and so faithfully did the Mendelssohn Quartet work together that its singing attained the precision of a single instrument, its shading made listening a delight and added greatly to the solemnity of church or memorial services.

The Dutch Club of our present Dayton is in a way a descendant of the old Mendelssohn Quartet. It made its appearance in 1902 as a male chorus, S. B. Hurlburt was the accompanist, afterwards Henry Ditzel, H. V. Lytle, the organizer. The first names on its roll were the familiar ones: Hyers, Bell, Loy, Kumler, Kiefaber, Bollinger, Trimmer, Emrick, Holland, Bimm, Gilbert, Gebhart, Legler, Kester, Crebs and Lytle. It was named the Dutch Club because after each rehearsal every member paid for his own treat. There were no rules except that every member should sing from his heart out.

The Women's Music Club of Dayton came into existence, later reorganized to take in men and rechristened the Dayton Music Club. Its object was to stimulate musical culture but to do it on a wider and more impressive scale. The membership at the present time of writing numbers close to five hundred, perhaps the best of its activities is to maintain a community music school where children who show talent are given lessons in piano, violin or voice at a nominal fee or none at all and by the best teachers. In case special aptitude is shown for a certain instrument it is purchased.

Another novel enterprise was inaugurated by Mrs. Edythe Drake Zuercher in the harmonica orchestra, in which two thousand children are regularly instructed and play on this humble and rather discredited instrument. It is not trivial and frivolous music either, that is produced, but sweet harmonized cadences.

The Dayton Music Club chorus gives its services at social centers and community welfare clubs, at the Dayton State Hospital, City Rescue Mission, Children's Home, Stillwater Sanitarium, Barney Community Center. The Mothers Singers Chorus was developed in 1928 under the untiring musical enthusiasm of Mrs. Charles Funkhouser.

The Dayton Choirmasters Club, a recent but potent enterprise grew out of a conversation sometime during 1927 between Rev. Don Copeland, former choirmaster of Christ Episcopal Church, and Scott W. Westerman of Grace Methodist Episcopal Church. Its most practical accomplishment is to maintain a free registration bureau for church musicians through

Don Bassett conducts the Dayton Civic Orchestra, 1927-1928 season. Now the Dayton Philharmonic, the orchestra has achieved national acclaim.

which singers and organists may secure positions and churches the leaders they desire. One result was a notable musical service in Christ Church where two hundred vested choristers, the united choirs of the city, moved down the aisle to the rhythm of the processional hymn. It was a lesson not only in music but in church fellowship, since the singers were of the Protestant, Catholic and Jewish faiths, all with one voice praising the Lord.

If emphasis has seemed to be placed on vocalization, it is not at all because there have been no instrumentalists in Dayton. For nearly forty years we have been moving toward the Civic Orchestra that is our present pride. In 1886 an orchestra of young Young Men's Christian Association members was organized by the leading violinist in Dayton, Herman G. Marsteller. He was succeeded by John S. Lytle and he by J. C. Eberhardt. In the early 1890s a few schools had orchestras among the pupils.

In the membership of the Young Women's League were eighteen women who played every week under the direction of Dr. J. Charles Reeve. Later, boys were admitted and concerts given at the league social functions, all on a purely amateur basis. When Dr. Reeve gave it up he was succeeded by Dr. Firth, and then by A. E. Fischman and for thirty-three years this modest group of music lovers continued their work.

In 1904 a small number of amateur musicians formed an orchestra to meet once a week at the homes of its members. It was then known as the "Morningstar Orchestra" after its leader . Tiring at last of their own amateurishness, they engaged the services of Mr. A. E. Fischman, a professional violinist and conductor, who gave his services gratuitously for a number of years. Then the organization was known as the Fischman Orchestra and held weekly rehearsals at the Young Women's League. After a while they rose to the dignity of giving concerts. At a program given May 11, 1916, Alverda Sinks, one of Dayton's most accomplished pianists, played Mendelssohn's G-Minor concerto with the orchestra accompanying, and included such composers as Schubert, Wagner, Nevin, Tschaikowsky. It was the first time in the history of music in Dayton that a local pianist played to the accompaniment of a local orchestra.

In 1920 the Fischman Orchestra was reorganized and the name changed to the Dayton Orchestral Club, which continued until it was absorbed into the present Dayton Civic Orchestra. It is wisely held to be an educational institution, and when a member is called to another city to play in orchestras, it is held to be more of a credit than a loss. The Cleveland Orchestra, the Damrosch Symphony Orchestra, New York, the Cincinnati

Symphony Association, all contain musicians who began practice in this little organization in Dayton.

Since 1920 its upholder and moving spirit has been Mr. B. B. Thresher. A musician himself he has made it one of his dearest pursuits. Together with Don Bassett, the director, Mr. Thresher has gathered musicians from far and wide. If scores were needed, he got them. If a place to rehearse was wanted he arranged for it. The present membership of seventy-two contains the best amateurs, professionals and semi-professionals.

Under Mr. Bassett's able leadership the standards of the orchestra have greatly augmented. From the twenty-five taken over in 1920, the membership now stands at seventy-two: first violins, fourteen; second violins, fourteen; violas, eight; cellos, eight; string bass, four; flutes, two; oboes, two; clarinets, three; bassoons, two; French horns, two; trumpets, two; trombones, two; tuba, one; percussion, one; harp, one. From a student group that was half play and half work the Civic Orchestra reached the dignity of accompanying the celebrated Westminster Choir.

For some time the orchestra rehearsed every Monday night at Steele High School. Then Mrs. Talbott generously offered the Runnymede Play House. Now the permanent home of the players is to be the Dayton Art Institute. At the end of each month of rehearsals a concert is given of purely local talent and of unpaid players.

In 1925 the happy thought struck someone to hold in Dayton a May musical festival, as has so often been done in Cincinnati. The first augury of success was when Nikolai Sokoloff, conductor of the Cleveland Symphony Orchestra, agreed to conduct. Practically all the musicians of Dayton rallied to the undertaking: six choirs and the Dayton Civic Orchestra in Memorial Hall.

The choirs were those of Christ Church under Rev. Don Copeland; St. Paul's Methodist Episcopal, Grace Storey Simmonds; the Westminster Choir; Central Reformed Church, Thomas Warner, Chare Ridgeway, accompanist; John Finley Williamson; Grace Methodist Episcopal Church, Harlan Haines; First United Brethren, George Kester; First Baptist Church, Gordon S. Battelle; the Choral Art Society of St. Mary's Church, J. C. Fehring. Also the voice pupils of the Alice Becker Miller School of Music; the Treble Clef Society, O. E. Gerhardt; and the chorus of the Women's Music Club, led by Mrs. Charles Funkhouser.

With the advent of the new century Dayton passed suddenly from the condition of being musically-starved and not knowing it to one of plenty. And the explanation of that transition lies in the fact that we had a real impresario in Mr. A. F. Thiele. In 1900 Mr. Thiele began importing celebrities and although it was an uphill road (his first venture netted him $400 on the wrong side of the ledger), he did at last succeed in putting it on a business basis. Besides managing many local musical affairs he brought to Dayton more than three hundred and fifty fine concerts. He also introduced the Russian Imperial Ballet and such world-known artists as McCormack, Galli-Curci, Kreisler and Schumann-Heink. In fact, for fifteen years Mr. Thiele fed Dayton with good music and slowly but steadily our appreciation grew.

In the meantime Dayton was progressing politically as well as musically. From the old Federal plan of government with its insufficiencies and limitations, Dayton had arrived at the modern plan of commission manager form, with Henry M. Waite at the head. His was the principle, belonging to the modern theories of community management, that things like music should be open to all and not reserved alone for people who had money. The Thiele offerings were fine but they cost money and only those who could pay large prices might enjoy them.

This Mr. Waite thought was wrong in principle and if European cities managed the best music for all, then an American city might. It was in a conversation with Mrs. J. B. Thresher that his idea found instant support. He acknowledged that his ambition was to have a civic music league which should present to the people the best artists at a low price. Her reply was that she knew two hundred women who would see it through: the Mozart Club, and it did.

Six hundred invitations were sent out for a meeting in the Young Women's Christian Association which, after an address by Mr. Waite on the advantages of community music, effected an organization calling itself the Dayton Civic Music League, with the slogan, "The world's best music at cost." The first president was Mr. B. B. Thresher, with Mrs. E. M. Wood and Mrs. Walter D. Crebs as vice-presidents. After three years of devotion to the cause, Mr. Thresher resigned and Mr. William G. Frizell was elected in his place.

The difficult thing the Civic League tried to do, it has most acceptably done. It brings to Dayton the finest artists, the finest concerts. Season seats sell from $3.50 to $10. Once they presented an extra concert with Fritz Kreisler at half a dollar a single seat. They paid McCormack $4,500, but sold tickets at the same low price. The secret is that Dayton has grown up musically. Singers face no more empty seats; guarantors no longer put their hands into their pockets. Two thousand and five hundred to 3,000 tickets are sold and it is numbers that turn the trick. The Civic Music League requires no guarantor and asks no favors. If there is a deficit it is carried along and made up next time. If a generously-minded person wants to buy a number of tickets and give them away he is permitted to do so. Dayton is one of the first cities to have a Civic Music League and others have borrowed the idea and the plan from us.

The artists' concerts brought by the league were not enough for those of scientific music knowledge to whom the symphony is the highest form of art. Therefore the Dayton Symphony Association was organized, the only one in a city of Dayton's size which maintains a strictly symphonic course of concerts. Those responsible for the venture in the beginning were Mrs. H. E. Talbott, who remains its enthusiastic president and promoter; Mrs. N. M. Stanley, Mrs. E. A. Deeds, Mr. W. A. Keyes, Mr. F. J. McCormick, Mr. Ferdinand Ach, Mrs. H. G. Carnell, Mrs. Charles F. Kettering, Judge B. F. McCann, Mrs. J. A. McMillan, Mrs. William B. Werthner, Mrs. Harvey King, and Mr. S. H. Carr.

What glorious concerts we have heard through the association! They have brought all the big orchestras in the country, not once but several times, and how cheerfully they have supplied the deficit, if any. Moreover they have kept the Dayton Civic Orchestra on its musical feet where it might not have succeeded in staying. Music like beefsteak takes money, and those who have it and are willing to give it, act as angels of mercy to a new kind of starving multitude.

During the three years that Walter Damrosch gave his famous young people's symphony concerts, Dayton heard them all and it was largely private generosity that did it.

In time Patricia O'Brien succeeded Mr. Thiele as impresario and business manager of the Dayton Symphony Orchestra, carrying on always his well-founded procedure. The milestones of her symphony concerts are the Philadelphia Symphony with Stokowski; the Boston Symphony Orchestra, Serge Koussevitzky conducting, and the return, after ten years' absence, of the New York Philharmonic. She also is responsible for the presentation of Mary Garden, Will Rogers, Paderewski, San Carlo Opera, Pavlova, and Galli-Curci.

We now come to a musical enterprise that has put Dayton on the map of the world almost as much as the invention of the airplane, and although it does not belong to us any more, it will always be a source of pride that the Westminster Choir had its origin in our midst.

It was in 1920 that John Finley Williamson assumed the leadership of the choir of Westminster Church and took up his work. He was a man of broad vision, the leading element in which was the conviction that church music needed to be improved. He abhorred the trumpery trash that went by the name of church music, the trivial singsong hymns, the paltry theology. He realized that worship, which is as much the function of music as of prayer, should be adequately framed in music that was high in form and purpose. So he selected only the best compositions for his chorus, and admitted to its ranks only singers who had consecrated their lives to the service of the church through the ministry of music.

In all these aims, in all these standards and ideals, Mr. Williamson found an immediate ally in Mrs. H. E. Talbott, for years the promoter, supporter and inspirer of all things musical in Dayton. Without her sympathetic aid and financial support the story of the Westminster Choir would have been a short one. It was she who fanned the flame Mr. Williamson kindled.

A musician of no small accomplishment, she saw in this enterprise a means of educating the public in more elevated standards of devotional music and an outlet for her own supreme vitality of purpose. Her home on the crest of the hill south of the city is a gathering place for musicians both professional and amateur. Her *Runymede Playhouse* holds delighted audiences for operas, dances and concerts. Either on her wide lawn on summer afternoons or in the Playhouse are large and frequent audiences in her debt for lovely programs.

In the augmented homestead where George W. and Eliza P. Houk made hospitality in the 1860s and 1870s, Katherine Houk Talbott carries on their example in the new century. The sixty-foot long music room, with its pipe organ and Mrs. Talbott on the console, holds frequent delighted audiences. It was a foregone conclusion that the Westminster Choir would appeal to her. She accompanied them on their American concert tours, she arranged for the European triumphs, if funds fell low she supplied them, if publicity languished she promoted it. She approved unqualifiedly of the standards set by its leader.

The choir was not only a choir, it was a school with the most rigid discipline. Four hours a day of practice for three whole years was the order of the day for their training. This bore fruit, as scientific devotion to an art always will. The Westminster Choir began to be known outside of Dayton and to be called upon for concerts. These fifty singers went to New York, Boston, Philadelphia, Washington, Buffalo and twice to Pittsburgh.

Walter Damrosch, not given to empty flattery, said: "The choir shows fine musicianship and work of an understanding character. It is second to none in this country or elsewhere, doing the most constructive work done in the last twenty years."

Nine thousand people heard the Westminster Choir in the New Coliseum in St. Louis; six thousand in Convention Hall, Kansas City. In 1929 (we are epitomizing for the sake of brevity), the Westminster Choir went on a grand tour to Europe. just before they sailed on the *Leviathan* they gave a farewell concert at Carnegie Hall and the New York critics gave them the highest praise. An official send-off was led by Mayor Jimmy Walker: down the bay they went accompanied by the enthusiasm of the greatest city in the world, and off for European triumphs.

Their first concert was at Royal Albert Hall in London, then to Manchester, Liverpool and Leeds, all of them centers of choir music, giving our singers a most hearty and appreciative welcome. Back for a second concert at Albert Hall. Then to Paris where they sang first at the Grand Opera House and later at the Trocadero and the Salle Pleyel.

At Vienna there was a grand reception held at the town hall with seven hundred guests, planned by the Austrian Government and Mr. Washburn, the American Ambassador. At Berlin seven thousand pairs of rapturous hands brought out twelve encores. The mayor at Hamburg welcomed them in a fine address. The *Budapesti Hirlap* said editorially: "Dayton is a relatively small town in the United States, but its choir is of outstanding artistic development and it is no wonder that it proceeds from one great success to another on its first European tour."

The sad sequel for Dayton is that for many and cogent reasons the choir is no longer a part of us. Mr. Williamson was called to be the musical director of Ithaca College, Ithaca, New York, and the choir followed him. Just before the move was made, a concert was given at the White House where the welcome and the appreciation were no less great than across the water. Dayton's send-off was a municipal banquet at the Miami Hotel where, on February 22, 1929, five hundred guests were present to express their appreciation, gratitude, and regret.

The present sponsors of the choir are Mrs. Herbert Hoover, Sir Esme Howard, British Ambassador; Father Finn of the Paulist Choristers;

Dr. Walter Damrosch; Dr. S. Parkes Cadman; ex-Ambassador to England Houghton and Mrs. Houghton; Ambassador and Madame Louden of France; Marguerite de Talleyrand; Frau Wilhelm Miklas, wife of the president of the Austrian Republic; Mrs. Charles Dana Gibson, New York; Baroness Von Klenner, president American Opera Association, New York; Serge Koussevitzky, conductor of Boston Symphony Orchestra; Countess Johanna Hartnaue, Austria.

Fifteen years before he died, Mr. John H. Patterson, moved by the idea that music ought to have an influence in industry, called to his aid Mr. G. B. McClelland, whose particular function in the N. C. R. business was to make men sing. At sales conventions he made them sing whether they had voices or not, and singing together is said to be a preamble to selling together. With his whoopem-up methods of conducting it is said that Mr. McClelland could bring music out of an audience of tortoises.

The idea, like most of Mr. Patterson's ideas, was a sound one and bore fruit. The N. C. R. chorus of eighty-five voices as it was later organized under the leadership of Albert Hartzell, did good work for six years and took part in the May Musical Festivals at Cincinnati. Of late years the Welfare Department of the National Cash Register Company in its big schoolhouse, holding 3,500 people, is filled every Sunday afternoon with listeners to some of the greatest artists in the musical world or to good local vocal and instrumental talent.

Saturday mornings are given up to the children who are entertained by the company and who, led by Mr. McClelland, learn to sing together, and in neither of these activities is there any charge to the public.

If the foregoing chapter has conveyed the impression that in the century since the Pleyel Society, all musical things in Dayton have advanced and improved, it is misleading. In one respect, and in the opinion of the writer, we have lost what we had and gone steadily backward. I will explain.

Sunday morning in the old Dayton days I used to go out under the trees in the yard (on the corner of Fourth and Ludlow) to listen to the bells. Sixty years ago Dayton was hailed in an encyclopedia as having more churches than any other town of its size in the country. If it had said "bells" it would be believable. For every church had a bell or a peal of bells or a chime. It was every sexton's duty to set them going at ten and again at ten-fifteen, and they were, to my distant memory, fine bells: some, deep-toned and vibrant, singing in an ever-increasing slow crescendo, "COME-TO-

CHURCH! COME-TO-CHURCH! COME-TO CHURCH!" Others, in a higher pitch and a more staccato measure said, "Cometochurch, cometochurch, cometochurch."

It was a peal of three from Emmanuel Church on Franklin Street that first made its appeal, followed by the First Presbyterian bell on Third and Ludlow, and the Reformed, farther up the street. Then the Lutheran chimes joined in from the brick tower on Main Street, the beautiful tower ruthlessly destroyed! These were a peal of three, swung by a rope, also a chromatic scale of bells struck with a hammer and upon which they sometimes played a hymn. It was entrancing if all were correctly tuned. If not, it was decidedly otherwise.

The German Lutheran on Wayne and Marshall and St. John's on East Third always came in with a sort of duet (the Lutherans like the Catholics being infatuated with bells). St. Joseph's on Second and Madison, had good bells, as did the Park Presbyterian Church on Cooper Park. We amused ourselves trying to identify them. Sometimes, when the wind was right, we thought we caught the faint tone from the far western edge of town, the Presbyterian bell on Summit Street, but this, like St. Mary's out on Xenia Avenue, was part imagination. Then, having heard from all points of the compass, the harmonies would die away, leaving the world to the silence of a summer morning: bees, chickadees, buttercups and the soft June sunshine -- *on the corner of Fourth and Ludlow!*

Where are all those bells now? Rusting in their steeples instead of telling people when it is time to get out their missionary money and put on their hats. It may be that the clocks and our individual consciences are enough for practical purposes, but how about the call to prayer? And if the bells should be resurrected, what chance would they have against the street noises of today? Then, the low buildings and wide open spaces permitted the dispersion of this really great ensemble; now, instead of lovely inspiring harmonies we get the shrieks of newsboys with the Sunday edition, the grinding of street car wheels, the honk of automobile horns and the overhead roar of a soaring airplane. Too bad !

18

The Great Flood

There was a time when Dayton citizens were justly sensitive about mentioning the flood of 1913, as sensitive as Californians are in connection with their great historical disaster, and for similar reasons. Now, for dissimilar reasons, they are willing to tell you all they know.

While engineering science has formulated no plan to escape earthquakes, it has to prevent floods. Through the Miami Conservancy plan the valley is forever secure from the horrible cataclysm which overwhelmed it in the spring of 1913. Everybody is safe and therefore everybody can afford to be frank.

A word as to the topography of Dayton is necessary to understand what happened to us on the night of March 24 and the morning of the 25th. The city lies on low ground surrounded by a sickle which is the Miami River. From the time the latter touches the northern confines of the older part of the town until it tangents off at the southern side it describes a perfect curve, literally nearly surrounding Dayton with water.

Just before it reaches the city its current is augmented by the volume of two more streams, Stillwater River and Mad River, which, though inconsiderable in themselves, when added to the channel of the large river do increase its potency. These three streams, together with Wolf Creek coming in from the west farther down, have a drainage area above Dayton of 2,600 square miles.

The destruction of former forests, the tiling of swamp lands and other improvements are all natural flood producers. When one of the great

Two of the best-known photos of the great 1913 Dayton flood: horses trying to swim against the raging waters at Fourth and Ludlow Streets; rescuers in NCR-made boats taking survivors to safety.

storms comes that periodically afflict our beautiful valley there is an insufficient run-off for the water at the rate at which it was precipitated. To those who can put two and two together no other explanations are needed.

The storm came and it lasted. For four days the rain came down and the streams of the valley, fed by the steady downpour, rapidly rose and poured over the levees. By all accounts it came suddenly but doubtless it was steadily gaining while people were asleep in their beds. Tuesday morning, the 25th, those earliest to appear found water in the streets, the gutters running full as they always did when the river came up. Householders gauged the height of their yards above the street and concluded they were safe.

What people did makes many an interesting story. Men went to market and never got home, being marooned in any business office they could reach. Some housekeepers, with a mind for possibilities, laid in a supply of firewood and drinking water. Others said: "The Miami River has never come into my house and it never will," since when they have acquired more knowledge of that temperamental stream.

When at last the surging waters reached the top of the levees and began to over-run they came with a rush. From the eastern limits of town appeared a yellow curling wave from six to ten feet high and meeting a similar wave coming from the north, swept over Dayton with awful suddenness and awful devastation.

It covered the street car tracks and then private lawns, bursting with a roar through furnace registers and filling lower stories of homes with a filthy soup that touched the chandeliers. Lovely parlors with inherited generations of mahogany, books, and carpets were immersed before the owners could lay a preventing hand.

Families raced upstairs and watched with fascinated concentration the rise of the water pouring through the streets where it at last attained a depth of twelve feet. All city noises were hushed; no cars moved, nothing was seen or heard but the steady rise of the water and the roar of the current as it swept around corners or through the inside of houses.

Happy those whose homes were high enough to keep the flood in the lower story! Thousands of people were marooned for three days and nights in the attics or on the roofs of their homes whither they had cut their way with a hatchet.

It was a time when the essential nobility of human nature, or its opposite, comes to the surface. Some varlets looted or asked big prices for

First flood, then fire; scenes of devastation were horrendous.

country produce. Others hunted out boats, stayed in them until they were soaked to the skin and worn out, in order that suffering people should be taken to homes where they could be cared for. Then Red Cross supplies came and the mariners in skiffs distributed canned milk, baked beans, bread, tinned soups and warm blankets wherever they were needed.

When the water receded and people could walk about in the streets, what a strange and transformed Dayton they saw. Wreckage piled almost to the roofs of the houses; overturned street cars, grand pianos, dead horses, waste lumber, asphalt pavement rolled into huge bales like a carpet; on every side ruin, waste, destruction, unspeakable filth and inconceivable property loss. Four hundred lives snuffed out and a hundred million dollars worth of land and buildings destroyed.

Did the citizens wring their hands and assume sackcloth and ashes? Not the least in the world. They broke up furniture to make fires in the grate, assembled what eatables the flood had spared and shared them with next-door neighbors; they went from door to door calling on citizens to form relief stations in the schoolhouses. Private cars in the suburbs collected bread, coffee, bedding and blankets and took them to the stations.

Fires were made, beds set up, pots filled with coffee or with potatoes to boil; ten to twelve hours a day they worked with faces so dirty that near friends failed to recognize each other and at the end fed themselves with a chip from a can of cold baked beans and went to whatever bed they could find, thinking "Never, never again, this sort of thing for Dayton."

After the militia appeared and martial law was declared, things went better. With great determination the citizens accepted both their individual and community losses, cleaned up the wreckage and reestablished their businesses. The militia patrolled the streets and enforced order. Every able-bodied man was put to work. Food was distributed and tents supplied for the homeless. Railroads and telegraph lines wrecked by the rush of water were rebuilt and communication restored, the last an inestimable blessing to the out-of-town Daytonians awaiting in other cities the news of their families.

The restoration period proved as good a story, though less picturesque, than the flood itself. People were hardly dried out than they began to make good "the promises made in the attic." Here was Dayton, beautiful, rich, powerful, our fathers' home and ours; should it be periodically threatened with the horrors we had just been through? Somehow, some way, some time, it must be prevented.

It would take money, then engineers, to solve an apparently unsolvable problem; it would take agriculturists and soil experts, architects and legislators and lawyers and enough official paper, it was estimated, to cover the continent from here to California.

First they raised a fund to enable engineers to study the problem as a whole, that is all up and down the valley, for there was no idea of wasting time on a piecemeal job. Well, they went to it and while they were studying plans and problems the citizens were raising money. A giant cash register on the courthouse corner showed each day's progress. It clicked around until the result showed that twenty-three individuals had contributed two million dollars.

There was an indirect advantage in that it gave people something to cheer about, which up to that time they had little reason for doing. Housekeepers with ruined carpets and books, cherished family treasures swept Cincinnatiwards, merchants with attractive and expensive stocks scooped out and spread in the mud, churches with organs, vestments, books and brasses destroyed, tried to minimize their sorrow when they walked past the courthouse and saw the mounting thousands rise.

The committee on flood protection was augmented by citizens from other counties, the personnel of which constituted the Miami Conservancy District and embraced portions of nine counties: Montgomery, Shelby, Miami, Clark, Greene, Warren, Preble, Butler and Hamilton. The first act of the committee was to employ the Morgan Engineering Company of Memphis and to put them in entire control of the job.

It then developed that not a spade-full of dirt, not even a blue print could be executed for the reason that there was no enabling law to fit the case. Cities could do things but not a lot of cities and counties cooperatively. Consequently the Conservancy Act of Ohio was prepared, chiefly by John A. McMahon and O. B. Brown, and passed by the Ohio Legislature, February 18, 1914.

The day after the signing of this act by Governor Cox, a petition was filed in the Court of Common Pleas of Montgomery County asking for the establishment of the Miami Conservancy District. Then followed a legal battle on the constitutionality of the law and it was not until June 28, 1915, almost two years after the flood, that the district was established by the court and the directors selected.

The plan decided upon was what is known as the retarding basin plan, which is this: At a certain place in the channel of each river a dam is built so solid that it seems just another long hill connecting at right angles the hills that make the river valley. This dam, in time of freshet, lets only enough water through to fill the normal channel of the river all that can safely be accommodated between its banks.

The rest is held back, "retarded" in a lake above the dam and, as the crest of the flood passes, it slowly takes its way down the valley, endangering nothing on the way. In addition to this there were to be other safeguards, such as deepening and straightening the channel, repairing and raising the levees, but the preliminaries to them all were to appraise the farms lying within the conservancy district and purchase them outright.

This, as may be imagined, was a long and sometimes painful job. Homes that had sheltered several generations of families had to be surveyed, appraised and taken possession of. In one case the whole village of Fairfield, up Mad River, had to be moved bodily to higher ground.

On November 25, 1916, the official plan was approved by the court; the appraisal roll was filed May 9, 1917; on September 13 they advertised the construction work; on December 3 they sold the first installment of bonds amounting to $15,000,000. All this time the general public, ignorant, as the general public always is in technical matters, had been screaming for accomplishment. "Five years" they bellowed, "and no dirt flying yet"! Now, if they have patience to read part 2 of the *Technical Reports of the Miami Flood Control Project*, they might gain some small idea of the multi-multitudinous arrangements, plans, surveys, sales, forms and specifications, drawings, court decisions, which had to be gotten over with before the first spadeful of dirt was excavated.

So the equipment was purchased and the actual construction period began on January 1, 1918. A flood forty per cent greater than that of 1913 was decided upon as the maximum to be taken care of by the flood prevention works. Never since the dams were built has there been that much increase over the flood of 1913 but as much as then went down has been experienced several times with not the slightest jeopardy to the banks, channel or abutting property.

The rains have come, the lakes have filled up, eighty feet deep on the upper side of Englewood dam, but the outlets have calmly accepted it, passed it slowly down the valley and Dayton has thought nothing about it. Storage is provided for a total of 847,000 acre feet of water under maximum flooding conditions.

Four railroad lines and several telegraph and telephone lines occu-

What the fire did to the buildings, the flood did to the pavements. As the clean-up began, plans were being made that eventually resulted in a massive, innovative, locally-financed flood control system that works; below, Englewood Dam, one of five that have kept Dayton flood-free.

pied rights of way in the basin area. In the case of the railway lines the rights of way were within the areas in which the dams were built. These public utilities are now relocated on higher ground wholly or partially out of reach of the backwater from the retarding basins.

The actual work as it faced the committee on January 1, 1918, consisted of the construction of five dams: at Germantown on Twin Creek, protecting Middletown and Hamilton; Englewood on Stillwater; Taylorsville and Lockington on the Miami; and Huffman on Mad River, all just above Dayton and protecting it and the towns below.

The quantities of material involved were large: 2,500,000 cubic yards excavation, 30,000 cubic yards concrete, 55 miles railroad tracks. This only to get ready for the real work of flood prevention. For this 8,200,000 cubic yards embankment in dams, 2,550,000 cubic yards embankment in levees, 5,330,000 cubic yards excavation in river channels, 162,500 cubic yards concrete in outlet works at dams, 89,000 cubic yards in walls and levee revetment.

The concrete, if put into a road, would make a sixteen-foot-wide highway from Cincinnati to Toledo. The earth removed, if put into ordinary two-horse dirt wagons drawn by teams, spaced far enough apart to allow the teams to walk, would fill a string of wagons long enough to go round the earth six times. To move such an outfit would take almost twice the number of horses and mules existing in the United States.

The organization of men to do the job was needed and not only men to do the actual digging, but accountants, storekeepers, cooks, buyers, warehouse men, chauffeurs, skilled mechanics and many others. The district early adopted a policy which guaranteed fair treatment, because of which the construction force stuck loyally to the job in spite of the war and the attraction of easy jobs at big pay that existed on every hand. The maximum number employed at any one time was 2,000; the minimum 750.

Equipment for the job called for 29 locomotives, 21 drag-lines, 200 cars, 63 automobiles, many miles of railroad track, 100 pumps, over 100 transformers, 73 miles of transmission lines. The men had to have a place to live, so five little villages were built to accommodate them and their families; 230 houses, 200 sheds, 5 mess halls, 5 stores, with running water and baths in dwellings and bunk houses.

As to supplies, the widely diversified construction required an amazing variety of articles. Millions of small tools, 70,000 tons of coal, 45,000 barrels of cement, 10,000,000 feet of lumber and 400,000 gallons of gasoline filled 7,800 carloads and several less than carload lots which if combined would make a solid string of cars reaching from Dayton to Cincinnati.

The purchasing, distributing and accounting of these articles was a job of no mean size. Railroad sidings freight, houses for sheltering the men, transmission lines over which to transport electrical energy and erection of equipment were undertaken first. As the progress on the dams depended upon the promptness with which the streams were diverted through the permanent conduits, these structures were started at the earliest possible moment. Of the five dams, that at Englewood was the largest, being 4,700 feet long (about nine-tenths of a mile), 415 feet thick at the base and requiring a volume of 3,600,000 cubic yards of earthwork moved.

The spillways were a vexing question since they were planned to be used only when a volume of water should come down the channel forty per cent bigger than in 1913 and it is quite plain we never will have a flood of that size. But it was decided that the dams could not contain the absolute element of safety which was promised the people of this valley unless these safety valves were included in the design.

There they stand, solid concrete assurances that should a flood come which, like Noah's, would cover all the face of the earth, the conservancy dams would still function. As highways cross the valleys on top of the dams, the spillways are all spanned by substantial concrete bridges strong enough to allow two twenty-ton trucks to pass each other.

The conduit tunnels which take up the ordinary overflow are ingeniously constructed. During flood stages, with the retarding basin above the dam nearly full, the water emerges from the conduit tunnels at high velocity. To break up this velocity a carefully designed structure built to utilize the hydraulic jump is placed at the lower end of the conduits. This hydraulic jump uses up energy when the water lifts itself in the standing wave, and the attendant pools also use up energy when the water swirls about within them. The water leaves the lower end of the structure quietly, at low velocity, and thus is eliminated one of the gravest dangers of a flood, the wearing away of the river bank on the outside of a curve.

The hydraulic excavation and the hydraulic fill methods were used in construction. The materials excavated were later used in construction. At the Lockington dam, gravel suitable for concrete mixing was found in sufficient quantity to furnish all the material needed.

The hydraulic fill method owes its origin to placer mining in the

West where it was at first developed. The natural borrow pit materials are thoroughly broken up by water and carried by moving water, at high velocity, to the outside edges of the embankment under construction, where the water, with its burden of material, is dumped on the outside edge.

The water, released from pressure, flows toward the center of the dam, over the sloping banks, by gravity. The rock drops out first, as the velocity of the stream decreases, then the coarse gravel, then the sand, until when the central portion of the core is reached, only the fine material is being carried along and deposited.

This fine material is semi-liquid mud just below the water-line of the pool but at greater depths it soon loses all the characteristics of a fluid and becomes a dense solid mass through which water will not percolate. It is this material which, when spread thickly over household possessions and not immediately removed makes later cleaning almost impossible. Added to the refuse of factories and cesspools, slaughter houses and paint works, it forms a concrete which requires nothing less than a pick to get out. When soft it entered the tiniest apertures in woodwork and furniture and even now, nearly twenty years after the flood, small particles of it will drop out of table legs and drawers to make despairing housekeepers ask "Will we never get rid of that flood mud?"

Channel improvement being a part of flood prevention, much work went into that at all the towns up and down the valley. The removal of sand bars, impeding trees and islands, the lengthening of bridges, the straightening of the bed of the river, the raising of the top of the levees and the revetment of banks were some of the improvements carried out. At one place the entire removal of a factory on each side of the river was accomplished to get the necessary width of channel. Every town had its special problem. Water and gas mains had to be lowered, bridges raised, two new bridges built, many railroad tracks shifted.

The handling, housing and feeding of the workers, the endless experiments to speed up and cheapen the work, the social significance of this great cooperative enterprise, the schools provided for the children in the camps are all complete stories in themselves and would make a larger book than this one. Interesting details are available at the Conservancy Building on Monument Avenue with other material for engineers the world over who come to Dayton to find out about flood prevention. In this building is carefully preserved the cost, down to the last penny, every conceivable item of preparation, whether legal or constructive, every problem and how it was solved; in fact it is happily not the flood which put us on the map of the world but our success in the prevention of floods.

For they have been prevented, and Dayton is as safe from loss by water as if she were situated in the middle of the Sahara Desert. On April 11, 1922, a severe storm poured its contents into the valley, all one day and well on into the night. In some places an inch and a half fell in less than two hours. Total rainfall for twenty-four hours was three and one-half inches and this on saturated ground.

Under the old conditions the danger mark in Dayton would have been eighteen feet at Main Street bridge. Actually, however, it only marked nine feet and six inches. Only thirty-two per cent. of the channel capacity was used and only four per cent. of the basin storage capacity utilized. Everything worked out according to plan. The water was carried through the improved river channels in the cities smoothly and swiftly; the familiar turbulent appearance in former floods being entirely absent.

At all of the dams the hydraulic jump worked just as it was intended to and only a few hundred feet below each of the outlets the water was flowing smoothly with no intention of scooping out soft banks. Practically no damage was done to property in the valley or to the works of the Conservancy District.

On June 8, 1924, a near-cloudburst caused a rainfall of over four and one-half inches over the upper part of the Stillwater water shed. The result was a rapid rise of Stillwater River and only the moderate stage of thirteen feet at Dayton. Englewood dam held back a volume of water which made a temporary lake covering 2,300 acres. No scraping off of rich loam from fields, no covering of other fields with gravel, no filling up of cellars in the towns, no tearing away of bridges and farm buildings to send them to Cincinnati on the crest of the flood. No wastage of stocks in stores nor crops in the barns, no ruining of carpets and household treasures, in fact nothing to worry about and nothing to regret. Thus have the forces of nature been conquered.

Of course we have our conservancy taxes to pay and will until we die. Some people object to doing this, which forces us to reflect that the conservancy plan lacked just one provision: a method of bringing to his senses a man who begrudges the outlay. It should provide for placing him for a certain number of days without sanitary arrangements, drinking water or food, for keeping a shovel in his hand while he removed several tons of offensive muck from the rooms of his house, meanwhile going without a shave or a bath. After such probation as this, wings wouldn't be quick enough to get him to the assessor's office.

As it is, the flood will always remain the Odyssey of Dayton. For in those four days Daytonians LIVED as they had never lived before. No volume of adventure could equal it. You may hear it when, on an evening before the fire or on a summer evening on a porch, even at this day, people happen to mention the flood. The very word opens the floodgates of narrative. No one's personal experience is like any other.

Those Daytonians who were out of the city when it happened feel as if they have lived in vain. For they cannot contribute. They hear, among other things, how an elderly maiden lady, full sixty years behind the ordinary fence-climbing age, crawled on a six-inch plank resting one end on her bathroom window sill, the other on that of her next-door neighbor, above a raging torrent of water ten feet below her and got there in safety.

Or how a family just beginning to set the breakfast table were surprised and fled to the upper story having only placed the butter-balls on ten individual plates. Three days afterward they arrived to view the scene. The dining table had risen on the flood until it touched the ceiling; then it slowly lowered itself, leaving ten butter-balls stuck tight. Or of the distracted mother who dropped her six-months old twins out of a skiff and found them again at the landing place where the next skiff that came along had rescued and placed them.

How the younger son of a family of refugees found a hammer and tacks and proceeded to drive them into the ancestral mahogany of his temporary hostess. Of millionaires standing in line to receive whatever a generous government could dole out to them and consuming dry bread and bologna sausage with relish. How a train-load of three hundred transient passengers were marooned in an upper room of the Union Station with nothing to eat but one box of chocolate creams and rainwater.

How one man showed a way of escape by walking three squares on aerial telephone cables and thirty people followed him. How an aged couple, marooned in a small house only one hundred feet from dry land and the swift current overturning every boat before it could reach them, were finally rescued by backing a freight train until the last car touched the house. Three minutes after they climbed up a ladder to safety the house bulged up on its foundations and left for the south.

How complete showcases filled with jewelry crashed through the windows of Newsalt's store and emptied themselves in the mud of the street. How an old couple, faint from cold and hunger, were carried out of their home on West Third Street, past a dead horse, a grand piano and a street car, all stranded on their front steps.

How fifteen hundred pianos were hauled to the river bank, kerosene poured over them and burned. How hundreds of poor horses swam and swam and begged with their eyes that people whom they saw at windows would help them and finally sank to the bottom. How the National Cash Register plant served two thousand seven hundred and fifty meals every day to refugees who lay thick upon the floors of the factory. How rescued old people died from exposure and babies were born in those halls and corridors. How sheds were washed away and one deposited on the roof of a small house.

Considered as a whole the flood was not an unmixed curse, for it carried with it new moral and spiritual appreciations. When families, having been separated and harassed by anxiety were finally united, they could hear the grand piano breaking the windows of the conservatory with complete equanimity. The wife of his bosom welcomed the husband of her bosom regardless of the fact that he had slept in his clothes on office chairs for four nights.

The flood took away from Dayton many precious things but it gave something in return: it illuminated those who were really precious.

(Ed. Note: For a full account of the flood and its aftermath, including the dominant role in rescue work and the Conservancy played by John H. Patterson, see *Keeping The Promise, A History of the Miami Conservancy District*, by Patrick Nolan and Carl Becker, Landfall Press, Dayton, Ohio, 1988.)

19

The Cradle of Aviation

During the closing years of the century just passed and the opening years of the present one, a germ of an idea was floating around both hemispheres seeking a human brain to give it an abiding place. Here and there, on rare occasions, it found temporary lodgement. Those who first offered it hospitality were marked men, for its mere possession was enough to make other people tap their brows and shake their heads dolorously.

For the idea was no more or less than that men might, at some future time, learn to fly in the air like birds; the most amazing, unbelievable, incomprehensible idea ever hatched and, of course, never to be entertained except by a simple-minded pipe-dreamers.

In the course of time this incredible idea came to Dayton and there it concluded to stay, because two minds instead of one took hold of it. It is an oft-told story about the "Wright boys," as they were called. How they became interested in a self-propelling toy brought home by their father to lessen the boresomeness of a childish convalescence.

This toy, when thrown into the air, instead of immediately falling to the ground fluttered and soared for some seconds before being overcome by gravity. How these brothers, being clever with tools, thought they could make one like it and did; how they made another larger one which also flew, and then a still larger one which did not fly at all, and how this very failure precipitated invention. The toy was a primitive helicopter only the makers did not know it, even the name not having been invented.

The mystery of the failure gripped their curiosity; why a contraption of a certain size would fly when loosed from control while another of the same construction but of double the size should fall ignominiously to the ground.

It is now well understood, even by laymen, that when doubling the size of their machine they should have quadrupled the power, a principle up to that time unguessed. They applied the principle to kites and kept on constructing, experimenting, inventing, all merely as an interesting recreation while the neighbors continued to tap their foreheads and commiserate with Bishop Wright for having such a worthless pair of sons. Suddenly their occupation ceased to be play and became work.

While European dreamers were hesitating, the Wrights went ahead and, with such scanty means that it seems impossible to believe, made a practical application of the flying germ-idea and perfected it. The world therefore never must be allowed to forget that the mighty science of aviation was born in the Miami Valley.

Lord Northcliffe, the great British editor and statesman, bore irrefutable witness to this fact when he came to Dayton in 1918 to bestow upon Orville Wright the medal of the Society of Arts and Science of Great Britain. "In spite of all contradictory evidence," he asserted, "Dayton is really the home of heavier than air flying."

If the brothers had begun as amateur dabblers they did not remain so. Omnivorous readers, they assimilated every book on the subject so far available; serious observers, they put every proposition to the test; with a colossal capacity for work they were at their shop laboratory from the earliest dawn. Their immediate objective was a study of the principles of wind currents: Mathematics of the Air. For, early in the enterprise, it was discovered that the mechanism of the flying machine was only half the story; the air, like the ocean, is full of inequalities which must be taken into account in navigation.

Their first help came from a system of logarithms worked out by Lilienthal, who was the first to discover that the great problem of flying rests upon figures. Four years were consumed in the study of these mathematical problems, finding many of them incorrect and working out the right ones on paper and in home-made wind tunnel tests before actual flying was accomplished.

Their uttermost plan at that time went no further than to construct a kite on the principle of the helicopter and operated by cords from the ground, which would remain in the air in winds having a velocity of from fifteen to twenty miles an hour. The world knows how they went to the barest, windiest, sandiest place in the United States, Kitty Hawk, on the North Carolina seacoast not far from Cape Hatteras. How they made a "glider" with ground ropes like a kite; and how, having made a machine that would stand up under the wind, they put a man aboard to guide it.

And how at last the day arrived when, with no ground ropes, with an improved engine and contributing winds, the clumsy machine, weighing seven hundred and fifty pounds, rose on the wind, stayed up for fifty-nine seconds and landed without wrecking. This was on December 17, 1903, an epoch-making date in the history of the world.

We remember now how the brothers came back to Dayton, got permission to use Huffman Prairie for experimental flying; how they minded their own business, kept to serious study, allowed no wildest guess to remain unanswered and took nobody except one or two clever mechanics into their confidence. At that day in Dayton not a soul knew anything about them or cared.

The few who suspected what they were aiming at quoted *Darius Green and his Flying Machine*. Because, of course, it was the wildest, silliest, most impossible of achievement and the most unproductive of human ambitions. If they had minded all this we never should have been able to keep an appointment for luncheon in Washington. But they were too busy and happy in their work to know they were being neglected. And the adulation, when it came, they accepted with equal serenity.

The following is in order of time an anticipation of twenty years. On December 28, 1928, the Rotary Club, of which Orville Wright had been made an honorary member, gave him a banquet and the president, Mr. George D. Antrim, invited as his guests some of the old habitues of the West Side who had seen the airplane in its doubtful youth. He recalled the early days when the Wright brothers were only bicycle repairers in a small shop on West Third Street and were tinkering on an old engine that they hoped one day might fly.

Three old neighbors were present, the barber who used to shave the brothers, the landlord who owned the shack they worked in and who sometimes had trouble collecting his rent, and a hardware man who, during the flood, tipped Orville Wright a quarter for helping him move a carload of nails out of a water-threatened cellar. These guests were invited to speak but for obvious reasons declined. There were two mechanics, however, Charlie Webbert and Charles Taylor, who had been foremost in bringing

The Wright brothers home in Oakwood. Wilbur died before it was finished, but Orville until his death in 1948. His father, Bishop Milton Wright, and his sister Katharine also lived here.

the airplane into being. On a street corner some days before, the former had told an eloquent story describing the first flight, and Mr. Antrim related in the original words the narrative to the Rotarians. Said Webbert, through the lips of Antrim:

Well, Sir, we pulled that fool thing around over the ground of Huff-man Prairie about thirty or forty times, hoisting it up on the derrick so it would get a good start, and we were all hot and sweaty and about played out. What was the use of wasting our time over such a ridiculous thing any longer? But once more we pulled her up again and let her go. The old engine seemed to be working a little better than ordinary. Orville stuck his head out and nodded to Wilbur and Wilbur turned her loose. And by God the damn thing flew. Round and round and round that field it went for thirty-one minutes. Some of the time he must have been a hundred feet up and every time he passed over us we all three threw our hats in the air and yelled our damn heads off.

The year 1908 was a notable one in the annals of the Wright brothers. First there was the accident to Orville on September 27, when in a flight at Fort Myer, Virginia, with Lieutenant Thomas Selfridge as passenger, the plane crashed. On the bank of its fourth circle a hundred and fifty feet up, a cracked propeller blade snapped the rudder wire and the plane wavered for a plunge. Orville, by lightning swift action, leveled the craft for a down glide but he had only seventy-five feet of elevation left and a defective front rudder.

Thousands of horrified spectators saw the crash and perceived the two men helpless upon the ground. It was indeed a tragic flight. Lieutenant Selfridge died a few hours later and Orville Wright suffered a broken leg and several fractured ribs, neither injury equaling in agony his mental suffering.

At this time Wilbur Wright was in France and Katherine Wright, the only sister, was teaching in the high school at Dayton. Upon the receipt of the telegram she closed her desk forever and took the train for Washington, where the strongest prop the brothers had in life sat at the bedside and cheered the patient with her hope and confidence.

There was abundant need for cheer. The family fortunes were low. Bishop Wright, the aged father, had retired from the ministry three years before; the united savings of both brothers and the sister were exhausted in perfecting the machine and the family home had been mortgaged. The United States Government was slow in making up its mind that the airplane was of sufficient importance to receive federal aid. And now, broken bones, grief and family separation.

However, "the darkest before the dawn." Four days after the accident Wilbur, at Le Mans in France, made a world record flight exceeding an hour and a half. Stepping from his plane, surrounded by thousands of excited spectators, he said calmly, "This will cheer Orville up."

This feat across the ocean was not only a message of fraternal love but proof to the world that the disaster at Fort Myer did not mean that the airplane was a failure or that it impaired the future of aerial transport. The French government awarded the heroes a substantial sum and the cable forwarded several thousand dollars to the convalescent in Washington.

Wilbur's triumphs culminated on the last day of the year when, by a world record flight of two hours and twenty minutes, he won the Michelin prize of four thousand dollars. (The Michelin Trophy itself is on display at Wright State University.) Not all the interest centered in his feats of aviation. To the ordinary Frenchman Wilbur Wright was a *rara avis*. He was austere and silent; he kept the Sabbath as his minister father had taught him; he used no tobacco, drank no wine, ate the simplest food and attended strictly to business.

But his letters home bubbled with enthusiasm. Since Orville was out of danger why should not Katherine come to France and act as her brother's "social manager"? She accepted the invitation. Orville followed later. At Pau the brothers organized an air school to train pilots for the French Wright Company. No textbooks were available, no theories of instruction worked out, no medical examination exacted to sift out the physically unfit. Teacher and pupil took their places in the open frame of a plane, rose in the air and took their chances.

It was then that European royalty woke up to what was happening. The King of Spain sent word requesting an exhibition flight on Sunday. A royal request is a command but not to the Wright brothers, who had taken the Old Testament seriously. They courteously replied that they would be pleased to entertain His Majesty on any week day. It was on a Friday, then, that the king and his suite arrived at the hotel, shaking hands vigorously with both brothers and expressing delight at their accomplishments. The royal visitor then inquired for the sister, who by this time everybody knew had stood so loyally by her brothers in all their achievements.

Katherine was over in a corner of the field taking her first lessons in curtseying under the tutelage of Lady Northcliffe, who had volunteered to instruct her in this essential of greeting royalty. When the crucial time arrived however, formalities were forgotten and Katherine met the king's reception in the truly American way of shaking hands. Alphonso was curious as a boy, running across the field, climbing into the seat by Wilbur and demanding to know the uses of the various parts of the mechanism.

The Emperor William of Germany, with his suite, was another visitor, and once interested beyond the honors due to himself, talked cordially for some time with the brothers and the sister. Edward VII of England, Victor Emmanuel of Italy, Prince Francis of Teck, Lord Haldane, Ambassador Reid, in fact the leading royal and political lights of Europe came from time to time to meet these Americans who were turning the world upside down.

To all of them the Wrights were serenely polite and politely explanatory, but they did no more bowing and curtseying and their manner was as if they were in the habit of meeting them all quite often in Dayton.

Now it was 1909 and the Wrights were back at home again. What could we do to match the glorious experiences of their foreign sojourn? For two whole days, June 17 and 18, Dayton did its utmost with speeches, bells, fireworks, medals and cheers to express, as best we might, the pride, affection and joy with which our hearts went out to them.

The first day began with the firing of a salute on the river bank and the blowing of all the factory whistles. John V. Lytle directed a band in Van Cleve Park, to usher in our patron saint, Jonathan Dayton, who advanced surrounded by heralds, an escort of Continental Soldiers, the city council, the board of education and members of the celebration committee. Jonathan Dayton made a speech, so did Leopold Rauh, president of the Chamber of Commerce; Ezra M. Kuhns, president of the city council; Conrad J. Schmidt, president of the board of education, and all the people cheered wildly.

The afternoon was ushered in by a parade drill of the Dayton Fire Department, filling Main Street from Monument Avenue to Sixth Street, and at 4:30 there was a review of troops. At eight in the evening all their fellow citizens had a chance to shake hands with Orville and Wilbur at the Young Men's Christian Association Building, then on the corner of Third and Ludlow.

Friday, June 18, the scene of festivities changed from the city to the

The first ambulance airplane.

Searchlight picks up plane in Wright Field demonstration.

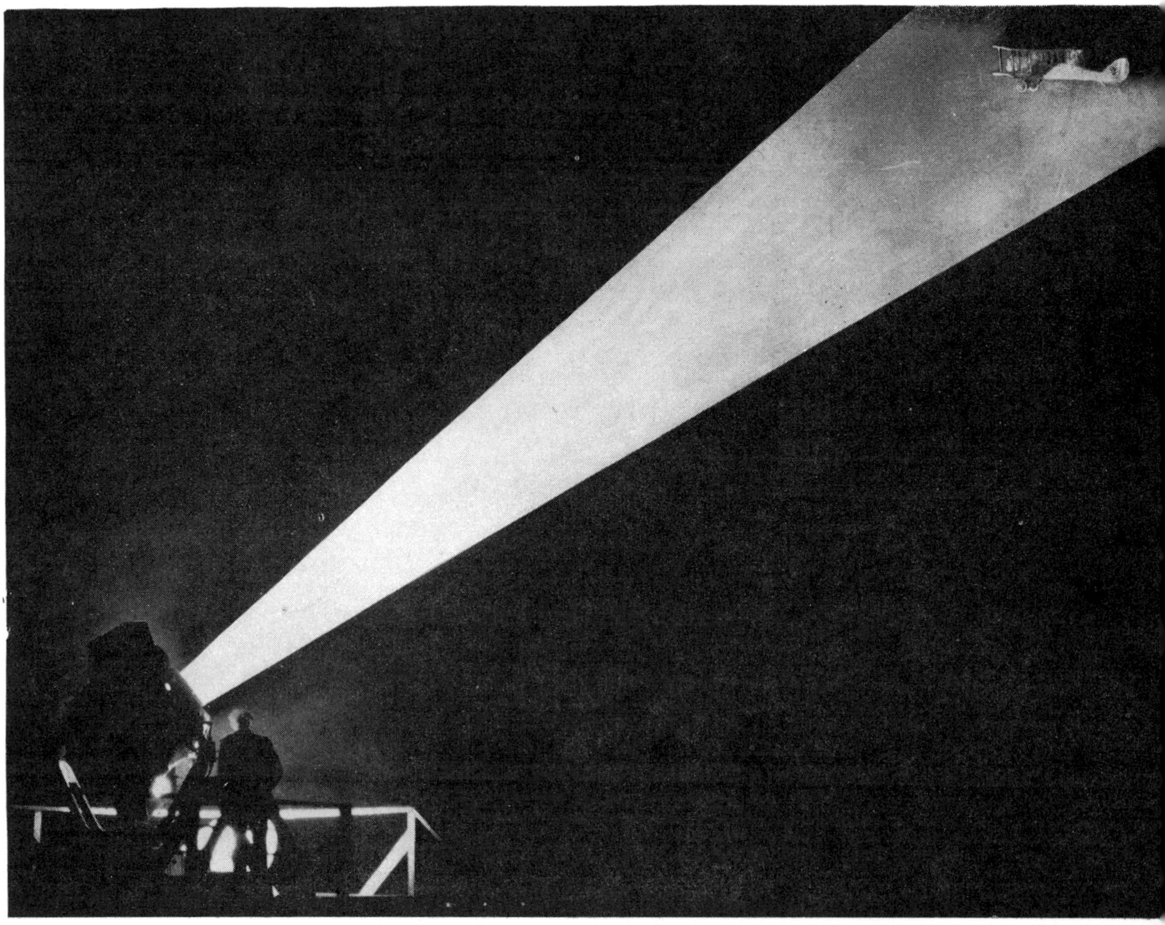

Fairgrounds where the people gathered as they had never gathered before. All the record breaking crowds for which Dayton has been locally famous in the past were outdone.

When Goldsmith Maid ran in 1873, when the Grand Army dedicated the Soldiers' Monument, the Centennial in 1876, and that earliest and most wonderful of all, the Harrison Log Cabin campaign in 1840 all paled into insignificance compared to the crowds assembled to do honors to the Flying Wrights. Rising tier on tier at the race track was a blossoming, blooming American flag composed of five thousand school children, some in white dresses, some in red and some in blue, to form a background for the speakers' dais.

Here sat representatives of the government at Washington and of the state at Columbus, but not a single king, nor emperor, nor foreign dignitary, just our city fathers and the two brothers with their sister and father. What an unprecedented thing to have the opening prayer made by Bishop Milton Wright, whose feelings probably surged up with pride and affection past all belief.

The now-yellow program records another item which challenges our credulity. It says: "Response by Messrs. Wilbur and Orville Wright." But we don't believe it. They were not the speech-making kind. Wilbur once said, when urged to make a speech, that it would be too much like a parrot, which talks a great deal but can't fly. The most oratory in which either of them ever indulged was to rise and bow and perhaps say, "thank you." But whatever they did, or did not do or say on this occasion, the great thing was to see them stand there so quiet and self-possessed (though rumor said blushing) and receive the greatest honors ever paid American citizens.

Three sets of medals were presented, one awarded by act of Congress, one by the Ohio Legislature and one by the city of Dayton. The managers of this celebration wisely determined to make it a lesson in history, therefore the really admirable transportation pageant which closed the day's proceedings.

On Main Street spectators saw on the leading float the first vehicle of transportation that the Miami Valley ever saw, the Indian canoe; after that the scow or pirogue, that ungainly vessel which brought our first ancestors up the river from Cincinnati in search of a new home. Then a Conestoga wagon with its accommodations for the pioneer family, the dog and the cow following slowly; next the canal boat with a stovepipe pointing aloft. From that to the wonders of steam transportation, the locomotive, the steamboat, the automobile, and finally and triumphantly last, the airplane.

One of the unrecorded but plainly remembered results of this great occasion was the large number of people who had always known that the Wrights would succeed in flying. There was no more tapping of foreheads and grave nods; instead, jovial and repeatedly expressed versions of "I told you so."

Thus far the history of aviation had been composed of equal parts of sentiment, experiment, enthusiasm, apathy and success. Flying was indeed wonderful but its fruits were thus far negligible and remained largely in the future. The fireworks, welcoming speeches and brass bands seemed to have exhausted our capacity.

Then and there Dayton should have established those facilities which every inventor needs to carry on his work. Had this been done, in due time we should have developed into the manufacturing center of the world's airplane production. It was with a gasp of incredulity that we suddenly perceived other nations outdistancing us. The French were making extraordinary strides; England was already giving more credit to some of her own workers than to the Wrights.

Then came the War and with it profound and saddening revelations. We found as Americans that we knew little about airplanes. We practically had none. In spite of Orville Wright's repeated declarations that the United States ought to appropriate a sufficient sum to carry on the work, here in Dayton we were at the tail end of the great and lengthening procession of air transportation.

The war had disclosed the value of the airplane for offense and defense. Germany was developing an aptitude for quick production and success in air fighting. There was no time to be lost. Throughout the country sounded the call "Build Airplanes! Airplanes will win the war!" But what uncharted territory it was, to be sure. Great factories would have to be built and highly skilled workmen assembled, mechanics who had not the slightest idea of the construction of an airplane. The demand was unique in the history of manufacturing.

It was the Dayton Wright Airplane Company that in this community answered the call. Foremost in this organization were Orville Wright, H. E. Talbott, H. E. Talbott, Jr., Charles F. Kettering, Thomas P. Gaddis, George Mead, Carl Sherer and G. M. Williams.

At that time the Domestic Engineering Company, manufacturing the Delco light, was just completing a mammoth concrete and steel building at Moraine City some miles south of Dayton. The largest structure of its kind in Ohio at that time, it was a thousand feet in length. This building was immediately taken over, its dimensions increased to two hundred feet in width and two thousand five hundred in length. Four more buildings were constructed before the housing of this unprecedented undertaking was complete.

The company was incorporated in July, 1917, and the roof to cover it completed. But what a task lay ahead! Much necessary raw material was not to be had. Linen for wings, oil for lubricating, spruce for framework, all had to be procured under the most extraordinary difficulties. Only five or six men in the company knew anything about the mechanism of an airplane, and not one of them had any experience in quantity production.

The force of mechanics numbered only forty, which number was rapidly increased to seven thousand men and women. Up to March, 1918, production was limited to the making of training planes of which five hundred were completed but as soon as the release from the government had been secured, enabling them to proceed with the manufacture of battleplanes, the pace was set for rapid work.

By the following July one thousand fully equipped battleplanes had been constructed; by October another thousand finished and the production rate definitely set at a thousand per month. It was no miracle, except it be the miracle of organization. In this case the secret seemed to be in a progressive system of manufacture by which no time was wasted in useless transfers from one department to another.

All raw materials, wood, metal, textiles, etc., entered the receiving room just at the south door of the factory; from there they passed, by an admirable trucking system, into the first department; from there, when transformed into the required part, into the second department, each being fitted as it went. The finished parts gathered at last into the assembling room at the extreme farthest end of the huge plant, emerged from the hands of the assembling force a complete airplane, ready for trial flight and shipment to France.

"Trial flight!" But that meant a place to fly them. And where should it be? Another hurry-up job for these doughty pioneers! So, behold three men in hip boots tramping the muddy fields north of town in search of space to fly airplanes.

Aerial view of Wright Field; early motto for pilots was "This field is small, use it all."

They were Orville Wright in the lead and following him Mr. Kettering and Mr. Smith. They were investigating a tract of level land west of the Troy Pike and east of the Miami River. The land belonged to the heirs of the Anson McCook estate and there were a lot of them. This tract and more of it on the opposite side of the river was purchased by Mr. Deeds and Mr. Kettering who offered to lease it to the city of Dayton on a basis of three per cent on the cost of the land with improvements.

This proposal was accepted by the city and an ordinance passed by the city commission June 17, 1917, authorizing the city manager to execute the necessary instrument. On April 1, 1917, the city took actual possession. The original idea on both sides in the beginning was to provide an amusement park for the citizens of Dayton but, when war necessities arose, other uses had to be arranged for. Eventually the southern part of the tract was leased to the government as a flying field and named after the "Fighting McCooks" whose record in the Civil War made the title highly appropriate.

Work was at once begun levelling the ground, vacating several streets and alleys, and removing sheds, trees, etc. The total area of McCook Field was 121.5 acres. (Pilots were told "This field is small, use it all.") Hangars were erected, office buildings provided and a tall fence built shutting out from the eyes of the curious whatever went on inside.

Many nationally known engineers and skilled mechanics were mobilized at the field for the purpose of pooling their aeronautical knowledge and making the results of their combined efforts available for the defense of the nation. A considerable portion of the development work on the Liberty engine went on at McCook Field. Skilled test pilots and engineers were employed to measure the performance and determine the adaptability of the new machines for the use of our armies in Europe.

Then the war stopped and the stopping was as great a jolt as the starting. Suddenly no more use for the high powered battleplanes that had been pushing forth from the big plant south of town under the stimulation of the big plant north of town. All was at a standstill. But not for long. The airplane had come to stay. The war was over but other uses called.

The history of civilization is largely the history of communication and transportation. We who have lived in the years since the end of the war have seen the airplane developed into a tool of everyday living. Mail air routes cross the continent and the post office has its air mail stamps. If Chicago is our objective and we are in a hurry we take a plane. Regular routes for daily use connect city to city. Airplanes take food and medical supplies to regions devastated by flood. Airplanes scatter insecticides over infected agricultural areas.

The Red Cross has its air ambulance like its motor ambulance, forest fires devastate large tracts of woods in the northwest but it is the airplane observation which first sees and reports the danger. In three years of aerial patrol in the state of Oregon the amount of territory burned over was reduced by sixty-two per cent. Aerial photography is another important phase of peace-time aviation in greatly facilitating mapping, surveying and city planning. The United States Coast Guard is finding aviation a great aid in carrying out its duties.

But all these things were as yet unfolded. Wise heads saw into the future but wise heads were few. The airplane was going to be improved, but the question was, who was going to do it? Dayton was logically the place in which to establish every facility, every stimulation, every impetus, only there was no one to make a start.

Appropriations must be from Congress. During the year of 1923-24 Great Britain appropriated more than three times as much as America did. Italy expended nearly twice as much. The United States ranked at that time, in aeronautical appropriations, about on a level with France and Japan, each smaller than the state of Texas.

The need for scientific development of aviation in America was the outstanding lesson of the great war. The engineering department of the United States Air Service came into being because it was a war-time necessity. It proved to be no less a peace time necessity.

Talk bubbled everywhere. Orville Wright declared that "When we entered the war we did not have in America a real fighting airplane. Individuals could not afford to develop airplanes at their own expense and the United States, before the war, was spending comparatively nothing for that purpose. We were fortunate in having the Allies help us in getting designs for our first planes. Development work cannot be done in the hubbub of actual warfare. The expenditure of ten million dollars before the last war would have saved the hundreds of millions that had to be spent to accomplish the same result after the war had begun. Economy demands that we keep abreast of the world in aeronautical research."

In 1922 General Dawes, director of budget of the Army Air Corps, had submitted to Congress a request for the appropriation of four million, two hundred thousand dollars for aeronautical research. When the bill came before the House appropriation committee that sum was reduced to two million, two hundred and twenty-five thousand dollars. It was recognized by air service officials that if the proposed reduction were made but a small part of the large aims of the air service could be accomplished.

At this point Mr. J. H. Patterson comes into the story. He had just returned from Europe, an old man enfeebled by his herculean efforts to make people understand the importance of the League of Nations. When the proposition was brought before him his clear vision grasped it at once.

That money spent in research was clear gain was evident to him from its part in the development of his own business, the manufacture of the cash register. Being asked by General Mitchell in what way the National Cash Register Company could influence Congress to appropriate the larger figure, Mr. Patterson's answer was prompt and practical. He commissioned two of his most trusted and efficient subordinates, John F. Ahlers and Horace W. Karr to go immediately to Washington armed with convincing ammunition for the senatorial mind.

They departed March 1, 1922 and stayed five weeks. They called on Senator Fess and the leading members of the lower House; they talked to the military affairs committee, to the House appropriations committee, and the Ohio delegation in Congress; they interviewed four hundred Congressmen and ninety-six Senators. The result of all this persuasive oratory was the appropriation of three million, seven hundred and forty thousand dollars to which the obliging Senate afterward added five hundred thousand more.

Highly gratifying, of course, but is only half the story as far as Dayton was concerned. For her public-spirited citizens wanted not only the money for the work but they wanted the work to go on where it had begun: in their own city. One of the many lessons taught by the war and one which was perhaps the more forcibly thrust upon our attention because of our previous attitude of apathy, was the absolute necessity for a continuing program of aircraft development. The appropriation of huge sums would, it was felt, be of little avail without a definite knowledge of what to build and how to build it.

This realization came too late to be of appreciable advantage in the war. In 1917, under the pressure of actual war conditions, the government realized that a central experimental plant was necessary and Dayton was chosen as the most logical location. The first practical difficulty was a lack of proper space. McCook Field had become quite inadequate. The smallness of the area and its proximity to the streets and homes of Dayton made

Propeller test facility, Wright Field.

Some of the early demolition bombs manufactured at the Field.

experimental flying highly dangerous. Dwellers in North Dayton did not want parachutes dropping into their radish beds or their ears assailed by the droning roar of engine testing.

The inference was inescapable. If Dayton wanted the research field she would have to produce for the government a suitable site. Eight miles east of the city lay the tract of land originally known as Huffman Prairie where, for the first time, "The damn thing flew." Part of this area lay in the retention basin above the Huffman conservancy dam, had been purchased of the Miami Conservancy District and used as a training field. This, the original Wilbur Wright Field, was a very important unit during the war and owed its selection for use of the air service to Colonel Edward A. Deeds, then head of aircraft production in Washington.

At the eastern extremity, near the village of Fairfield, a number of buildings had been erected where war supplies in large quantities were stored. It was known as Fairfield Air Depot. The proposition, as it finally took shape, aimed at buying the Wilbur Wright Field, the Fairfield Airport, and in addition five hundred and fifty acres to the southwest in Montgomery County, the original tract being in Greene County. Between the two tracts lies a high ridge comprising several acres on which it is hoped, at some future time, to erect a suitable memorial to the Wright Brothers. From this elevation can be seen the original wooden hangar used by the brothers in their early experiments. (Ed. Note: This memorial was constructed; it was dedicated on August 19, 1940, Orville's 69th birthday.)

That portion of the land lying in Montgomery County was equipped with buildings to house the various projects carried on at McCook Field and eventually became known as Wright Field. The original Wilbur Wright Field was rechristened to honor the memory of a Dayton boy who gave his life to the cause and is called Stuart Patterson Field. (Ed. Note: The entire complex became known as Wright-Patterson Air Force Base in 1948.)

This in brief was the plan, the recounting of which has gotten ahead of its own chronology. The mere statement of the idea was enough to set a campaign in motion. John H. Patterson had died, but he left a son, Frederick Beck Patterson, whose interest in flying was due to the fact that he had held a commission as lieutenant in aerial photography during the great war.

The first step towards the raising of the money was to organize the Dayton Air Service committee with the following personnel: President, Frederick Beck Patterson; vice-president, Frederick H. Rike; secretary, Ezra M. Kuhns; treasurer, W. M. Brock; board, W. R. Craven, Valentine

Winters, H. H. Darst, I. G. Kumler, Colonel Frank T. Huffman, Colonel E. A. Deeds, G. W. Shroyer, F. J. Ach, J. C. Haswell, H. W. Karr, Edward Wuichet, George B. Smith, H. D. Wehrley, John F. Ahlers, and C. E. Comer.

Calling to his assistance the citizenry of Dayton, Mr. Patterson outlined a plan which included, as its main feature, the acquiring of five thousand acres of land to be presented to the government free of charge for the establishment of a research station. The National Cash Register Company led in publicity work, the papers loyally did their share. It was insisted upon that no less than thirty other cities, and especially Detroit, with Selfridge Field, were competing strongly for the honor. If this opportunity were allowed to pass, Dayton, the logical cradle of aviation, would forever take second or third place. The greatest honor we could bestow upon the men who had invented the airplane would be to make secure the plan for centering all the activities of aviation in Dayton.

For two heated days everybody thought and talked Wright Field. Not a man was left unapproached. All the arguments were aired; all our civic loyalty was drawn upon. When the final count of contributions to the fund was made it showed that Dayton had "gone over the top" to the tune of $425,673. F. B. Patterson sent the following telegram to Major-General Mason M. Patrick, chief of the United States Air Service:

Our public spirited citizens today subscribed sufficient money to buy the new site for the government's aviation experimental field on the eastern boundary of Dayton. Enough money was raised to pay for the five thousand acres in the proposed gift and a sufficient amount to be used as a nucleus for a memorial to the Wright Brothers. The spirit which dominated the campaign will ever mark the attitude of Dayton toward the United States Air Service. Our citizens will always extend a hearty hand of fellowship to its members.

So now, Wright Field being definitely established, what, after nine years, are the conditions and accomplishments? First it is the home of the Materiel Division of the United States Army Air Corps. The interested observer sees two runways, each one mile long, grass covered. There are three hangars of steel and concrete construction having a total area of 86,300 square feet with a plane capacity of seventy-five.

Twenty-nine buildings house the Materiel Division activities, including administration building, main laboratory and radio, power plant, wind tunnel and propeller laboratories with a total floor space of 2,200,000 square feet. 'These are the physical characteristics. The Materiel Division is divided into six main engineering sections: Airplane, power plant, equipment, armament, materials and lighter than air (balloons).

No flying is taught at Wright Field. It is a vast laboratory for experiment and the production of all that concerns the art of flying. The airplane branch deals primarily with the military airplane structure. Before a new type of airplane is completed, all its parts are tested to learn their actual strength values. There is a wind tunnel laboratory where small models are tested. Wright Field uses two such tunnels, a large one and a small one. Propellers are developed in this section and Wright Field possesses the largest propeller test rig in the world. Propellers up to forty-five feet in diameter may be whirl tested.

The aircraft engine forms the kernel of activities in the power plant branch, the constant aim being for higher power without increase in weight. A new cooling system, permitting great reduction in the size of the radiator, is an important development. A supercharger for supplying the engine with sufficient air pressure for operation in very high altitudes; the obtaining of a higher standard fuel and oil have resulted in much engine improvement.

Equipment Laboratory: Hundreds of projects of special interest are under way all the time in this department. Parachutes, field and airlighting equipment, aviators' clothing, oxygen apparatus (to enable the flier to breathe in an altitude above 17,000 feet), photographic supply, including an aerial mapping camera with five lenses are among the products in use here. Also a flight tutor in which the embryo pilot may learn quickly how he will react to the different positions of an airplane, and the gyro pilot, an instrument which keeps the airplane stable on its course without the aid of the pilot, are two enormously important inventions.

Materials Branch: This department is used for testing all materials used in the air corps: wood, sheet steel, wire, cloth, fuels, oils, paints, varnishes, fabrics, rubber goods, all must come up to the necessary aircraft standard. Common enough materials, all of them, and easy to procure in peace time; but every piece of an airplane is of uncommon material, perfect to a degree never before demanded. And a man's life hangs on every piece.

Where a material which would be necessary in time of war, such as parachute silk, is not available in quantity in this country, effort is made to obtain a substitute which may be domestically produced. During the war, when linen for airplane fabric was unobtainable in sufficient quantity, this laboratory developed a mercerized cotton which proved better for the purpose than linen. It also invented an aluminum alloy for use in cylinder heads of air-cooled engines. Innumerable small parts such as tires, wing-ribs, metal and wood wingspars, cables, and propeller blades are the subjects of ceaseless experiment.

Armament Branch: The war uses of airplanes include the carrying of bombs, guns, cannon and ammunition and it is this department which controls offensive and defensive operations. Instruments for the accurate dropping of bombs upon definite objectives, taking into consideration the speed of the plane, its pitching and yawing, the speed of the wind and the trajectory of the fall of the bomb have all been developed. Gun sights, machine gun synchronizers (a timing device which makes it possible for the pilot to fire dead ahead through the rotation of highspeed propellers) are undergoing constant improvement. Pyrotechnics, including signal and lighting flares, are handled by this branch.

The Hangars: But all these technical elements in aircraft production are of less interest to the casual visitor than the giant hangars with the airplanes equipped and ready to be rolled to the flying line. Virtually every type of military airplane is represented: training planes, bombardment planes, observation planes, attack planes with guns mounted in the wings, light pursuit planes, transports for carrying troops and supplies, photographic and ambulance planes.

Machines that were undreamed of fifteen years ago are here like steeds in a stable, ready for the race. Wright Field is the testing ground of new planes for the Army Air Corps, the only one of its kind in the United States. A group of special test pilots are stationed there to ascertain of each new plane its speeds, rate of climb, its "ceiling," in short, just what it will do in the air. This taking up of an untried plane is pioneering of the most venturesome kind.

Although the risks are ever present, thousands of test flights have been made without accident. In other instances aviators have lost a propeller, landed planes that caught fire in the air, taken to parachutes to save their lives or sometimes, in dreadful disaster, given up their very existence for their work.

The amazing history made by Wright Field pilots would fill a volume. Major R. W. Schroeder flew to 33,113 feet through 67-degrees below

One of the first aerial photographs of downtown Dayton.

zero to set a new world altitude record. Lieutenant Louis Meister landed his plane in a tree to break the fall when his engine failed. Captain A. W. Stevens established a record for a high altitude jump, going over the side of the plane at 23,894 feet. Lieutenant J. A. Macready on September 5, 1924, made a world record when he lifted his machine to 32,400 feet. Lieutenants Macready and Kelly stayed up for thirty-six hours for another world record.

We can best conclude this chapter by the estimate of General Patrick Hurley, Secretary of War, which he paid to Dayton when he landed at Wright Field on a recent flight from Tulsa, Oklahoma to Washington: "There is no question that Wright Field is the nerve center of aeronautics in the United States and that it is the greatest air and air-equipped experimental station in the world."

(Ed. Note: Wright-Patterson AFB is still the nation's aeronautical nerve center although the requirements have grown so large that some of their functions have been disbursed throughout the country. In terms of personnel it is the largest air base in the world.)

Index

Thruston, Robert A. 82
Titsch, Robert 240
Toulmin, Harry A. 225
Treaty of Greenville 26, 30, 50
Turner, James 185
Turner's Opera House 147
Turpin family 251
Turpin, James 118, 248
Twightwees 21

Valentine, Grace 235
Vallandigham, James L. 225
Van Ausdal, Isaac 126
Van Buren, Martin 75
Van Cleve Park 39
Van Cleve, Benjamin 7, 26, 31, 33, 39, 48,
    83, 85
Van Cleve, John 7, 54, 65, 82, 95, 130, 218,
    244, 247
Van Cleve, Mary 28, 30

Waite, Henry M. 257
Wallace, Don 235
Walters family 143
Walters, J. A. 126
Walters, Jefferson 250
War of 1812 51, 89, 202
Wayne, Gen. "Mad Anthony" 25, 26
Webbert, Charles 279
Weber, Sara C. 233
Webster, Elmer R. 240
Wehrley, H. D. 294
Welsh, Dr. James 92
Weng, Siegfried R. 235, 241
Werthner, William 7, 224, 231
Westminster Choir 256, 259, 260
Whitmore, Robert 244
Whitten, Mary 48

Wight, Collins 95
Wilbur, Rev. Bacchus 83
Wilhelm, Paul E. 235, 246
Wilkinson, Gen. James 26
Williams, G. M. 286
Williams, John Harbert 93
Williams, John Insco 227
Williamson, John Finley 259
Williougby, A. J. 187
Wilt, A. D. 231
Winters, J. H. 126, 167
Winters, Valentine 111, 139, 231, 294
Wolf, Billy 161
Wolf's crackers 122
Women's Music Club 253
Wood, E. M. 167
Wood, Mrs. E. Morgan 250
Wood, Mrs. George 90
Woodhull, Mrs. Roger 88
Woodland Cemetery 65, 131, 134, 149
Worman, John 248
Wright brothers home 280
Wright, Bishop Milton 281
Wright, Katherine 281
Wright, Orville 231, 240, 278, 286
Wright, Wilbur 281
Wuichet, Charles 224
Wuichet, Edward 294
Wuichet, Eugene 167
Wuichet, Mrs. Abby Lytle 246

Xenia 22, 60

Young Women's League 255
Young, Rosamond 15

Zwinak, John 235